ANTHROPOLOGICAL PAPERS

MUSEUM OF ANTHROPOLOGY, UNIVERSITY OF MICHIGAN

NO. 38

THE ADMINISTRATION OF RURAL PRODUCTION IN AN EARLY MESOPOTAMIAN TOWN

BY

HENRY T. WRIGHT

Contributions by

Sandor Bökönyi
Kent V. Flannery
John Mayhall

ANN ARBOR

THE UNIVERSITY OF MICHIGAN, 1969

© 1969 by the Regents of the University of Michigan
The Museum of Anthropology
All rights reserved

ISBN (print): 978-1-949098-10-5
ISBN (ebook): 978-1-951519-32-2

Browse all of our books at
sites.lsa.umich.edu/archaeology-books.

Order our books from the University of Michigan
Press at www.press.umich.edu.

For permissions, questions, or manuscript queries,
contact Museum publications by email at umma-
pubs@umich.edu or visit the Museum website at
lsa.umich.edu/ummaa.

PREFACE

THIS monograph presents a simple idea about a particular type of community, and exemplifies this idea with data from one such community. It is important to first discuss the history of the idea and the difficulties involved in discussing it, given the present state of research.

I developed an interest in the relation between communication and organization in 1963 when I was reading in Amazon warfare under the guidance of Professor Elman Service of the University of Michigan, Department of Anthropology. Professors Aram Yengoyan, of the same department, and Amos Hawley, of the Sociology Department, encouraged me to attempt a quantitative model involving such relationships in simple societies. In 1965 Professor Lewis R. Binford of the University of Chicago subjected this model to a well-deserved, devastating critique. I allowed this interest to languish.

Meanwhile, Dr. Robert McC. Adams of the University of Chicago encouraged an interest in early complex societies, and offered me the opportunity to do fieldwork in Southwest Asia. In the fall of 1965, my wife and I went to Iraq and took up residence in the British School of Archeology with the kind permission of David Oates and Jeffery Orchard, respectively its director and secretary. It was my intention to conduct an archeological survey in order to locate evidences of the earliest irrigation agriculture on the Tigris-Euphrates alluvium. Toward this end we spent three months in the Iraq Museum with the permission of the Director-General of Antiquities, Dr. Faisal al-Wailly, and the Director of Museums, Dr. Faraj Basmachi, under the tutelage of the Director of Excavations, Mr. Fuad Safar.

In January, 1966, with the aid of Mr. James Knudstad, of the Oriental Institute's Nippur Expedition, Mr. Nicholas Vester, and Mr. Julian Wootten, we began an archeological survey in the vicinity of Ur. During this operation we were accompanied and aided by the guards of Ur, Hajji Hussein Abboud and Mahsen Nais. The tribal leader of the area, Sheikh Muhammed Manshet, and the Inspector of Antiquities, Mr. Wail al-Rubie, were of great assistance. After a month of fieldwork it became clear that there were few visible evidences of early settlement.

Several new objectives were considered. The study of a settlement pattern of the first phase of the Early Dynastic, roughly contemporary with the Ur Archaic texts, offered the possibility of pursuing my interests in communication and early complex societies together: deductions about the administration of the rural economy, based on archeological evidence of this economy, could be checked with the administrative texts. In March, 1966, Professor Robert J. Braidwood, accompanied by Mrs. Braidwood, Professor Halet Çambel of Istanbul University and Professor Bruce Howe of Harvard University, visited the rural site we proposed to excavate, and approved the project. Mr. Safar and several of his staff also visited the site and offered helpful suggestions.

The joint sounding of the Iraq Directorate-General of Antiquities and the Oriental Institute began in early April and ended in early May. Mr. Ghânim Wahida was the co-director. The work crew was led by two skilled Shergati field workers, Khalaf Jassim Saleḥ and Hussein 'Ali Saleḥ. The archeological problems encountered in this brief effort are described in Chapter IV.

Upon return to Baghdad, my wife and I took up residence in the house of the Annual Professor of the American Schools of Oriental Research in Baghdad, Professor Theresa Howard Carter, and began the analysis of the artifacts from the excavation. Miss Mira Ter-Minassian was our laboratory assistant. After the necessary counts and measurements were recorded, the artifacts were packed and placed in the care of Dr. Basmachi. Samples of various artifact types were sent to Chicago.

The analysis of these samples began in September, 1966, in Professor Braidwood's laboratory in the Oriental Institute. Various specialists participated in this analysis. Dr. Wilhem van Zeist of the Institut Biologisch-Archaeologisch in Groningen studied most of the plant remains. Professor Robert Stewart of Sam Houston State College examined the impressions of grasses for traces of disease. Dr. Kent Flannery, then of the Smithsonian Institution, and Dr. Sandor Bökönyi of the Hungarian National Museum both studied the mammal remains. Dr. Karel Liem of the Field Museum of Natural History examined the fish remains. Dr. Robert Marschner of Whiting Research Laboratories of the American Oil Company conducted a study of the petroleum artifacts. Miss Anne Miller of the University of Michigan conducted ceramic firing experiments on clays from the excavations. I proceeded with an analysis of the types of artifacts and the horizontal and vertical distribution of these on the site.

During the fall of 1966, I began to study Sumerian under the direction of Professor Miguel Civil of the Oriental Institute. As the analysis of the artifacts approached a conclusion, the analysis of the Ur Archaic Texts was begun. The monograph embodying these analyses was written during the summer of 1967.

As one might expect, the data of ethnography, survey, excavations, and tablets do not allow a really rigorous test of my hypotheses about the administration of the economy in an early complex society. Now let us consider some of the reasons for this inadequacy.

Certain ethnographic sources are discussed in Chapter II. These are neither geographically comprehensive, nor topically well-rounded. For instance, it is not possible to assemble adequate statistics on the relationship between house type, house density, and population density, a key relationship in the study of settlement patterns. Beyond this simple level of observation, which is more the province of the cultural geographer than the anthropologist, it is not possible to assemble comprehensive data on traditional subsistence, crafts, or decision-making, to name a few topics of interest in my work. Furthermore, it seems unlikely that many cultural or social anthropologists would be interested in collecting data for the use of archeologists. It will probably be necessary for archeologists to do these studies themselves. Until proper ethnographic surveys are done, efforts such as that which follows will be founded upon a small and perhaps unrepresentative body of ethnographic and geographic data.

The data of archaeological surface survey is introduced in Chapter III. It seems clear that the survey method at present has definite limitations: certain brief periods of time are characterized by distinctive, durable, and ubiquitous artifacts, while the intervening periods are not. Thus it is difficult to do population trend studies over short spans of time. More relevant to this monograph is the probability that some settlements are totally obscured by later settlement, silting, or river channel erosion. The first two problems can be solved with a program of drilling, and the latter can to some extent be accounted for if the locations of later channels are known. In my study, rural settlements are so small that failure to record half of them would not significantly affect the inferences about the labor force. A more fundamental problem is the skeletal character of a settlement map. Given such a map, the land between settlements must at present be interpreted with modern analogy. We desperately need a method which provides direct evidence of rural land use. Mollusks, plant pollen, and fossil soils are all possible sources of evidence. To assume an analogy in place of such evidence is unsatisfactory indeed.

The evidence from archeological excavations is by present standards of reasonable quality. A wide range of recovery procedures and a relatively unbiased sampling design was attempted. The major problem is the small size of the sample. Judging from the range of variation in modern villages of the region, at least a ten per cent random sample of a rural settlement could allow assessment of the characteristics of the settlement. In addition, a number of settlements should be investigated to allow assessment of the range of variation in settlement. My three per cent sample of one site is probably unreliable.

The evidence drawn from the Archaic Texts is also unsatisfactory. Only a small sample of fragmentary tablets is available. Were more tablets available, more extensive biographic information, more administrative terms, and more statistics would be available. The administrative arrangements might prove to be more complex. In addition, and this is true of any documentary evidence, the archive sampled may not have much to do with the activities of interest. Fortunately the Ur documents are concerned primarily with agriculture, though we cannot be certain that they are fully representative of agricultural activity in the region. Because of this uncertainty, it is wise not to utilize the Ur texts in such controversies as that over the proportion of temple vs. non-temple control of land. Another problem is one of the intelligibility of the documents. Even Sumerian of the second millennium B.C. is not fully understood. Furthermore, the connotation of forms shifted as the language developed. As the language is traced back, the large archives needed to conduct contextual checks on connotation become less common. The general meaning of the more common signs and sign groups in the Ur Archaic Texts is clear but the specific connotation is often not. Some of the less common signs are of unknown meaning. In addition, the precise equivalents of the units of measure are unknown. Nevertheless, though one cannot say exactly how much of a certain type of barley is being recorded, he can say that an approximate amount of some type of barley is being recorded. Such general interpretations are sufficient to fulfill the objectives of this monograph. Full understanding and actual readings of the Archaic Texts will require the discovery of more textual material and the expenditure of many years of philological study.

Given weaknesses in every aspect of the data, the reader may well wonder why I even attempted to propose and test a formal hypothesis. There are two simple answers to this query. First, to consider the problems without providing a satisfactory answer may encourage others to collect the missing data. Second, to consider the data in any formal framework, however dubious the result, may help to reveal new insights, in this case unnoticed aspects of the organization of early Mesopotamian states.

The manuscript has been examined by Robert McC. Adams, Robert J. Braidwood, Miguel Civil, Lloyd Fallers, Lewis Binford, and Aram Yengoyan. The final product profits from many of their constructive comments.

My thanks are due those listed above and those whom I was unable to mention who contributed to the development of my ideas and the carrying out of the project. Responsibility for the errors is my own.

Contents

List of Figures xi

List of Tables xiii

I. Theoretical Considerations and Methodological Consequences 1

II. Subsistence and Settlement on the Southern Alluvial Plains of Iraq 7

III. Early Dynastic Ur: The Context 25

IV. A Rural Community 43

V. The Archeological Evidence of Rural Production 89

VI. The Documentary Evidence of Rural Production...... 99

VII. The Rural Economy: A Summary 117

Appendix

I. The Statistics of Artifacts From Sakheri Sughir 123

II. Faunal Remains From Sakheri Sughir by *Sandor Bökönyi* and *Kent V. Flannery* 143

III. The Dentition of Two Human Burials From Sakheri Sughir by *John Mayhall, D.D.S.* 151

References 159

List of Illustrations

Figure   *Page*

1. Lower Iraq 8
2. 'Ubaid Period Settlement in Southern Sumer 26
3. Settlement in Lower Iraq during the Early Third Millenium. . . 29
4. The Ur Enclave during the First Phase of the Early Dynastic Period.. 34
5. The Town of Ur during the First Phase of the Early Dynastic Period.. 37
6. The Town of Ur during the Last Phase of the Early Dynastic Period.. 38
7. Sakheri Sughir 44
8. A Section of the "Canal Sounding"..................... 45
9. A Section of the "Deep Sounding" 46
10. The Excavations at Sakheri Sughir 48
11. Details of Work Area and the Long Oven-IB 51
12. Details of the Rectangular Structure-IIB 53
13. Chipped Stone Artifacts 57
14. Bitumen Artifacts 60
15. Ceramic Artifacts 62
16. Conical Cups and Stone Bowls 64
17. Bowls 66
18. Jars 67
19. Jars 69
20. Vessel Fragments 70
21. Other Vessels...................................... 72
22. Profiles of Conical Cups 73
23. Stratigraphic Distribution of Cup Base Types............. 76
24. Schematic Plan of the 'Ubaid Cemetery................. 82
25. An Exercise Text and a Goods Deposit Text 101
26. Two Goods Allotment Texts and a Land Survey Text........ 102
27. A Land Allotment Text 103
28. A Personnel Text and a Miscellaneous Text.............. 110

xi

List of Tables

Table		Page
1.	Some Characteristics of Four Modern Iraqi Settlements	23
2.	City Names on the Archaic Seal Impressions.	32
3.	The Attributes of the 'Ubaid Graves in Woolley's Chronological Groups.	80
4.	Head and Face Orientation of the 'Ubaid Graves	81
5.	Orientation in the Areas of the 'Ubaid Cemetery	83
6.	The Association between Jars and Cups in the 'Ubaid Cemetery	83
7.	The Association between Vessels and Rare Items in the 'Ubaid Cemetery	84
8.	The Placement of Objects in the 'Ubaid Graves	84
9.	Numbers of Items in the Areas of the 'Ubaid Cemetery	85
10.	The Placement of Items in Graves in Areas of the 'Ubaid Cemetery	86
11.	The Association between Orientation of Face and Number of Vessels	86
12.	Portions of Domestic Animals in the Areas of Sakheri Sughir.	92
13.	Activities and Decision Variables.	98
14.	Artifacts in the Provenience Units at Sakheri Sughir	125
15.	Conical Cup Bases	128

I
THEORETICAL CONSIDERATIONS AND METHODOLOGICAL CONSEQUENCES

IN 1949 Julian Steward's paper "Culture Causality and Law: A Trial Formulation of the Development of Early Civilizations" drew the attention of American anthropologists and archeologists to the similarities in the developments of early civilizations. At that time it seemed likely that a general theory which would explain these general similarities could be approached with a minimum of research. The model of Wittfogel (1938, 1957) seemed particularly amenable to rigorous test. In the late fifties a number of field workers attempted to test his hypothesis that major irrigation works require complex coercive administrations and thus cause the development of states. Differences of opinion have arisen over the interpretation of these tests. Adams rejects Wittfogel, arguing that " . . . irrigation merely forms a subsidiary part of a functionally interdependent network of subsistence techniques, political hierarchies, and economic relationships. Our task of understanding this network will not be advanced by isolating irrigation as the primary, independent causative agency" (1965:76). Sanders, on the other hand, accepts Wittfogel's hypothesis, arguing that " . . . two primary characteristics of the ecological system of the Central Mexican area in 1519 were the primary stimuli toward the evolution of civilization in that area, hydraulic agriculture and economic symbiosis" (1965:194). Though there is certainly real disagreement here, both men would probably agree that there is a relationship between the complexity of the subsistence economy and the complexity of the administration which directs it. Clearly this relationship deserves further study.

In this monograph I will consider the economy and administration of a single urban system over a limited span of time. An "urban system" will be defined as (1) a spatially bounded set of activities, (2) maintaining a population, (3) each of which is performed only by an ascribed subgroup of the population. The term system here emphasizes that the activities are inter-related through exchanges of material items, energy in the form of labor, and information.

Let us consider the definition in more detail. First, the definition emphasizes sets of activities. Second, given the biology of a human population, it follows that a portion of those activities will involve the production of food, crafts goods, and architectural constructions. Furthermore, a portion of the activities must be concerned with the movement or circulation of produced items to people other than those who produced them (and vice versa) and with coordinating the various movements of all items. Third, the definition distinguishes between urban systems and other systems on the basis of degree of division of labor. If each of the activities crucial to population maintenance is performed by a special clearly-defined group, then the hypothesis which will be developed in this study should be relevant. If the activities are not so performed then the system is not complex enough to be characterized as an urban system. Of course it is possible, and given the seasonal nature of many productive activities it is likely, that individuals could belong to a number of ascribed subgroups.

This definition is a denotative one defining my area of interest. It does not say anything about "cities" as dense population clusters. It does not say anything about the "state" as a coercive political form. It does not say anything about "civilization."

Now let us consider activities related to the movement of produced goods. Steps in movement can be: (1) exchange between two parties, (2) the contribution of all parties to a common pool and provisioning of all parties from this pool, and (3) the competition among a number of parties with an item for the patronage of a receiving party. The parties involved in movement can vary in the size, composition, and location. An item may move through several steps, not necessarily all mediated in the same manner. Also, no two items necessarily move through the same sequence of steps. Thus, the movement of items to people (or vice versa) in an urban system can be complicated.

The coordination of a series of movements requires information about items produced, information about the requirements of individuals or units in the population, and a means of arriving at decisions on the basis of such information. It must be emphasized that coordination could be effective with incomplete information or partially nonrational means of decision-making. Furthermore, it is possible, even in differentiated systems of the sort being discussed, that particular types of movement and production require little or no coordinating activity. Thus coordination can be complicated too.

Two questions can be raised at this point: (1) What is the relation between production and the organization of the movement of the produced items? (2) What is the relation between the movement of produced items and the coordination of this movement? The first question is difficult to handle because in early urban systems both production and movement are usually attested directly by archeological evidence, often by the same evidence. For example, plant food remains are seldom recovered from the fields where they were produced. They are usually found in storage or cooking areas to which they had been transported. Thus they are simultaneously evidence of production and movement. One way to deal with hypotheses about this relation would be to study the movement of a type of good in a sample of urban systems. This is not possible with the presently available data. Consequently hypotheses about this relation may be offered in this study, and they may be assumed to be correct for heuristic purposes, but they will not be tested. In the case of the second question, since movement is archeologically evidenced but coordination is directly evidenced in contemporary texts, it should be possible to predict in the case of a single urban system the organization of coordination activities from the archeologically evidenced movements, and to test such predictions with the texts. With this possibility in mind, I sought archeological evidence of production and movement near the Early Dynastic city of Ur in southern Iraq because I knew an unanalyzed body of contemporary texts was available for study.

The problem is therefore, given my assumed definition of an urban system and delineation of production, movement, and coordination activities, what additional definitions and assumptions will I need to generate hypotheses about the relation between the first two sets of activities and the last?

First, let us consider the organization of individuals into decision-making groups. Simplest is an "individual decision": a single person considers the range of possible moves and their outcomes, then chooses a move or combination of moves. Another possibility is a "concensal decision." A group of individuals each having information on a situation present solutions, then they argue until all agree on one solution. There are a number of possible ways of coming to agreement, but to my knowledge there are no good comparative studies of this sort of decision-making. It seems likely that the time consumed in making a decision is in direct proportion to the number of relations between group participants, which would be the factorial of the number of group participants. When time is restricted then a moderated decision may emerge: one individual in the group receives all the solutions and reduces them to a solution with which all agree. Very similar to this is a "hierarchic decision" in which one individual receives information from others in the group. There are many possible variations here. The hierarch may receive partial decisions or condensed information rather than simple information. He may convey not one decision, but a specific decision to each member in the group. He may convey decisions to a group different from the group from which he received information. Nevertheless, all varieties of moderated and hierarchic decision must have essentially similar limitations: time consumed in making a decision would increase in proportion to the number of relations between the central figure and people in a group. The ultimate limit on these types of decision making and on an "individual decision" would be the ability of a single individual to handle all the information coming to him. This ability depends on the "type of problem-solving" he is using and his "capacity" to process information.

If the number of sources of information increases beyond the capacity of an individual, then either information necessary for an effective decision must be ignored or there must be two individuals handling the decision, and a moderated or hierarchic decision will appear. When the capacity of the central figure is exceeded, then two groups with two levels of decision will be necessary and a third level will be necessary to coordinate these two groups. Thus as the amount of information about possible moves and outcomes and the number of sources of information increases, the number of levels of decision making can be expected to increase. Such an increase might be obscured by "labor redundancy," having more than enough decision makers, so my hypotheses based on this correlation will have to assume that within any urban system the degree of labor redundancy in all productive activities is similar.

Second, let us consider types of problem solving. On the one hand, there are situations in which all the outcomes of the possible decisions are known. In the simplest case, the choice is of a single move from a set of moves. The solution involves reviewing the possible outcomes and picking the move with the best outcome. In a more complicated case the choice is between the combinations of moves that can be drawn from a set of possible moves. Recently mathematicians have devised linear programming theory in order to find the optimal combination of moves in such situations. On the other hand, there are situations in which only the probabilities of the possible outcomes of each move are known.

In the simplest case the choice is of a single move. The solution involves reviewing the probabilities and choosing the move most likely to produce a beneficial outcome. This should require somewhat more solution time per given number of moves than the simplest case in the first type of problem solving mentioned above. In a more complicated case the choice is between possible combinations of moves. In another more complicated case the move or moves desired are the ones which are most likely to produce gain with a minimum risk of loss. Recently mathematicians have devised game theory in order to find optimal moves in some of these more complex situations.

In the above paragraph, I did not discuss situations of either general type in which information on the outcomes or probabilities of outcomes is only partially available or unclearly defined. Does the relative decrease in amount of information allow faster decision making, or does hesitation cause even slower decision-making? There is evidence to suggest that in at least some situations, the choices conform to an optimizing model in spite of ambiguity. Central Ghanian land use (Gould, 1963), and Jamaican fishing techniques (Davenport, 1960) have been shown to conform to game theory solutions. Full information on productive and climatic variability was unavailable to the decision makers in these two cases. We can assume that, if a given situation occurs repeatedly, even if complete information is not available or the problem-solving procedure is not conceptualized as recent mathematicians have formalized it, then through the repeated successes and failures of the various moves, an optimal problem-solving technique of the appropriate type will be approached.

Third let us briefly consider the capacity of individuals to process information. The term capacity implies that either, given a certain speed of information handling, only a certain amount can be handled; or given a certain amount to be handled, it can only be handled at a certain speed. Most measures of human performance vary in the same person from time to time, and from person to person. There is evidence that within a particular ethnic group and in a particular problem situation, information capacity does not vary greatly (Quastler, 1955; Pearce, 1961). I shall assume that this variability is insignificant for purposes of this study.

In the above discussions of decision making, four interrelated variables have been noted: (1) the number of separate sources of information about the problem, (2) the number of possible moves and their outcomes, (3) the problem-solving technique, (4) the capacity of an individual to handle sources and moves, given the problem-solving technique. While a specific problem-solving technique is usually unknown in archeologically evidenced situations, the general type of problem solving, that is whether outcomes or probabilities of outcomes are to be considered, can be inferred from the type of movement or production about which decisions are being made. Furthermore, given the same general type of problem solving in two cases in the same cultural milieu, one can assume that the specific techniques would be similar. Likewise, the capacities of individuals can never be known archeologically. If experiments in various types of problem solving in various cultural situations had been performed, we might be able to assume a capacity. In the absence of well-controlled experiments, we might assume that in a single cultural milieu capacities for a single type of problem solving are roughly similar.

If one is willing to assume similar capacities, similar problem-solving techniques, and similar labor redundancies; then he can deduce that: (1) if the number of sources of information and alternative moves are similar in two cases, then the number of levels of decision making in a coordination activity will be similar, or (2) if the number of levels of decision making are different in two cases, then the case with the greater number of levels of decision making will have a greater number of sources and/or moves. These are the general hypotheses to be tested in this study.

Obviously many elaborations on this line of reasoning are possible. Nevertheless, the first step will be to attempt to infer the movements of items, the type of problem solving, and the number of sources of information and number of moves from archeological and ethnographic evidence; and to deduce from these inferences and from the first general hypothesis which movements would have coordinating activities with similar levels of decision making. These specific hypotheses will then be tested with the written evidence. From the residual written evidence one can infer which coordinating activities do have different levels of decision making. From these inferences and from the second general hypothesis he can deduce which production or movement activities would require different quantities of information on sources and moves. These specific hypotheses can be tested with the residual archeological and ethnographical inferences of the first step. The above outlined system of assumptions, definitions, deductions, and hypotheses will have been tested in several ways, and the available evidence on our single urban system will have been exhausted. If the hypotheses have not been rejected, then further elaborations of the line of reasoning may be suggested and further hypotheses proposed.

II

SUBSISTENCE AND SETTLEMENT ON THE SOUTHERN ALLUVIAL PLAINS OF IRAQ

INTRODUCTION

IT would be senseless to describe in detail the modern environment and ethnography of the area in which the urban center we will study was located. Both have altered fundamentally several times since the third millennium B.C. Instead, I will describe a range of soil-plant communities known to occur in southern Mesopotamia. Then I will describe a series of traditional subsistence techniques related to these communities and their implications for labor and coordination. Next, I will consider some of the structures built to aid in subsistence. Finally, I will discuss some factors affecting land use and settlement distribution today, and processes of change in those factors.

Several types of sources have proved especially useful. Recently published monographs on the flora (Guest, 1966), mammals (Hatt, 1959), and fishes (Khalaf, 1961; Mahdi, 1961) contributed to the first section. A general geographical study of the Middle Euphrates (see Fig. 1) provided some background and invaluable specific information on settlement pattern (Al-Barazi, 1961). An agro-economical study of the Hilla-Diwaniyah area of the Middle Euphrates (Poyck, 1962) provided figures on many aspects of production. Ethnographies of an agricultural group in the Middle Euphrates (Fernea, 1959) and a marsh community on the Lower Euphrates (Salim, 1959) provided additional figures, detail of subsistence techniques, and clear description of social organization. I have supplemented these works with my own few ethnographic observations on Lower Euphrates communities. Though additional evidence would be welcome and a comparative ethnology of the alluvial plain would require many more ethnographies, we are fortunate to have as much as we do.

GEOLOGICAL BACKGROUND

To the southwest of the alluvium is the stable Arabian Shield. To the northeast are the mountains first folded and thrust up in

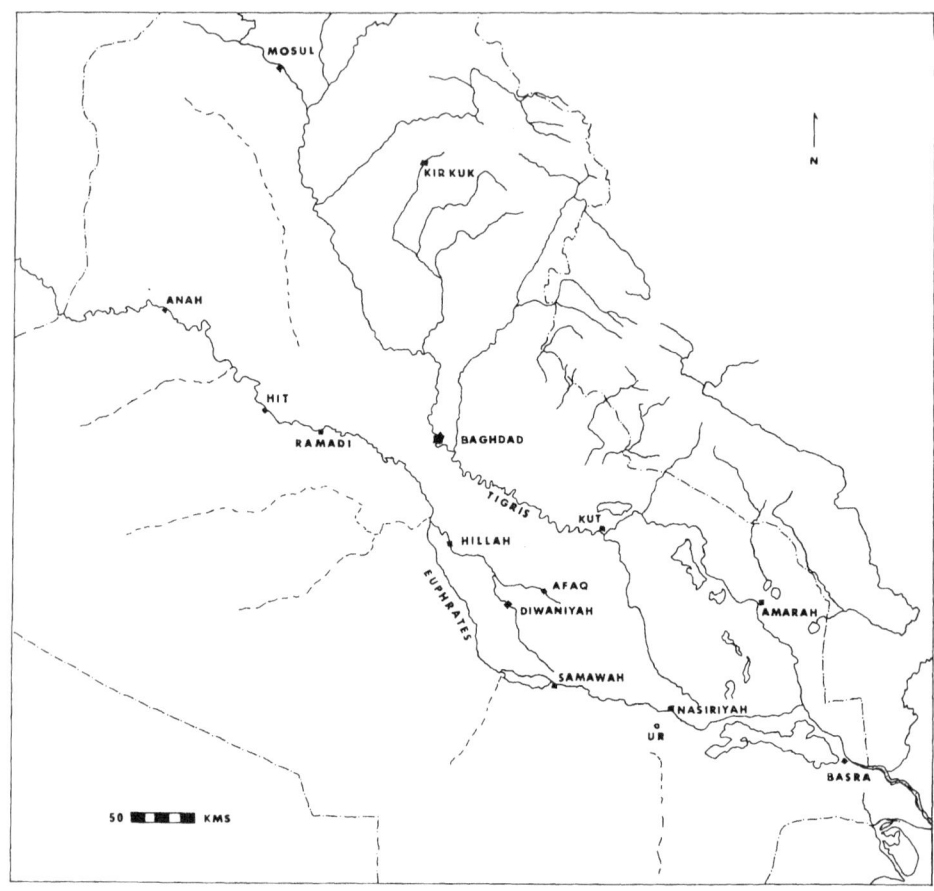

FIG. 1. Lower Iraq. Modern towns and rivers are shown.

the Cretaceous period. Sediments eroded from the products of this first period of mountain building were deposited where the Zagros Mountains and the Tigris-Euphrates Valley are located. As the Zagros were folded and thrust up during the Miocene and Pliocene periods, increasing thicknesses of coarser and coarser sediment were deposited. The earth's crust gave way and the area now the lower alluvium of Iraq became a depositional basin. The detailed history of this basin is not available.

At the last glacial maximum, the sea was over a hundred meters below its present level. The Tigris and the Euphrates must have been deeply entrenched below the flood plain surface which was graded to the sea level of the previous interglacial period (Voute, 1957). This surface would have subsided throughout the glacial period even though it was not receiving sediment.

The entrenched valleys of the twin rivers would have filled with sediment as sea level rose to its present level.

By 5000 B.C. a complex arrangement of estuaries, lakes, marshes, levees, both newly deposited and remnant alluvial plain, and braided river channels would have developed. This time the change in river gradient would have moved to the head of the alluvium and the maximum amount of sediment would have been deposited on the upper alluvium as it is today (Adams and Harris, 1957). Localization of sedimentation would result in limited subsidence and faulting. The continuing rise of the Zagros may have complicated the picture further by lifting the northeast side of the basin and tilting the southwest side downward, in addition it may have pushed the basin southward against the Arabian Shield causing minor upthrusting of ridges around the edge of the basin.

Over the last seven thousand years diking has maintained channels long after nature would have abandoned them; artificial canals have distributed silt widely around these channels; and irrigation has raised the water table and caused the formation of saline soils. Thus agriculture has left relatively high areas of alluvial desert. When the wind blows on the light, denuded soils of the abandoned channels, sand and silt dunes are created. When these man-made factors compound the varied natural situation on the surface of the Euphrates geosyncline, then the physical environment becomes so complex that it yet defies detailed interpretation.

SOME BIOLOGICAL COMMUNITIES OF THE ALLUVIUM AND ITS ENVIRONS

The fundamental biological division is between desertic and riverine environments. Within the former the southern desert and the better watered and more saline alluvial desert can be distinguished. Within the latter, the river edge and the marshes can be distinguished.

The Southern Desert

The Southern Desert stretches for hundreds of kilometers to the south of the alluvium until it grades into the more arid Saudian Desert. It is a rolling country of seasonally flooded wadis and depressions and low stony ridges. At least 20 different plant communities grow there, most of them flowering in the winter or spring. Five particularly widespread and useful types of vegetation are detailed below:

1) The most common association is dominated by *Haloxylon salicornicum* (rimth), a broomlike shrub, but contains other small shrubs and herbs. The community generally covers about 20 per cent of the soil, which is a calcareous sandy loam.

2) The second most common is dominated by *Rhanterium epposum* (arfaj) a small shrub, which occurs with *Plantago sp.* and a variety of small annuals. The community generally covers about 40 per cent of a sand or sandy-loam soil. This community is much used and abused for grazing and fuel collecting.

3) *Zizyphus numularia* (sidr), a thorny shrub, and *Lycium depressum*, a small shrub, dominate another rich community of annual herbs and grasses found in silty wadi floors. Also good fodder and fuel, the dominant species is protected by the herders' belief that it is "haunted" (Guest, 1966).

4) Another community, dominated by *Artemesia herba-alba* (shih) a small shrub, contains many spring-maturing herbs and late summer-maturing shrubs, mostly chenopods. This doubly good grazing vegetation is rare in the Southern Desert but is very common in the Western Desert.

5) Excessive grazing will degrade any of the above communities into a surface covered with *Stipa capensis* (sama'a), a spike grass, with some *Astragalus spinosus*, a small spiny shrub. The former provided good grazing for sheep and goats in wet years.

The fauna of the Southern Desert was, until the eighteenth century, relatively rich. Among the large herbivores were the onager (*Equus hemionus*), various species of gazelle (*Gazella sp.*), and the Arabian hare (*Lepus arabicus*). The large carnivores are still diverse: the wolf (*Canis lupus*), three species of foxes (*Vulpes vulpes, V. rupelli,* and *Fennecus zerda*), the rattel (*Mellinova capensis*). The Indian desert cat (*Felix libyca iraki*), the caracal (*Felix caracal*), and the cheetah (*Acinonyx jubatus*) occurred until recently. Presumably they subsisted in part on domestic sheep and goats.

In summary, the Southern Desert provides extensive grazing in the wet season from November to May.

The Dunes

Sand and dust dunes occur in the larger depressions in the Southern Desert, and near abandoned channels on the alluvium. Most impressive, however, are a belt of probable Pleistocene age extending for almost three hundred kilometers along the southern

SUBSISTENCE AND SETTLEMENT ON PLAINS OF IRAQ 11

edge of the alluvium. The belt is over ten kilometers wide and some dunes are more than 40 meters high. The characteristic plant community is dominated by *Haloxylon ammodendron* (ghada) a small tree, and *Callignum comosum* ('irta) a shrub. The former can reach a height of five meters and so might serve as a timber supply as well as a fuel supply.

Alluvial Desert

The alluvial desert is a product of human activity from both a geological and biological point of view. Unfortunately, little is known about the plant communities of its southern portions. Three types of communities can be distinguished:

1) *Abandoned levees:* In areas with higher water tables, low thickets of *Prosopis farcta* (shauk) and *Alhagi mannifera* (agul) both deep-rooted shrubs, occur. Otherwise *Stipa capensis* (sama'a) with *Lycium depressum* ('arsaj) a shrub, and various annual herbs occur. These provide some grazing in winter.

2) *Dry levee slopes and flats:* In moderately saline areas *Sueada baccata*, a spiny shrub; *Nitriara retusa*, a bushy shrub; and *Tamarix sp.*, here a shrub, thrive. They are poor grazing. More saline areas are barren or support an occasional *Aizoon hispanicum*, a salt-loving annual.

3) *Seasonally flooded depressions:* Such depressions occur in the Southern Desert, but are more frequent and more important on the alluvium. Most useful are the large and relatively salt-free depressions. These support a lush growth of perennial grasses and herbs. Unfortunately no botanical information is available on these important grazing areas. Various communities around saline depressions have been studied and defined but since none of them are good grazing, they are not worth discussing.

The fauna of the alluvial desert is degraded and poorly balanced. Large herbivores are rare and carnivores and other mammals often dwell in former human habitations and sometimes prey on human crops and domestic animals. The major herbivores were the onager and gazelle. The minor ones were and are the European hare (*Lepus europaeus*), porcupine (*Hystrix indica*), and badger (*Meles meles*). The carnivores were and are the wolf, fox (*Vulpes vulpes*), jackal (*Canus aureus*), hyena (*Hyena hyena*), the cheetah, and the small Indian mongoose (*Herpestes auropunctatus*).

In summary, the alluvial desert provides some accessible areas of good grazing even in summer. Some of its predators feed on domestic animals.

River Levees

The vegetation of the uncultivated levee top (Ahrash) is usually tangled thickets of *Tamarix sp.* (Tamarisk), *Salix acmophyla* (a willow), and *Populus euphratica* (a poplar), all trees, with *Rubus sanctus*, a thorny shrub, and *Glinus loitoides*, an herb, covering the ground. If undisturbed for long periods pure stands of *Salix* or *Populus* can develop. This vegetation is usually cleared off and replaced by *Phoenix dactylifera*, the date palm, or by vegetable gardens.

On uncultivated levee backslopes, behind the levee top, are dense thickets of *Prosopis farcta*, *Glycyrhiza glahra* (wild licorice) and *Alhagi mannifera*, all leguminous shrubs with deep roots.

The levee thickets served as cover for limited but dangerous fauna: the fallow deer (*Dama mesopotamica*) and the European hare were the large herbivores. The wild pig (*Sus scrofa*) was and is very common. Among the carnivores were lion (*Panthera leo*), the swamp cat (*Felix chaus*), the jackal, and the Indian mongoose. The long-eared hedgehog (*Hemiechinus auritus*) also occurs.

In summary, the levees without modification probably served as a source of wood products. Their soils are excellent.

Marshes

Marshes are of two types: seasonal and permanent. Seasonal marshes often occur in abandoned canals or canal seepage areas scattered throughout the cultivated area. Various reeds, grasses, and sedges such as *Typha*, *Juncus*, and *Scirpus* dominate these areas. *Cyperus rotundus* and *Phyla nodifera* live on the damp banks. These small marshes can provide fodder, material for baskets and mats, and edible tubers.

The permanent marshes occur in areas of recent downfaulting or river channel readjustment. These are dominated by high stands of the reeds *Phragmites communis* and *Typha sp.* A tremendous variety of floating plants, bottom-dwelling plants, and mud-bank plants also grow here. These large marshes provide fodder, cane, reeds for mats and baskets, and a variety of wild foods. Fish resources will be discussed later.

Mammalian fauna include the wolf, wild pig, the common otter (*Lutra lutra*), and the Iraq smooth coat otter (*Lutragale perspicillata*). A large migratory bird population lives here in the winter.

SUBSISTENCE AND SETTLEMENT ON PLAINS OF IRAQ 13

General Summary of the Biological Communities

It should be clear that southern Iraq contains considerable, though seasonal and widely scattered, natural grazing vegetation, and bountiful, to some extent year-round, sources of wild animals and birds. Soils of the levees and levee slopes are generally light and relatively salt free.

The related component areas of the southern Iraqi environment are large and to some extent separate. Groups utilizing all the available gathering, planting, and grazing resources must either move seasonally from area to area or must divide into specialized segments exchanging local products with each other.

TRADITIONAL SUBSISTENCE PRODUCTION OF THE PLAINS

Grain Agriculture

Wheat and six-row barley are the major traditional grain crops of southern Mesopotamia. Soil fertility is maintained if half the cultivable land is left in fallow. Thus the land must be reallocated to some extent every year. It could be plowed just after harvest in May in order to seal in the remnant winter moisture with a powdery layer, or it could be irrigated so the livestock could graze on the stubble and weeds. It is plowed and cross-plowed in parcels of several hectares with an ox or donkey-drawn scratch plow in September or October. Then it is seeded and braked. The fields are subdivided by dikes into lots of about a hectare. These dikes prevent the irrigation water from moving rapidly over higher areas and flooding lower areas. Plowing and diking are always coordinated group activities.

Irrigation water is applied every three weeks if supply is unreliable as in gravity flow canals, or every five weeks if supply is reliable as in lift arrangements. This task requires few individuals but must be carefully scheduled.

Grain is harvested in April and May. Every available laborer must work long hours either cutting with a hand sickle, collecting sheaves to dry, or in threshing. If the grain is to be divided, it is done at this time. It is then transported to storage.

Productivity varies considerably. Increases in the salinity of the soil is met by increasing the proportion of salt-resistant barley production. Decrease in fertility is met by increasing the amount of seed per hectare. Between 300 and 1200 kilos of barley per hectare are produced. On tenanted estates an average of 900 kilos of barley and 870 kilos of wheat per hectare are produced, allowing for pilfering and field loss. On small farms an average of 720 kilos of barley and 520 kilos of wheat per hectare are produced. This is in part a function of larger fallowing ratios and the fallowing of large contiguous areas on the estates. Seed varies from 80 to 200 kilos per hectare but averages 120 for barley and 92 for wheat (adapted from Poyck, 1962:38-50).

I have no information on flax cultivation.

Vegetables

These are grown the year-round. Melons and cucumbers are available in summer. Cucumbers, beans, onions, and garlic are available in winter. Cucumbers, onions, okra, and eggplant are available in spring. Many poorly-known herbs and green vegetables are also grown. Of the above, onions, garlic, okra, beans, and herbs are storable. Vegetables are generally grown in small plots in silty levee soils. They require considerable individual attention but no coordination.

Orchards

Orchards must be continually tended and must be watered every ten days. Dates can grow in almost any soil, even saline soils. Other fruits require light, salt-free levee soils. The histories of these plants are not known. It is possible that dates became a mass-produced fruit only in the second millennium B.C. (Civil, personal communication). The special pollinating and fruit protection techniques may not have been necessary before that time. Pomegranates, apricots, plums, pears, peaches, and apples are possible traditional orchard crops. These crops require intensive labor but no particular coordination.

Sheep and Goats

These animals are grazed on the stubble in the fields immediately after harvest. Through the summer they eat straw and the dried weeds and stubble on specially irrigated fallow and waste land or on canal and pond beds. With the first rains in October or November they graze on the uncultivated waste lands, either alluvial desert or stony desert. When the barley shoots are six- to nine-weeks-old, stock can be grazed on the shoots with only minor damage to the final crop. Supplementary feedings of 30 to

50 kilos of barley are given to the animals in the winter if large areas of waste are inaccessible.

Each year a herd will increase by about 30 to 35 per cent. The ewes and she-goats bear young from February to April. This per cent of the herd can be eaten every year, but there should always be enough young to replace those of the old that are eaten.

Modern ewes and she-goats produce from 20 to 35 kilos of milk in a three-month lactation period. A sheep produces about 1.5 to 2.5 kilos of wool a year, while a goat produces 1.0 to 1.5 kilos of hair per year.

Sheep and goat herding can be conducted in several ways. First, the stock can be kept in flocks of 20 to 40 animals by small groups. These are grazed near the cultivated land by boys. Second, stock can be kept in larger flocks by groups who specialize in herding. These go south into the desert with the first rain and return to summer homes and campsites during March and April. During the summer these graze in flooded fallow and waste areas. The advantage of this second pattern is that it allows exploitation of an immense natural pasture and therefore allows the production of more meat. On the other hand, it removes a large block of the adult population from full participation in the agricultural economy. In addition it requires coordination of the larger flocks and of the distribution of animals. The first pattern avoids these problems but it is only feasible on a large scale if there are small settlements scattered across the countryside. If the second pattern is dominant, there should be few remains of animals of nine- to eleven-months-age and no animals of ten-months-age on the settlements, because they will have been in the desert during this period in their lives.

Cattle

These are grazed on straw, flooded fallow land, and wasteland. In the summer they must be grazed in the shady orchards. They are seldom fed supplementary grain. When a cow is neither pregnant nor lactating it is kept in a herd with a bull. When pregnant or lactating it is often kept in a byre and hand fed straw or greens by the children. Male calves are soon eaten. Every rural family strives to keep a few cows in order to provide a domestic milk supply. A cow provides between 350 and 400 kilos of milk in a three- to six-month lactation period. Dung is collected and used for fuel.

Poultry

The domestic chicken, at present an important contributor to Iraqi diet, was probably introduced in the first millennium B.C. Ducks and geese, doves and pigeons, and other birds were traditionally kept, but little is known about the care they require or their productivity.

Draft Animals

Since the horse, camel, and domestic water buffalo probably came into general use in the second millennium B.C., we will not consider them. Teams of oxen, onagers or donkeys were traditionally used in plowing and harrowing. Several workers are necessary to manage such teams. The team animals are fed supplementary grain. Donkeys are often used as pack animals. Whether wheeled vehicles were more commonly used for bulk transport before this task was taken over by camels is not known.

Fishing

Hundreds of species of fish live in the coastal, riverine, and lacustrine waters of southern Iraq. Though several lists of species are available, the ecology of these fish is poorly known. The species reported as edible by Khalaf (1961) are as follows: there are two anadromous shad living in salt water but swimming up the fresh rivers and canals in the fall to lay their eggs (*Hilsa ilisha, Nematalosa naus*). There are two carp ranging up to 2.0 meters in length, which live solely in fresh rivers and lakes (*Barbus grypus, B. xanthopteros*). There are also smaller carp and a catfish ranging up to .3 meters in length in these waters (*B. sharpeyi, B. luteus,* and *Silurus triostegus*). Doubtless many of the less common fresh-water fish are edible, but there is no record of it. There are four large species of up to 2 meters inhabiting both the Gulf and the tidal (though not necessarily brackish) estuaries (*Polydactylus tetradactylus, Epihephelus taurina,* grouper, *Scomber guttatus,* and *S. comersoni* (Spanish mackerel). Twelve smaller species .2 to .8 meters in length also live in these waters: (*Sillago sihama,* a smelt; *Pomadasys argyreus,* a grunter; *Acanthopagus berda,* mud bream; *Gevres punctatus; Otolithes ruber,* a drum fish; *Drepane punctata; Scataphagus argus; Rachycentrum canadus,* a sergeant fish; *Caranx sexfasciatus,* horse mackerel; *Platycephalus indicus,* flathead; *Pseudorhombus indicus* and *Pseudorhombus arsius,* flounders; and

Cynoglossus lugus, a tongue fish.) Whether this greater concentration of species in the estuaries is accompanied by a greater total population of fish is not known. In addition the exact habitat preference of many of these fish, and thus the possible ways of catching them, is not known. Both ecological and ethnozoological studies are desperately needed.

There are at least three traditional ways of taking fish. One is with a hook. This is at present a small boy's occupation. Another is with a spear, the activity of solitary men in the day or two men with a light at night. The other is with a net. This requires a minimum of two men and a boat. It can be profitable to combine a number of nets and boats. At present this is done between February and April on the permanent lakes with groups of eight or ten men. Coordination is necessary both for the operation of the net and the speedy distribution of the fish, but the details of this are unknown (Salim, 1962:100).

Fresh fish are eaten more frequently between October and May when the weather is cool. Fish are dried after a fashion, and kept for considerable periods of time.

Game

Firearms replaced most traditional hunting techniques several centuries ago. Which of the many possible techniques is used to hunt animals like gazelles, onager, oryx, fallow deer, or any of the smaller mammals and the fowls is not known.

The pig was, until recently, hunted in the thickets and marshes with spears and pikes. It is likely that these weapons were also used as a defense against the larger carnivores noted previously.

TRADITIONAL CRAFTS

In considering subsistence, it is possible to eliminate from the ethnographic record most practices introduced since about 1000 B.C. and to profitably discuss the ethnographic data on all techniques which might be archeologically evidenced. For several reasons this is not desirable in the case of craft. (1) The natural resources of the crafts are flexible and in some cases the techniques of handling them change continuously. An exception is reeds, a rather complex skill performed in marsh communities. Modern and ancient reed products are indistinguishable. This craft is described in some detail by Salim (1962).

Otherwise it is difficult to speak of a basic complex of crafts. (2) In most cases, the craft resources themselves do not limit the organizations which handle them to the same extent as the subsistence resources. (3) In any event, the ethnographic record of the crafts is generally even poorer than that for subsistence activities.

TRADITIONAL CONSTRUCTION FOR SUBSISTENCE PRODUCTION

Buildings

Field shelters, storehouses, pens, stables, and so on, are necessary in subsistence production. Their construction and maintenance requires considerable skill and labor.

There are three broad traditional means of construction. One is mud construction. On the alluvium, straw-tempered, often saline mud is piled up about twenty centimeters each day until the walls are at the desired height. A small multiple room house takes two men about two weeks to build. With semiannual re-plastering such a structure can last for about fifteen years, but is normally abandoned in about ten. The salinity of the mud causes rapid cracking and spalling of the walls. Because walls deteriorate rapidly, the techniques of northern "tauf" construction such as special settling and curing of the mud and special plasterings would be a waste of effort and are not commonly used.

Another traditional means of construction is with mud brick. The bricks, which can be made by a variety of techniques, are usually made and dried on a canal bank, a source of relatively salt-free mud and water. They are carried by donkey to the construction site where a specialized builder and a few laborers lay them. Baked bricks can be used in the foundation, watertable, or doors, and ceramic drains can be inserted. Plastering and replastering protects the walls. The lifetime of such a building depends on the speed with which salt is drawn into the foundations by capillary action. This in turn depends on the dampness and salinity of the building site. In any event, this form of construction requires considerable labor and coordination.

The roofing of these two types of buildings is similar. Beams at present either poplar or split palm logs, are laid from wall to wall. A layer of reed mats is tied down and a layer of reeds is placed over it. Then mud is poured on top of the reeds. This must be replenished every few years and must be torn up and totally rebuilt when the weight of the roof becomes too great.

Another type of traditional construction is with cane and reed mats. A field hut can be built of these materials in a matter of hours. Larger buildings require the help of a specialized builder. The structures are supported by a number of cane arches, to which reed mats are tied. The time consumed in construction is a function of the number of arches and the elaborateness of the weaving and typing of canes and reeds. A reed structure has a life expectancy of ten years at most.

The above statements are all rather gross and all based on casual observation and interviewing. Studies are needed of the canons of present day mud and mud brick architecture and of the social organization of construction groups.

Banks and Ditches

Agriculture on the alluvium depends on the manipulation of water. Banking is undertaken in order to prevent the river from destroying fields and settlements and to prevent it from changing its course and forcing the abandonment of settled areas. The river tends to fill in its bed and thus eventually rises to a point well above the surrounding plain. The raised levee facilitates gravity irrigation and allows such irrigation to be conducted over a larger proportion of the year. On the other hand, should the break in the bank get out of control, the greater potential energy of the higher river will cause rapid enlarging of the break. Thus, banking leads to a greater probability of disaster, and requires more planning and control. Unfortunately, little information is available on the labor required in bank construction. In addition, it is not possible to study the affects of banking alone, since it always occurs together with ditching.

Flood irrigation has the disadvantage of always flooding the field nearest the bank, thus encouraging soil saturation and salt deposition. Ditching directs water to particular fields, and thus mitigates this. There are several important physical limitations on ditching. In the first place, as the water leaves the larger natural channel and enters the smaller artificial channel, its velocity drops. The heavier particles can no longer be carried and they are dropped immediately. Thus, the majority of silting is near the intake. This raises the bed of the canal and cuts off the volume of water reaching the outer fields. It does not necessarily affect the water supply of the inner fields, and the users of these fields have no particular reason to clean the canal bed. In the second place, the users of the inner fields have first choice of the water. It is possible that they would divert all of it through their fields and deprive the outer field users (see Fernea, 1959: 10-18 for a longer discussion).

From a social point of view canals can be divided into those external to farming units, constructed and cleaned by organized groups of men not necessarily connected with the nearby land; and those internal to farming units, constructed and maintained by small local groups of farmers at a leisurely pace. The construction of the large canals can occur gradually as groups of men extend the ditch a little farther each year. They must, however, be cleaned by a directed group, or else the greater amount of silt around the intake will not be removed. According to Fernea, the 900 farmers supported by a main canal a mile and a half long with an intake of 340 cubic meters per hour could clean the canal in one or two days. This group was called together by the Shaykh, who gave small gifts to those present and wrote down the names of those absent. The small ditches could be constructed quickly and cleaned at a more leisurely pace. Men spent forty to sixty hours cleaning these, over the course of as many as twenty days (Fernea, 1959:143-48).

At each branching, flow must be regulated. This can be done by limiting the size of the gate or pipe and by limiting the time it is open. If water is scarce, somebody must decide the size and time ratios, or self-help and conflict will prevail. Examples are known where conflict over water has broken social groupings down to the level of extended families (Fernea, 1959:142).

Canals are maintained until it is difficult to throw silt out of their bottoms. Then a new channel is dug beside them. Otherwise, canals are maintained until the fields around them become too salty. Then the immediate area must be abandoned. Both of these processes depend upon local conditions.

POPULATION, ECONOMY, AND SETTLEMENT

We have considered a variety of categories as discrete phenomena. Now let us consider some of them in an integrated perspective.

Subsistence and Population

Diet in southern Iraq includes grains, fruits, vegetables, milk products, meat, and fish. It is certain that these categories are in various ways interdependent: the animals benefit grain fields with their droppings; milk products and vegetable oils are used in the summer when meats and fish are difficult to store; orchards protect flocks in summer; and so on. Unfortunately quantitative data on most of these aspects of subsistence production are lacking, and one is forced to treat the integrated subsistence complex as if grains were dominant and other things were purely supplementary rather than necessary.

At present, in the Hilla-Diwaniyah area, a family of six needs six hectares of land to be supported without lowering the fertility of the soil. Of these six hectares, three are in fallow. The other three produce no less than 1500 kilograms of grain, of which the family members directly consume no more than 600. The remainder is used as fodder, seed, or as an exchange medium for other goods and services. This last output goes to an unknown extent to nonfarming craft and transport specialists. Therefore, six hectares actually support more than a family of six (Poyck, 1962:60-71).

Farmers who sharecrop for their land must produce enough to feed themselves after the crop is divided. Since they are members of estates, they profit by more efficient fallowing and water allocation and produce more crops per hectare, as was noted above. Should their share be fifty per cent then they should cultivate slightly less than twelve hectares, simply to survive. The additional six hectares, however, supports, when distributed, more than one nonagricultural family because such families are not feeding much livestock, and are exchanging their own products for the goods and services for which a farmer would exchange grain.

Thus to assume that every six hectares of cultivated land will support one family provides a minimal population estimate.

Let us consider a single hectare of well-cultivated land, half of which is in fallow and half of which is under barley. On the average, 450 kilograms of barley would be produced. Eleven per cent, or 60 kilograms, of this must be set aside for seed. Sixteen per cent or 75 kilograms must be fed to animals (Poyck, 1962:53). At least 25 per cent or about 115 kilograms can be assumed to be lost in storage. This leaves 200 kilos for consumption. Thus a hectare of cultivable land could support a maximum of about two adults. If budgets of loss in transport and storage were available and traditional diet were known, then the maximum number of people who could be supported with a hectare could be more accurately measured.

Subsistence and Labor

We have noted or implied that the following activities require group labor: plowing and seeding, harvesting, canal digging, canal cleaning, bank building, brick construction, and net fishing in lakes. In addition, the following activities require the regulation of quantity and timing: land reallocation, plowing and seeding, crop division, canal cleaning, water allocation, brick construction, the allocation of pregnant cattle, large-scale sheep herding, complex net fishing in lakes, and fish distribution. Of course, there are no doubt other activities of these types which we have missed. In addition there are other activities at which large groups could be employed or in which coordination would be useful, but neither of them are imperative: canal digging, sheep and goat shearing, and crop transport are examples.

Let us consider a labor problem, grain cultivation, in detail.

The limiting factor in traditional grain cultivation is harvest. A hectare requires two man-days of labor during the height of harvest activity, a period of about twelve days (Adams, 1965:15). Thus, a single laborer can cultivate and harvest up to 6.0 hectares. In independent farming 0.6 hectares is average, while in share crop farming 2.0 is average (Poyck, 1962:35). I suspect that when Iraqi farm families move to field huts to work from dawn to dusk, they do so not because they have a great deal of grain to harvest, but because they wish to remove the grain as soon as possible before a damaging change in weather.

Population and Settlement

Adams, in *Land Behind Baghdad* (1965), assumed that two hundred people lived on each hectare of settled area. This figure is reasonable for settlement pattern studies based upon surface survey, but for detailed studies of partially excavated settlements of a single period, a detailed reconsideration is warranted.

In Table 1, data on four settlements in the southern alluvium are given. The bulk of these data are from Al-Barazi (1961, Table 22). The first row is from my own observations of a village very much like the one I excavated. The first column is roughly estimated from air photographs presented in Poyck (1962).

Before consideration of this table, note that in this area there are now two distinct types of settlements in terms of household size. There are those whose sizes range from 6.5 to 7.4 people per household and tend to be about 7.25. There are those

TABLE 1
SOME CHARACTERISTICS OF FOUR MODERN IRAQI SETTLEMENTS

Settlements	Area in Hectares	Population	Houses	People/Hectare	Houses/Hectare	People/House
Sayeh South	6	96	16	16	2.7	6.0
B'dair	24	1587	282	66	11.0	5.6
Daghghara	23	2965	530	129	23.4	5.6
Diwaniyya	195	33204	3799	170	19.4	7.3

Note: Sayeh South: a settlement near Nasiriyyah; B'dair: a settlement on the Lower Daghghara canal, near Afaq; Daghghara: a settlement on the Upper Daghghara canal near Hilla.

whose sizes range from 5.2 to 6.4 people per household and tend to be about 6.0. The former type, as exemplified on our table by the city of Diwaniyya, have a predominance of large planned streets with modern concrete housing. The latter type, as exemplified by the first three settlements on our table, have unplanned streets and traditional mud-walled compounds. Since this traditional type more closely approximates the architecture of the third millennium B.C., I will not consider the second type any further other than to note that population density is a partial function of architectural type and that to assume a general figure for all times and places on the alluvium is very much an heuristic device.

Turning to the first three cases on the table, one can note that even with so few cases, certain relationships stand out. First note that, though architecture is controlled, density varies immensely. Second, note that as one would expect, population and number of houses are linearly related. These two closely related pairs show a general rank correlation. None of these variables, however, show a linear relationship to area. This is probably because, as settlements increase in population, houses are constructed closer and closer together. It is difficult to test this idea with only three cases. For our purposes it suffices to state that in order to estimate population, we will have to consider the size and distribution of housing units in the case of each settlement.

SUMMARY

This chapter has presented the minimum data and relationships between data which we must draw from the natural history and ethnography of Iraq if the various aspects of the economy are to be inferred from the archeological record.

III

EARLY DYNASTIC UR: THE CONTEXT

IN this chapter I will present some background information on Ur, the specific case to be considered. I will discuss the following topics: (1) the history of the region of Ur; (2) the geography of the entire Tigris-Euphrates alluvium during the period at which the case is being considered; (3) the detailed geography of the vicinity of Ur during this period; and (4) the economic and social organization within the town itself. Rural organization, the major focus of this work, will be dealt with in detail in the next chapter.

SOUTHERN SUMER IN THE THIRD AND FOURTH MILLENNIA B.C.

Settled communities existed in Southern Sumer long before the outlines of economy and society became clear (Lloyd and Safar, 1948). In Late 'Ubaid times at about 4000 B.C., two, perhaps three, branches of the Euphrates flowed through the region of Ur and Eridu.[1] The small town of Ur was on the northern branch. The small town of Eridu was on the southern branch. Six-row barley, emmer wheat, and flax were grown in irrigated fields (Helbaek, 1960). Baked clay sickles, a common Late 'Ubaid and Uruk agricultural tool are distributed along channels within bands about five kilometers wide (see Fig. 2). This requires only small irrigation canals. About 400 square kilometers were within the cultivated bands. The remaining 1200 were alluvial desert or marsh. In total there were about 50 hectares of settled area suggesting a population of about 10,000 and a population density of about 25 people per square kilometer. Slightly more than half lived in small rural settlements. Surface remains indicate that considerable food preparation and ceramic manufacture occurred on these settlements. None has been adequately excavated. Slightly less than half the population lived in towns at Ur and Eridu. Only the peripheries of the former have been investigated (Woolley, 1956). In the latter, there was a temple on a platform in

[1]The settlement pattern data discussed in this section are unpublished data collected by the author in 1966.

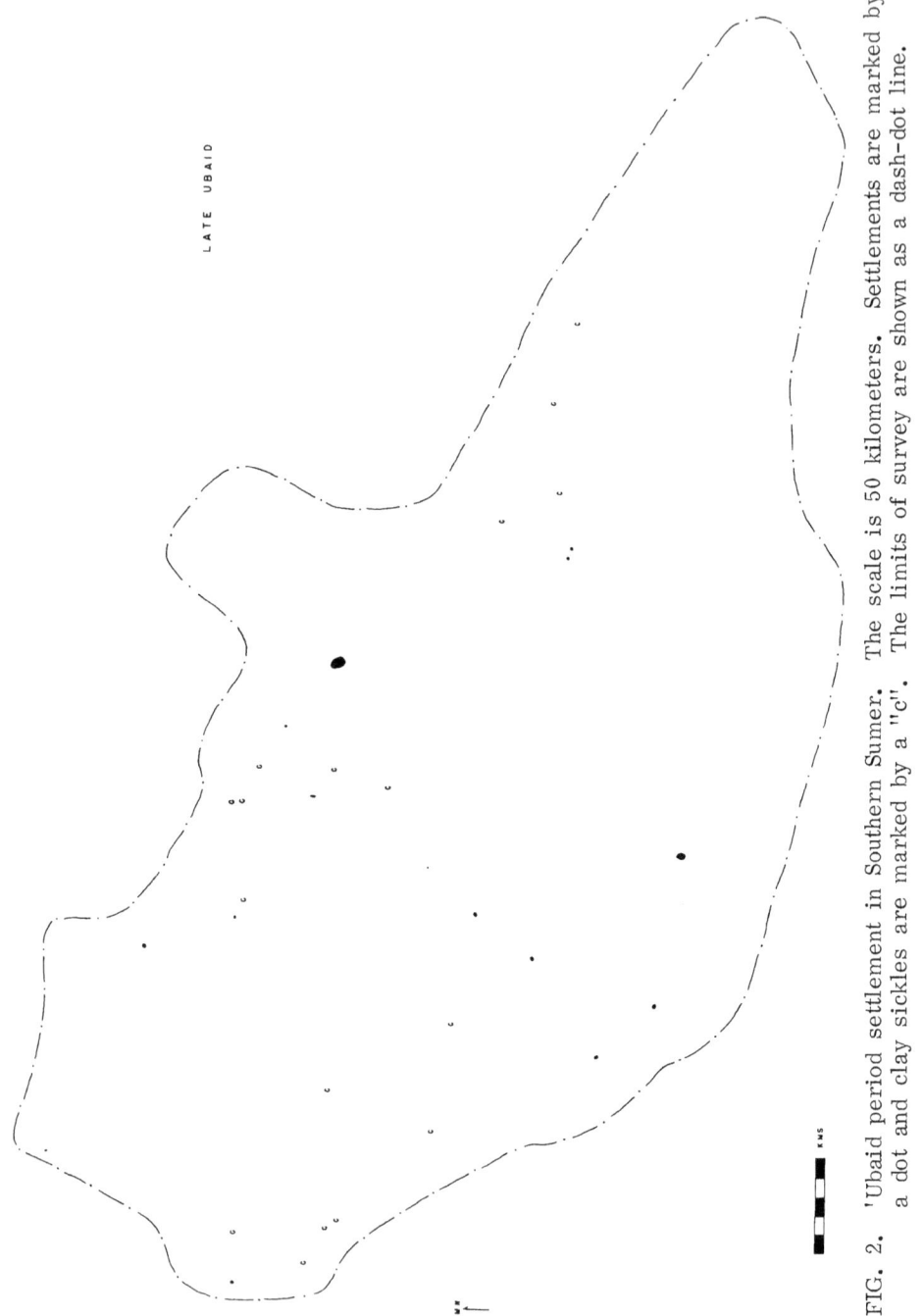

FIG. 2. 'Ubaid period settlement in Southern Sumer. The scale is 50 kilometers. Settlements are marked by a dot and clay sickles are marked by a "c". The limits of survey are shown as a dash-dot line.

the central part of the town. Around this were substantial mud-brick buildings. In the lower surrounding town were less substantial mud-brick houses (Lloyd and Safar, 1947; 1948; Campbell-Thompson, 1919). Small sailing craft probably moved goods up and down the river channels (Safar, 1950). There is little indication of funeral ritual differences indicating differences in rank (Safar, 1950). Thus, though little is known about social and political organization, some of the gross economic and demographic features of traditional Mesopotamian life were established by this time.

In the succeeding Uruk period, of about 3500 B.C., there were changes in settlement pattern. Eridu became a large town. Ur, judging by the excavated remains, was unimportant. It is possible that the Ur channel decreased in size. Small rural settlements are rare. One was spread out along a canal bank for several hundred meters. The scarcity of rural settlement may be due to their very small size and consequent covering by alluvium. For this reason I am hesitant to present population estimates.

In the succeeding Jemdet Nasr period, about 3200 B.C., Ur regained its importance (Woolley, 1956), and Eridu was largely abandoned (Lloyd and Safar, 1947). A village upstream from old Eridu became a small town with public buildings and craft areas. The great temple of Nanna at Ur was founded by this time (Woolley, 1939). Rural sites are hard to recognize and site sizes are difficult to measure because their ceramics are easily "masked" by similar later types. Once again population estimates would be misleading.

During the succeeding first portion of the Early Dynastic period, to be discussed in detail subsequently, the old Eridu channel was largely abandoned. Settlement was restricted to a 90 square kilometer enclave with an estimated population of 6,000 people, about 66 people per square kilometer. The towns of Ur and Sakheri contained the great majority of the people.

In the later portion of the Early Dynastic period, about 2400 B.C., Ur appears in history as a small centralized state. Ur may approach its later 50 hectare size implying a population approaching 10,000. The old rural settlements upstream from Ur were abandoned, but administrative buildings (Safar, 1950) and rural centers were built in the Eridu area and a ten kilometer canal was built to the northeast of Ur. One of the four sites along this canal exhibits only small quantities of the usual refuse. It may have been a rural estate. The few documents recovered from Ur (Burrows, 1935), the elaborate grave series from Ur

(Woolley, 1934), and the temple at 'Ubaid (Hall and Woolley, 1927) illustrate the social stratification in the city and the political and military organization of the First Dynasty of Ur.

Only three towns survive into the period of the Empire of Agade of about 2200 B.C. This represents a nadir in southern Sumer. By 2000 B.C. the area quickly recovered to become the political center of alluvial Mesopotamia. This is not relevant to this brief introduction.

SETTLEMENTS OF THE ALLUVIUM *CA.* 2800 B.C.

To further elucidate the context of the case in point, let us consider some aspects of the cultural geography of the entire alluvium during the very end of the Jemdet Nasr period, and the first phase of the Early Dynastic period. The work of the Iraq surface survey is especially useful in this endeavor for several reasons. First, ceramics distinctive to the period form a large proportion of the ceramic complex, are durable even when exposed to surface weathering, and they are easily recognized when present. Second, while levels of the later Sargonid or Ur III periods are often eroded away, the deeper Early Dynastic levels are often just being exposed. Thus, in the surveyed areas, the record of settlements is amazingly complete.

The surveyed areas are shown in Figure 3.[2] Four main areas have been intensively surveyed: (1) the Eshnunna-Tutub area totaling about 8,000 square kilometers (Adams, 1965), (2) the Sippar-Nippur area totaling about 3,000 square kilometers (Adams, 1958), (3) the Uruk-Larsa-Umma area totaling about 6,000 square kilometers (Adams, personal communication), and (4) the Ur-Eridu area totaling about 2,000 square kilometers. The first is the only area of the Tigris drainage examined. The former middle and lower Tigris flood plain has not been examined. The latter three survey areas are centered on the ostensible former main course of the Euphrates (Jacobsen, 1960). Only small segments of the former southern branch through Borsippa and Marash, and the early northern branch through Lagash have been examined in any detail.

In some surveyed areas, settlement of the first phase of the Early Dynastic is in small enclaves. In the first mentioned area,

---

[2]The settlement map for the first phase of the Early Dynastic period of the northern alluvium have been constructed from site and artifact field notes kindly made available to me by Dr. Robert Adams.

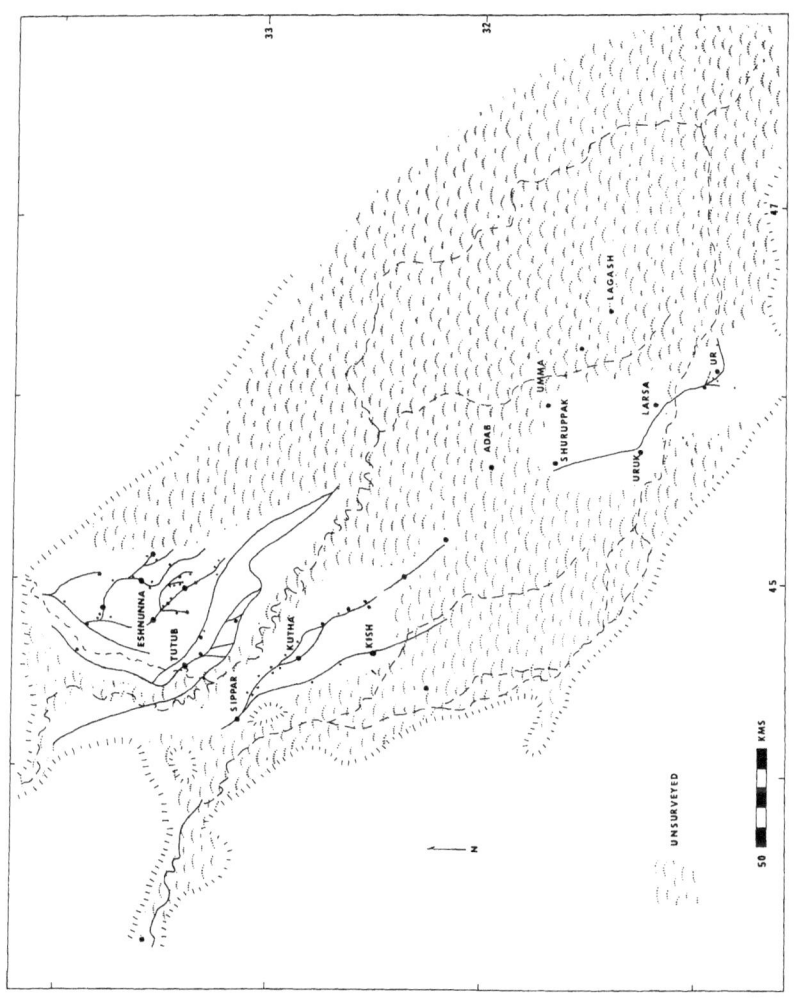

FIG. 3. Settlement in Lower Iraq during the early third millennium. Modern channels are dotted and ancient channels are solid. Large dots are large towns, medium dots are small towns, and small dots are villages.

the modern Diyala region, there are two enclaves. The larger is on a system of small canals southeast of Eshnunna. Here four large towns are on the periphery of an enclave containing four small towns and sixteen villages or hamlets. Three of the large towns were upstream from the other settlements in the cluster. The smaller enclave is on canals south and east of Tutub. It contains one large town, three or four small towns, and a village. The large town is upstream from the other settlements. North of these two enclaves near the Jebel Hamrin there is a scatter of settlements of various sizes. Whether this is a result of intense cultivation in the area of the last century or whether this represents a former sparse distribution of settlements is not known.

In the second mentioned area, a portion of ancient Akkad, there are no separate enclaves. Two types of patterns may be arbitrarily separated. To the north and east of Kutha toward Sippar are eleven village and hamlet-sized settlements strung along the main channels of the Euphrates. Kutha and Sippar are probably large towns. There are no definite small towns. Below Kutha is a pattern composed of a string of at least four small towns and two villages along a main channel of the Euphrates.

Data from the third mentioned area, a portion of Central Sumer, has not been analyzed in detail.

In the fourth mentioned area, a portion of Southern Sumer, there was a single settlement enclave around Ur. This will be considered in great detail later. It contained a large town and a small town on the main channel. There were three small hamlets scattered between these towns on the channel and on subsidiary canals.

From the above discussion one thing is clear: no two settlement areas are alike in pattern. There are likely to be a number of factors underlying these variations: (1) the type of water situation—a few main channels, as in Akkad, as opposed to a rami fying set of smaller and smaller channels as on the Diyala; (2) th position in a cycle of land use—relatively new, as around Tutub, or developed, as around Eshnunna. Demonstrably old enclaves, in decline during the first phase of the Early Dynastic, perhaps exist in Central Sumer, but maps are not yet available; (3) the ratio of types of cultivation—areas of predominant intensive cultivation, especially orchard crops, as opposed to areas of predominant extensive cultivation, especially grain. There is as yet no archeological evidence on this point. (4) Brigandage—smaller enclaves would be less able to defend themselves against marauders and one could expect few small hamlets or villages in them. Such is the case around Tutub, below Kutha, and around Ur, all of which are small enclaves.

Very little is known about economic relations between enclaves in this period. The principal imports into the alluvium included bitumen, flint, copper, alabaster and similar stones for vessels, and basalt and similar stones for grinding slabs. Two large towns on the fringes of the alluvium are associated with the first two of these imports. Tell Aswad, on the Middle Euphrates just above the alluvium, exhibits asphalt debris in quantity on the fresh-cut river bank. Perhaps this town was the center for the exploitation of the bitumen sources at Hīt, a short distance up the river. Tell Abū Rāsain, the only large town in the northern Diyala region, has concentrations of worked flint on its surface (Adams, 1965). Perhaps this town was on a route by which flint was brought from sources in the Zagros. Doubtless there are other towns through which these materials, and others listed above, were carried to the alluvial communities.

Evidence on the distribution of goods between major towns is provided by a series of seal impressions from Ur (Legrain, 1936). These result when the seals of storehouse keepers are impressed into the still soft clay caps on containers. These particular sealings have the signs of seven towns, some of which tend to occur with each other more than would be expected by chance alone. Table 2 shows that Ur and Larsa, Larsa and Adab, and Adab and Keš tend to occur on a single seal. The map of Figure 3 shows that these associated towns tend to be close to each other and in direct water communication. A system by which a storehouse in a town is related to those in several nearby towns, and which can build up into chains of interrelated towns stretching from one end of the alluvium to the other, is implied. Absent from the seals are other relatively important towns: Umma, Lagash, and Kish. These and other towns may belong to other systems of linked storehouses. It is unfortunate that there is no evidence indicating what material or product was being sealed into the containers.

Nothing is known of the political relations between enclaves of settlement during this period.

In summary, at about 2800 B.C., the Tigris-Euphrates alluvial plain was traversed by at least four major river channels with numerous smaller tributaries and offshoots. On these channels were a number of small settled and cultivated enclaves and areas each including one or more towns of various sizes. Scarce materials such as petroleum, metals, and stones were imported onto the alluvium from the surrounding regions through trade centers on the alluvial edge. These resources, and most probably

TABLE 2

CITY NAMES ON THE ARCHAIC SEAL IMPRESSIONS

Seal Number	City						
	Ur	Larsa	Abad	Keš	É. Anna	(Bird)	(Snake)
398	X	X	X	...	...	...	...
400	X	...	X	X	...	...	...
401	X	...	X	X	...	...	...
402	...	...	X	X	...	...	...
404	X	...	...	...	X	...	...
407	...	X	X	...	X	...	...
410	X	X	...	...	X	...	...
412	...	X	X	...	...	...	...
413	...	X	X	...	...	...	...
414	X	X	...	...	...	...	X
415	...	X	X	X	...	X	X
416	X	X	...	...	X	...	...
417	...	X	...	...	...	X	X
421	X	X	...	...	...	X	X
424	...	...	...	...	...	X	...
429	X	X	...	...	...	...	...

City	Ur	Larsa	Abad	Keš	É. Anna	(Bird)	(Snake)
Ur	...	6/9	3/9	3/9	3/9	1/9	1/9
Larsa	6/11	...	5/11	2/11	3/11	3/11	3/11
Adab	3/8	5/8	...	4/8	1/8	1/8	1/8
Keš	3/5	2/5	4/5	...	0/5	0/5	1/4
É. Anna	3/4	3/4	1/4	0/4	...	0/4	0/4
(Bird)	1/4	3/4	1/4	0/4	0/4	...	2/4
(Snake)	1/3	3/3	1/3	1/3	0/3	2/3	...

products of the alluvium itself, were distributed from enclave to enclave by water under some type of intercity exchange arrangement whose economic and political structure is not known.

UR AS AN URBAN SYSTEM *CA.* 2800 B.C.

It is not yet possible to describe any early Mesopotamian settlement enclave in detail or to propose and test hypotheses about any urban system as a whole. In this section I will briefly describe the settlement pattern of this enclave as a whole, and present what is known about the organization of activities in the town or Ur. This will provide background for our detailed consideration of the organization of the rural economy.

The enclave of settlement around Ur occupies the northeastern edge of the area surveyed in 1966. The formerly inhabited land to the south around Eridu was largely abandoned alluvial desert, with old canals and depressions filling with water only in spring and with only a few small settlements surviving. Fifteen kilometers to the south were the great dunes and beyond these the stony desert. The southern margin and the upstream end of the enclave are well studied. If the downstream end is considered to be the effective walking limit from Ur, then the enclave was a small one of 9000 hectares.

Five types of features occur within this enclave: the first is the channel of an ancient water course. At least one of the many channels visible on the air photographs dates to the Early Dynastic period. This comes from the northeast and bifurcated at the town of Sakheri. These two marks then disappear under the silt cover left by later cultivation. The main channel probably curved around the southwest side of Ur, since the site was more built up on this side, and flowed northeast into areas not yet investigated. Evidence of a small canal not definitely visible on the air photos was excavated at the village of Sakheri Sughir. The possible canal ran from west to east. Prior to or during the early stages of the village's occupation, a channel was dug south of the site, but it was allowed to fill with sand and refuse. During the later stages of the site's history, the mound dropped off abruptly to the north. In addition, this slope of the mound received great lenses of clean silt, in volumes out of all proportion to the quantity of mud-brick construction in the area. It seems probable, though not proven, that a small canal ran along this side of the mound. By analogy with the bifurcation at Sakheri and the small canal at Sakheri Sughir, I have shown similar canals branching off the main channel of the Euphrates on the conjectural map of the enclave (Fig. 4). The actual pattern was doubtless more complex.

The second type of feature is the town site. The major town, Ur, may have covered about twenty hectares. This is based on the assumption that the southeast end of the mound was not settled until late Early Dynastic times, when much secular housing on the northwest end was replaced by public buildings. There is no direct evidence of this. The site was definitely reveted on the southeast, and may have been completely surrounded by a low wall. Urban land use as revealed by Woolley's excavations, will be discussed below. The minor town, Sakheri, was up the main channel to the northwest of Ur. Surface traces of the period cover eight hectares. Air photos reveal a complete town wall,

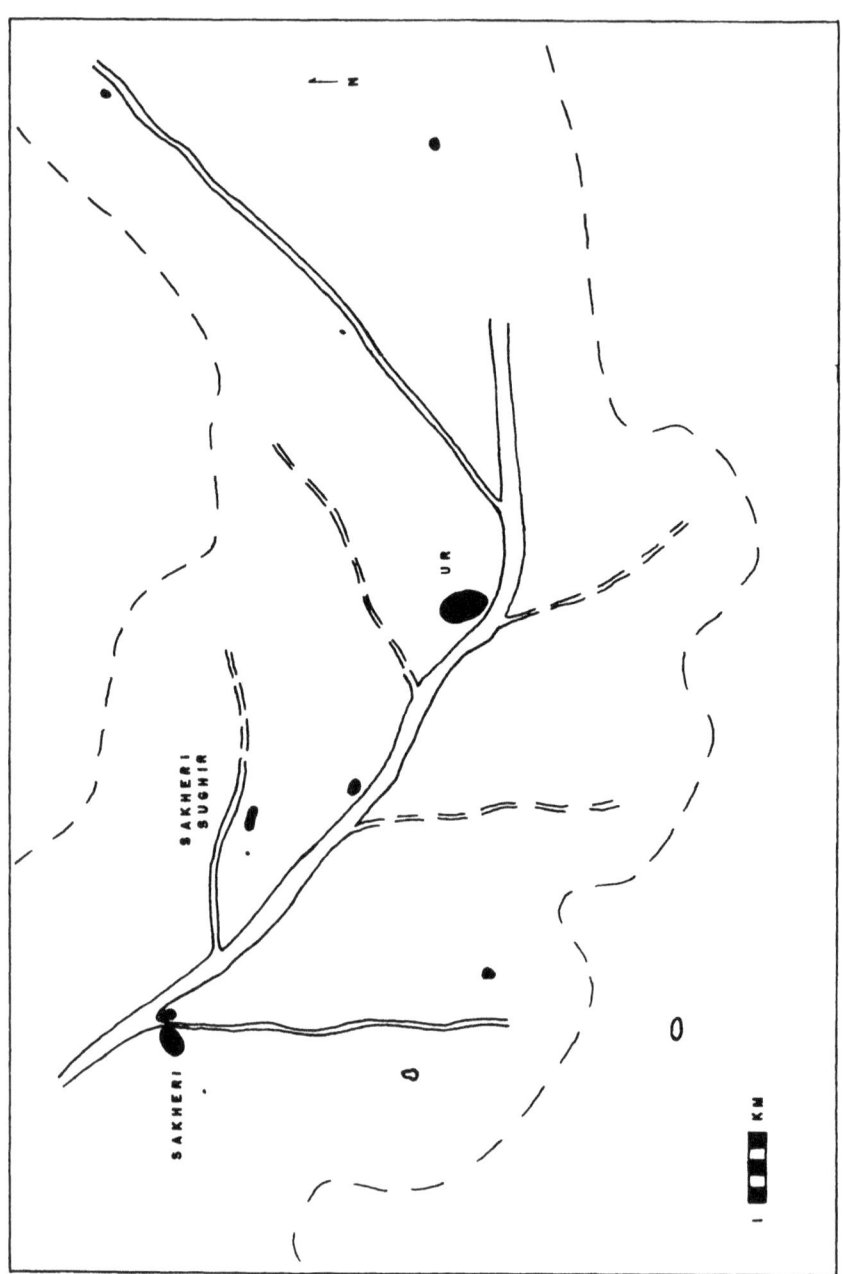

FIG. 4. The Ur enclave during the first phase of the Early Dynastic period. The dashed line is the probable outer limit of cultivation, solid circles are settlements, open circles are cemeteries.

but its date is unknown. Concentrations of very large jar sherds, kiln wasters, and baked plano-convex bricks suggest storage areas, craft areas, and public buildings, respectively. Little more can be said without excavation.

A third type of feature is the village or hamlet site. The three such sites in this area are less than two hectares in size. As will be discussed in the next chapter, structures were widely scattered on these sites and they rose only slowly, never exceeding a few meters in height. Thus some may be invisible below the later alluvium. One of three in the area under consideration, the site of Shaman, is probably on the main channel halfway between Ur and Sakheri. Though the situation is obscured by much later debris, the village probably covered about one hectare and contained ten dwelling compounds. To the north is Sakheri Sughir, sounded by a joint operation of the University of Chicago Oriental Institute and the Iraq Directorate General of Antiquities in 1966. It covers an area of one and a half hectares in the middle of the first phase of the Early Dynastic period. It could have contained 15 dwelling compounds. To the southwest of Shaman was a small unnamed hamlet site. It is triangular in shape and covered four-tenths of a hectare. It could have contained three compounds. These three sites, one south of the main channel, one north of the main channel, and one on that channel, are roughly halfway between Ur and Sakheri in an area not within convenient walking distance of either town.

A fourth kind of feature can be called a "rural center" in absence of a clear understanding of the activities conducted in it. One of these is known at Tell 'Ubaid. It is located on the north end of the 'Ubaid period village site. It was excavated by Hall and Woolley (1927) and reinvestigated and considerably clarified by Delougaz (1938). Most of the known remains date to the final phase of the Early Dynastic period. Leveled by this later building activity was an earlier oval compound with a series of rooms facing inward to the court. There was a single entrance from the outside. Presumably the later temple platform obliterated some kind of shrine in the center of the court. A few fragments of possible lexical texts suggest that scribes worked here, at least in later times. It is not certain that this oval compound is from the first phase of the Early Dynastic period, but since a cemetery of that phase occurs on the south end of the mound of 'Ubaid, and since the complex was founded no later than the preceding Jemdet Nasr period, such seems reasonable.

A fifth type of feature is cemeteries. Two are known. Both are on natural sandy knolls with evidences of prehistoric occupation.

One is at 'Ubaid. It will be discussed in detail in the next chapter. Another is southeast of 'Ubaid and southwest of Ur on what must have been the fringes of cultivation. This unnamed and completely eroded site was littered with fine stone bowl fragments more reminiscent of the burials at Ur than those at 'Ubaid. It may have been a cemetery for the town dwellers of Ur.

These various types of features must have occupied much of the 9000 hectares in the enclave. In addition, it is likely that sites of earlier periods, flooded areas, and salty areas removed more land from cultivation. Assuming one-third to be thus eliminated by analogy with comparable modern situations (Poyck, 1962), 6000 cultivatable hectares would remain.

It would be difficult to consider the organization of an urban system as a whole without adequate samples of observations on the craft and political centers. In the following paragraphs I will summarize the little that is known about such areas.

Between 1920 and 1932 the site of Ur was extensively investigated by the British Museum and the University of Pennsylvania under the direction of Sir Leonard Woolley. He attempted to reveal the main temple area as it was around 2000 B.C. Only limited areas of the Early Dynastic settlement were revealed. These remains are shown in Figures 5 and 6. In addition, some of the clay tablets provide information relevant to the organization of activity in the town.

First let us consider urban land use. Four general types of land use can be described. The first is for temple areas. These are elaborately planned complexes often with an outer wall surrounding utility rooms of various kinds and an inner court and shrine or shrines often on a raised platform. The temple and ziggurat of Nanna at Ur is a particularly large example. When probable storerooms, kitchens, guardrooms, and shrines are eliminated from consideration, there is dwelling room for no more than twenty attendants in this mammoth complex. Since the structure of the first phase of the Early Dynastic was destroyed down to its foundations there is no artifactual debris of this period reported. The debris in the duplicate later Early Dynastic structure is predominantly sealings removed from storage containers, bits of inlay and statuary which probably once decorated the complex, and weapons fragments—clay "sling missiles," spear points, and a bitumen mace head. The latter item is now used on shepherds' staffs. Ceramics are rare. The large size of the possible kitchens suggests that on occasion many people were fed at once.

EARLY DYNASTIC UR: THE CONTEXT

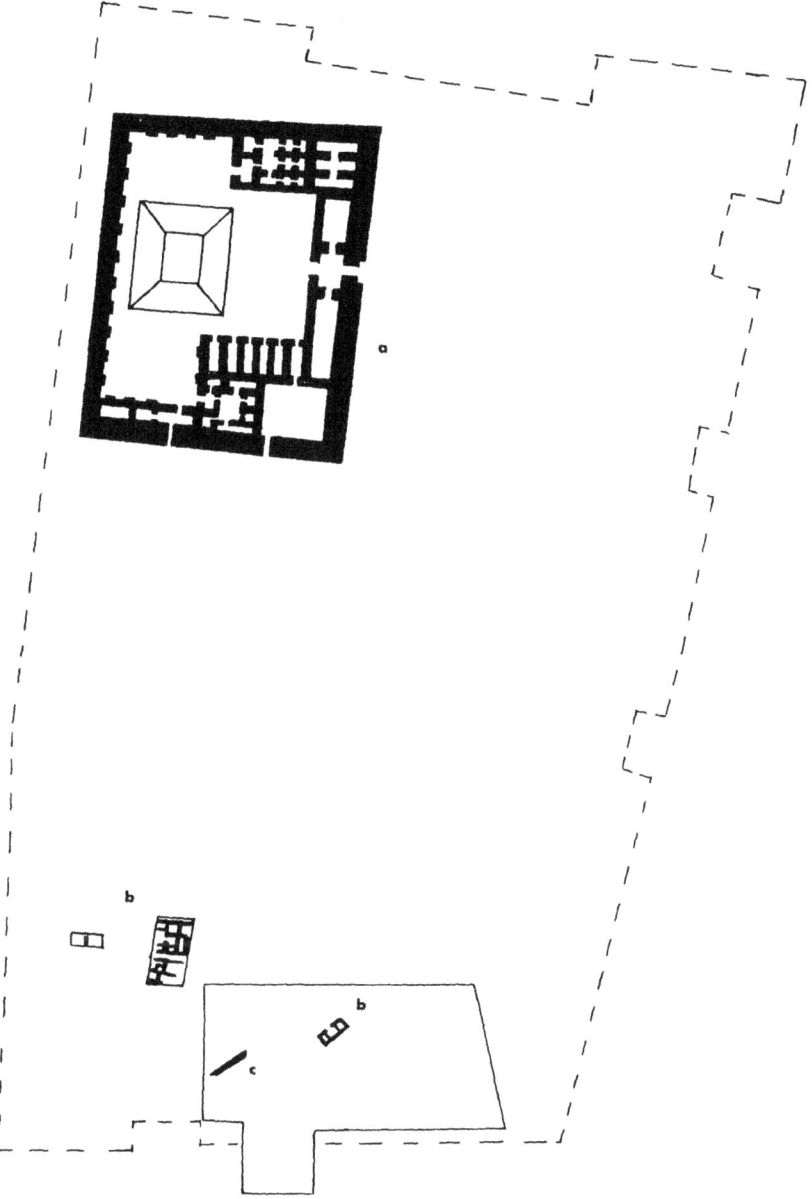

FIG. 5. The town of Ur during the first phase of the Early Dynastic period. The dotted line marks the borders of the Neo-Babylonian: *a*. the Temple of Nanna; *b*. small buildings; *c*. a fragment of a revetment around the town.

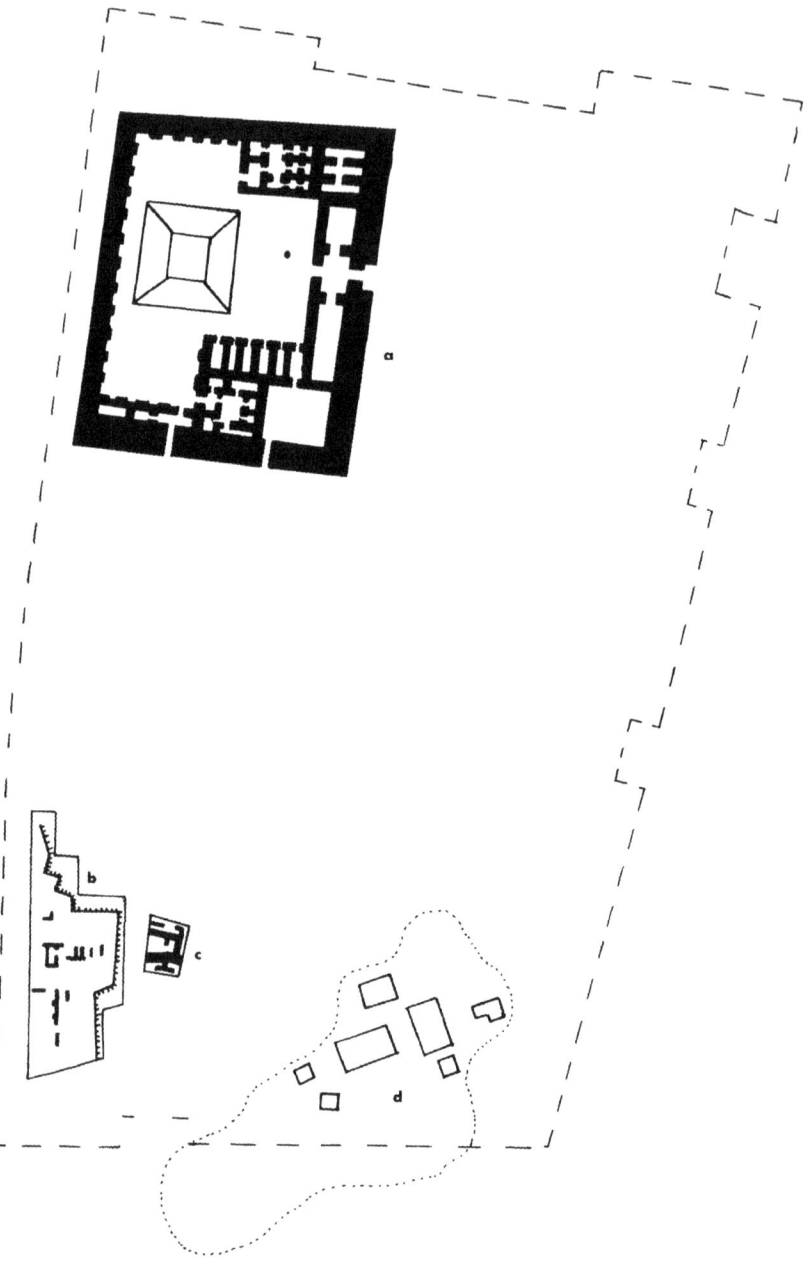

FIG. 6. The town of Ur during the last phase of the Early Dynastic period: *a*. the Temple of Nanna; *b*. planned structures on an earth platform; *c*. large buildings; *d*. the royal cemetery.

EARLY DYNASTIC UR: THE CONTEXT

A second use for town land is for large secular building complexes. Though such buildings must have been the source of the many tablets and container sealings thrown over the southeast revetment, the area southeast of the Nanna temple where they probably stood was not adequately investigated. The better examples of such buildings of the later Early Dynastic period were found above the smaller structures discussed in the next paragraph. These structures show much variation. One complex has massive outer walls and light, irregular, interior partitions leaving small rooms. Another complex has planned, but rather light construction with large courts and a variety of rooms. In these structures, ovens, braziers, and discarded bone suggest some cooking activity. Small ornaments are relatively frequent. Seals, seal impressions, accounting tablets, and a variety of unique finds occur. Small cups and unspouted jars are common. Very large jars seem to be distinctive to this type of structural complex. This type of complex is most poorly understood and probably most crucial to understanding how towns were organized. It is possible that this type of structural complex contained such things as high status dwellings, servants' quarters, storerooms, workshops, and so on.

A third use for town land is for small secular building complexes. Several levels of such architecture were investigated on the southeast side of the mound. Rooms are small and closely packed. Allowing three rooms to a family of six, densities of three hundred people on a hectare would be possible. Grinding stones, braziers, jewelry, and other unique small finds occur. Conical cups and small unspouted jars are common. Medium- and large-sized spouted jars seem distinctive to this type of structural complex. The absence of ovens in these structures is striking. Presumably these are the dwellings of the working population.

A final use of town land is as location for a dump and cemetery. Apparently only the steep edge of the mound outside the town's revetments was used for these purposes.

In the absence of adequate architectural information, 200 people per hectare are assumed for the towns. Ur would have had 4,000 inhabitants. Sakheri would have had 1,600 inhabitants. Having seven people per rural residence unit, about 200 people would have lived in rural settlements. Assuming that some rural settlements were not located in the survey, the Ur enclave would have had about 6,000 inhabitants.

From the artifacts found in these various areas, the practice of the following crafts at Ur can be inferred:

a) throwing and firing of ceramics

b) cutting of stone bowls (the cutting head of a rotary drill for rounding out the inside of stone bowls was found on the dump)

c) smithing of copper vessels

d) hand spinning (spindle whorls were found)

e) seal cutting.

The many other crafts that must have existed can only be directly demonstrated through better samples and better methods.

Some of the texts provide evidence, direct or indirect, of production and administration in the town itself. First, however, a description of the findspot and the character of the tablet sample is necessary.

The tablets were found with the seal impressions in the strata of burned debris on the southeast slope of the town. These strata at times coalesced into one stratum, and fragments of a single tablet sometimes appeared in both strata. Thus the strata seem to result from the clearing away of a single, burned structure or group of structures. Presumably most of the tablets were written in the space of a few years.

The tablets were studied by Burrows (1935). Of the 375 catalogued by him, about 220 are large enough to be useful in a study of content. Very few of these are undamaged. Most are small portions of the original text. The bulk of these involve rural production. They deal with land, grain, animals, reeds, trees, fish, or food allotted to individuals who are connected with these products in some way. These will be considered in Chapter VI.[3]

Here we will consider (1) scribal activity itself, (2) some specialists and officials mentioned in passing in the texts, and (3) some groups of people who apparently had special duties in the town.

The presence of scribes is clearly demonstrated by the existence of texts, however, there is no definite reference to the scribal craft in the texts. Nevertheless, certain points are clear. First, the mixture of economic and practice texts suggests that scribes were trained in the place of business. Some texts are merely practice markings. In addition, there are a number of sign lists including the names of statuses, fish, gods, and feasts,

---

[3]The following modified system is used for transcribing Sumerian: When the reading of a syllable is known, it is written with lower case letters, when not, it is written with upper case letters. When the proper order is known then the syllables are separated by a period, when not, they are separated by a colon.

which much have been used in training. Second, scribes recorded literary compositions in spite of the simplicity of the writing system. One fragment is from a work about Abzu, the personification of the Deeps, and various birds. This is the oldest reported literary fragment (Biggs, 1966:79). It is possible that such efforts represent a hobby or pastime of the scribes.

There are no texts which explicitly deal with other town specialists or craftsmen in any organized way. Nevertheless, when two individuals having the same name are mentioned in a text, then they are distinguished by some additional appellation. Often this appellation is the name of the man's craft or specialty. Burrows collected the names of eighty of these specialists. Eliminating those referring to administrative or ritual positions and those whose meaning or context are not clear, eight remain:

šidim.gal	chief bricklayer
nagar	carpenter
simug	smith
nu.kir$_x$(SAR)	gardener
muḫaldim	cook
en.giz	kitchen supervisor
MUNU$_3$.MÚ	maltster
a.zu	physician

Several important buildings are mentioned. The AB was an institution with a large storehouse and a staff. A temple for Nanna is not mentioned in the texts, though its archeological remains are clear. It may be that the AB was the temple of Nanna, but was not given its later name until it was necessary to distinguish the AB or Ur from that of other towns.

The é-gal, the palace, is also mentioned. Though officials of the lugal, the resident of the palace, are mentioned; and though a number of personal names refer to the lugal, there is no convincing direct reference to this personage. It is possible that at this time Ur had no resident lugal but was subordinate to that of another town. If the lugal were less important, however, than he later became, it would be difficult to tell his title from his personal name. This role is poorly understood.

It is likely that many of the texts listing rations of food and other items, and listing groups of people, in fact refer to the organizing and provisioning of people working in the town. However, in only a few examples is there any indication on the tablet that such might be so. Four possible cases are listed below.

The AB.—Text 50 records the giving of bread of the AB to various people. Two loaves go to one individual and five to another. Five or six go to the female servants of the AB. These people may have cared for the storehouse, or performed some unknown activity connected with the institution.

Text 95 records the exchange of 73 gur of grain (NINDA$_2$x BAPPIR.sa$_{10}$) from the AB and the allotting of 94 gur of grain for eating (še.kú) to three important people.

The Temple of Inanna.— Text 72 records the disposition of bread associated with the goddess of Innana. Of the thirty loaves, eight of them are actually offered to the goddess. The rest are apparently given to various people. Perhaps these are the custodians of the temple.

Text 93 records a similar disposition of bread to a number of groups in addition to Innana and her associates. The É.AN, the house of the god, and the ki:GEME$_2$, the place of women, and various individuals and office holders also received bread.

Several additional texts dealing with the AB and with Innana are known. The above examples serve to illustrate this type of text relevant to town activities.

SUMMARY

The context of the rural economy of the enclave around Ur in the first phase of the Early Dynastic is generally clear: On the southern alluvium there was a trend toward fewer and larger settlements. Ur was a larger town in a small cultivated enclave. The town was tied to others up the river in some sort of exchange relations. The town had a few surrounding smaller settlements. There were some central institutions—a storehouse, various temples, and a palace—in some way interrelated. A variety of officials and craftsmen worked in the town. The organization of these statuses and institutions is unclear, and will remain so until more contemporary documentation is available. Nevertheless, the organization of rural production can be studied without complete understanding of town organization.

IV

A RURAL COMMUNITY

IN this chapter I will consider a rural community: its physical structure, its technology, and its inhabitants. While it is clear that only a small segment of the agricultural work force lived in such rural settlements, we can be certain that evidence from such a settlement pertains to rural laborers. On the other hand, it is difficult to ascribe any domestic structure in a town to either town or rural laborers.

INTRODUCTION

Fieldwork at the small site of Sakheri Sughir was previously described in the preface. The position of the site in the settlement pattern was discussed in Chapter III. In the following pages the types and distributions of features and artifacts are discussed. The artifact count is presented in Appendix II.

The ancient settlement is now marked by an irregular scatter of potsherds, 250 meters from east to west and 110 meters from north to south. Much of this scatter results from eroded peripheral dumps of later Early Dynastic times. During the period of interest, the middle portion of the first phase of the Early Dynastic period, the site was about 230 meters by 70 meters, or about 1.5 hectares. At this time the site was about one and a half meters above the plain level. The initial occupation was probably near the beginning of the Early Dynastic period. The final occupation was perhaps during the middle phase of the Early Dynastic period. At this time the little mound may have risen as high as three meters. Two processes have all but obliterated the mound: irrigation of the first and second millennia B.C. deposited silt on the plain and raised its surface about two meters. Erosion lowered its summit, leaving only the peripheral dumps of the later occupations. The site is virtually invisible (see Fig. 7).

The site was selected from among the three between Ur and Sakheri because it is in danger of obliteration by expanding modern cultivation.

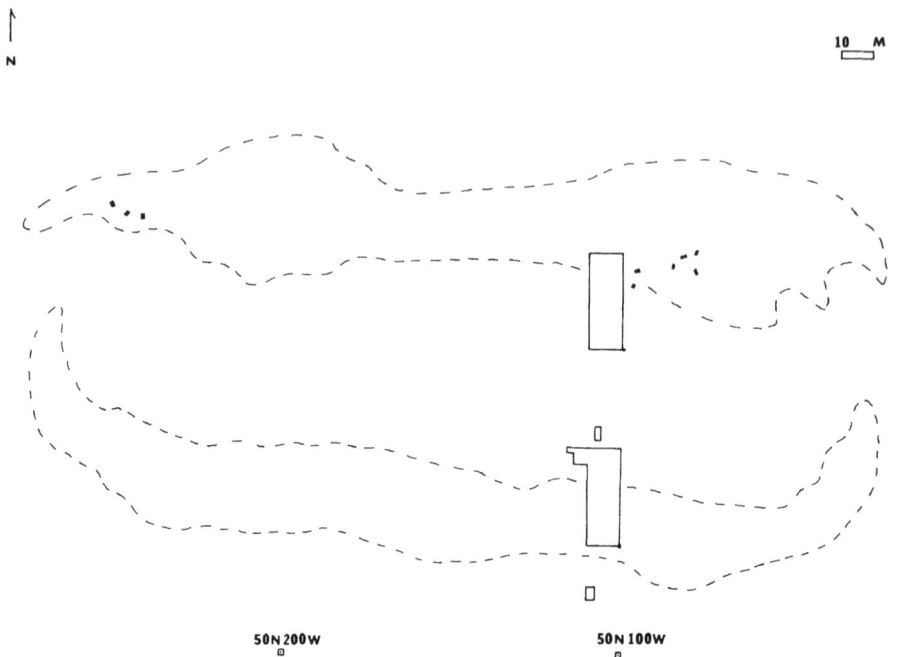

FIG. 7. Sakheri Sughir. The dotted line encloses the concentrations of sherds marking dumps; the solid-lined rectangles are excavations; the small black rectangles represent baked bricks.

The original plan of excavation was based on the erroneous assumption that recognizable architecture would be found immediately below the surface. I intended to clean two ten-meter-wide strips across the site from north to south along two randomly selected lines, completely exposing the uppermost level. In fact 30 centimeters or more of weathered debris had to be removed before mud construction was recognizable. Only two 10 by 30 meter blocks in one of the strips could be investigated. About three per cent of the middle Early Dynastic I settlement was examined.

Separate sets of stratigraphic numbers were assigned to the two blocks. Two small soundings were carried down to the Early Dynastic plain level—one, to the south of the site, provided information on the original plain level and on the characteristics of irrigation deposited silts. As mentioned in Chapter III, direct evidence of a shallow ditch running along the south edge of the settlement was found. A section showing this ditch and an overlapping sequence of irrigation sediments and former sabkhah soils

(Buringh, 1960:83-99) is on Fig. 8. The other small sounding, known as the "deep sounding," was in the north block. This revealed the following stratigraphic sequence from top to bottom with altitude measured in meters above the arbitrary field datum (see Fig. 9).

- O: A number assigned to all features originating from strata now destroyed; that is, from above the present surface at +3.85 m.
- O/I: 3.85 to 3.45 m. Red-brown silt-clay with fine columnar fracture.
- I: 3.45 to 3.35 m. In the deep sounding this stratum appears as a scatter of sherds in the base of the above described deposit. To the north, as will be detailed in the next paragraph, this stratum can occur as one or more compact floors each overlain by brown silt-clay containing many sherds.
- I/II: 3.35 to 3.10 m. Red-brown silt-clay with coarse fracture.
- II: 3.10 to 2.85 m. Brown silt-clay containing sherds.
- II/III: 2.85 to 2.75 m. Dark brown silt-clay with few sherds.
- III: 2.70 to 2.40 m. The deep sounding penetrated this stratum at a point where some complex architectural feature had been

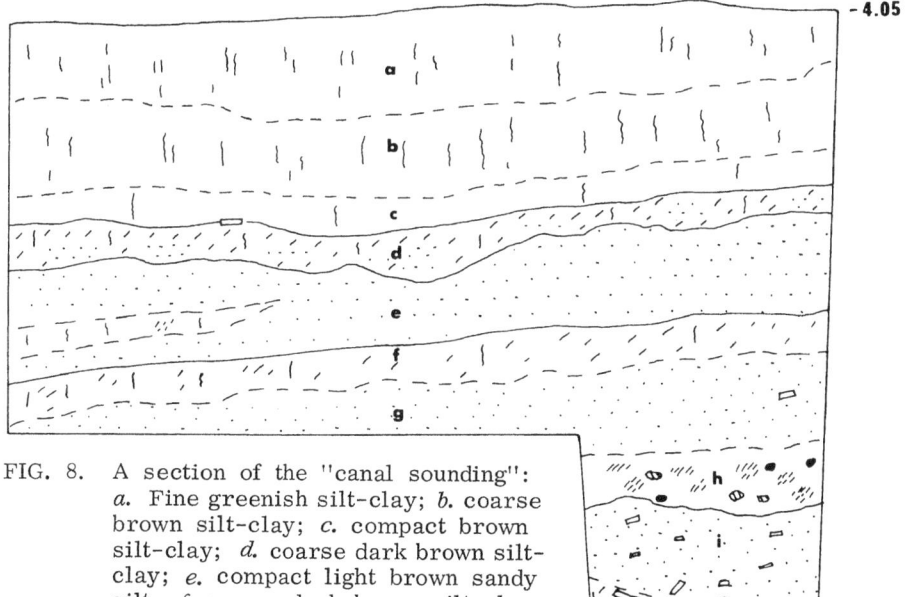

FIG. 8. A section of the "canal sounding": *a.* Fine greenish silt-clay; *b.* coarse brown silt-clay; *c.* compact brown silt-clay; *d.* coarse dark brown silt-clay; *e.* compact light brown sandy silt; *f.* coarse dark brown silt-clay; *g.* compact light brown sandy silt; *h.* dark brown silt-clay with charcoal and brick fragments; *i.* greenish sandy silt; *j.* mottled dark brown and gray silt-clay; *k.* compact light brown silt-clay.

built. On the west side of the square there was (from top to bottom) a compact floor with rectangular hearth, a puddled clay deposit bordered by lightly-baked bricks, and another complex floor. East of the brick border there were five compact floors of various colors.

IV: 2.40 to 1.85 m. The sounding penetrated this stratum at a similarly complex point. On the south wall the footings of poorly bonded plano-convex mud-brick wall were found. North of this wall (from top to bottom) was a layer of mud-brick fragments, a solid layer of packed mud brick, a compact floor, a layer of dark brown silt, and, finally, another compact floor.

V: Below 1.85 m. The upper .08 meters was composed of mottled red-brown and gray silt-clay containing a few charcoal flecks. Below an irregular but definite interface there was a deposit of light red-brown silt with occasional clay lenses. This was tested to a depth of 30 cm. without finding further evidence of human occupation.

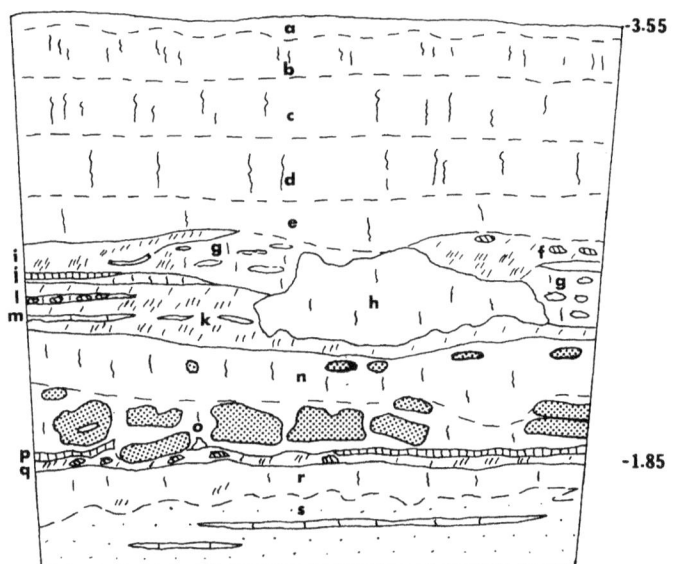

FIG. 9. A section of the "deep sounding" (the uppermost twenty centimeters are not shown): *a.* Disturbed; *b.* fine red-brown silt-clay; *c.* coarse red-brown silt-clay; *d.* compact brown silt-clay with sherds; *e.* dark brown silt-clay; *f.* dark brown silt-clay with charcoal and burnt clay; *g.* compact puddled light brown silt-clay; *h.* compact puddled red-brown silt-clay; *i.* brown silt-clay with charcoal and burnt clay; *j.* greenish silt; *k.* dark brown silt-clay with charcoal; *l.* light brown silt-clay with burnt clay; *m.* light brown silt; *n.* red-brown clay with sandy sun-dried brick fragments; *o.* plano-convex sun-dried brick in brown clay matrix; *p.* greenish sandy clay; *q.* dark brown silt-clay with sherds; *r.* mottled red-brown and gray silt-clay with some charcoal; *s.* light red-brown silt with clay layers.

The general pattern of occupational deposition seems to be one of isolated architectural remains with complex arrangements of walls, floors, and both external and internal special features. These remains are separated by open areas covered with sediment, washed and reworked from the piles of architectural debris and canal cleanings. Horizontal scatters of sherds in such deposits would mark relatively stable surfaces contemporary with periods of architectural repair. Since architectural complexes could shift from place to place in time, the sequence of strata could appear to be very different in different places. With these factors in mind, let us consider the depositional history of the small part of the site that the sounding happened to penetrate.

The relatively coarse oxidized deposit of stratum V was probably laid down near the bank of a channel. This slight levee may have been cultivated prior to occupation. The first occupants built and occupied a room. When this was abandoned, the room was packed with used mud brick. Another structure of some kind was built on the resulting mound. A hearth on a puddled mud platform was built on a floor in this structure, but gradually floors built up around the platform hiding it from view. This structure was leveled, and constructing shifted from the area. A scatter of refuse, a layer of weathered mud brick and canal cleanings, another layer of refuse and yet another layer of weathered debris were all deposited in this spot.

The upper levels of both the north and south blocks were extensively investigated. In the north block there was architectural continuity from floor to floor so each floor and the debris above it were labeled as subdivisions of a single stratum, from top to bottom in Ia, Ib, and Ic. Ic was investigated in only one small area. Ia and Ib coalesced into a single floor throughout much of the block. In the south block the floors showed no significant structural continuity so the deposits were labeled as separate strata; from top to bottom, I, II, and III. The floor of Ib in the north block dipped down from north to south. If it continued at its observed dip it would meet the floor of stratum III in the south unit. Thus some of the features in the south unit are later than those in the north unit. (See Fig. 10 for a simplified presentation of the north-south section.)

FEATURES

Since there were few features and no two were alike, each will be described verbally in a brief paragraph. First the

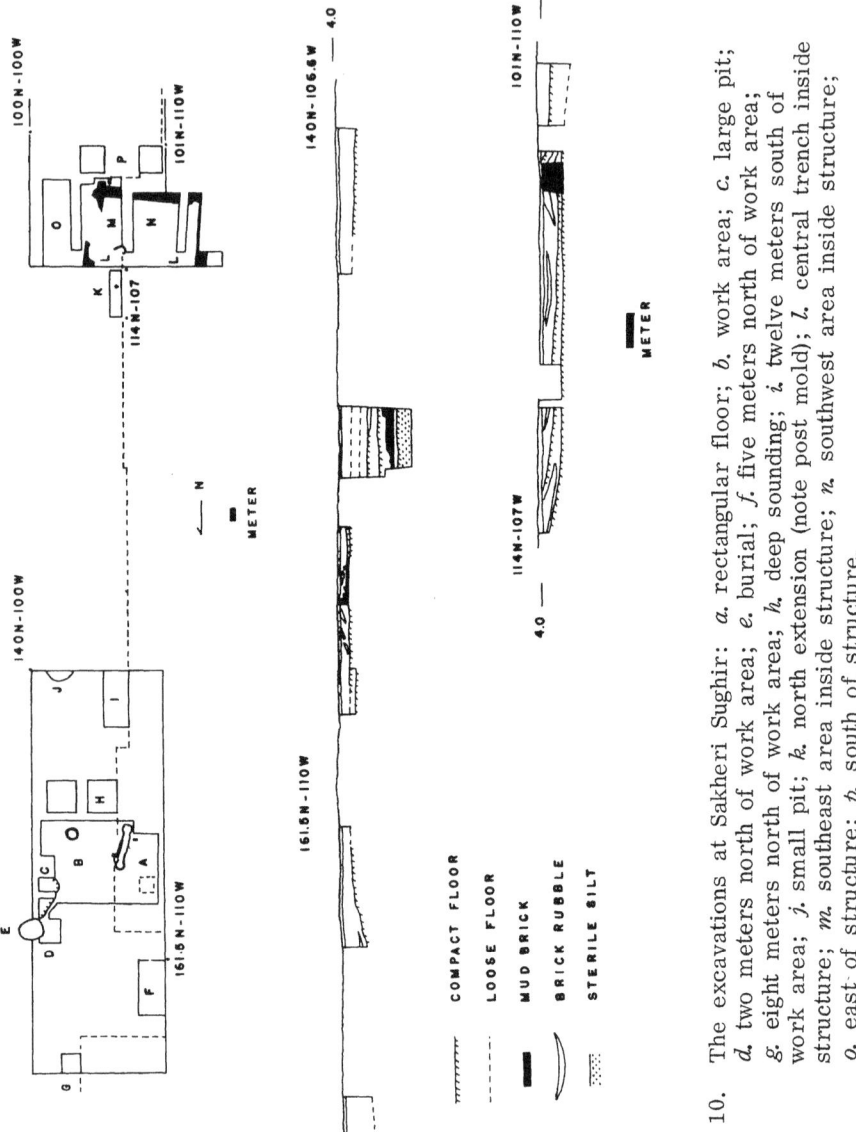

FIG. 10. The excavations at Sakheri Sughir: *a.* rectangular floor; *b.* work area; *c.* large pit; *d.* two meters north of work area; *e.* burial; *f.* five meters north of work area; *g.* eight meters north of work area; *h.* deep sounding; *i.* twelve meters south of work area; *j.* small pit; *k.* north extension (note post mold); *l.* central trench inside structure; *m.* southeast area inside structure; *n.* southwest area inside structure; *o.* east of structure; *p.* south of structure.

features of the north block, then the features of the south block, will be described. Finally, the plan of this part of the settlement in successive intervals of time will be discussed. The stratum number and location of the center or of the limits of each feature are given in parentheses.

Child Burial (0; 159.4N-100W).—In a pit 1.45 by 1.15 meters and more than .5 meters deep, are the articulated remains of a child of about nine years age.[1] It was loosely flexed on the right side, with spine roughly east-west, head west, face south, arms bent to bring the hands near the face, and legs slightly bent at hips and tightly bent at the knees. West of the head were a group of vessels including a large straight rim-spouted jar with reserve slip decoration (Fig. 9), a medium straight rim-spouted jar (Fig. 9), and four wide conical cups, one of which covered each jar and two of which were west of the jars. Northwest of the skull was a small ledge-rim jar (Fig. 9). North of the body was a narrow conical cup. Also north of the body by the left elbow was a denticulate sickle blade. This grave group provides a useful datum for correlation with the 'Ubaid cemetery.

The North Block

Small Pit (0; 140N-102W).—Only the edge of this refuse-filled depression was investigated. It is probably about 2.5 meters in diameter and more than .30 meters deep.

Rectangular Floor (Ia, Ib, between 152.3 and 156.9N; 104.7 and 109.4W).—A compact dark silt clay floor separating into two floors to the east. The north, west, and south edges are relatively straight and face the cardinal points. There is no definite eastern edge. The long oven (see below) blocks the southeast corner of the floor. On the south edge of the floor near this oven was a partially baked remnant of a mud-brick wall, one brick wide. This suggests that the regular south, west, and north edges of the floor were surrounded by a thin wall. There was a fragment of a grinding slab near the north edge on the floor. In addition there was an earlier rectangular hearth and a later circular hearth on the floor (see below).

Long Oven (Ia, Ib; 153N-105.8W).—This complex feature had two main parts, a long hearth and a wall footing.

The main part of the wall footing runs from north-northeast to south-southwest. It is one brick wide and, as preserved, four courses high. Floor Ib stops against the southeast edge of the wall. Floor Ia seems to continue over the third course. The bricks of the fourth course are laid on this floor at right angles

[1] This is called Burial 2 in Appendix III.

with spaces, perhaps air intakes, between them. At the northern end there is a corner. A short thick segment of wall runs southwest. It is composed of two thin walls one brick width thick separated by a small space. The plano-convex bricks and the mortar of all these wall remnants were baked: those near the oven are hard and yellow-brown; those farther away are soft and red. A pile of fragments of such brick was found three meters northwest of the oven on floor I*b*. These probably result from a rebuilding of the oven before floor I*a* was constructed. Among the fragments was a baked fragment of wall, one brick length thick laid in herringbone pattern.

The long hearth is northwest of the wall. The central portion was 2.85 meters long, 1.60 meters wide, and .20 meters below floor I*b*. The primary fill of the hearth is a dark-brown silt clay. Above this is a thick deposit of gray ash resulting from burnt straw. The outer edge of the hearth is a hard baked yellow clay. It is possible that this was the base of a vault which arched over the hearth. At either end of this central hearth is a shallower, ill-defined ash-filled hearth which rises and expands to meet the floor (see Fig. 11). There is little to indicate the exact function of this feature. Mr. Fuad Safar has suggested that it was a small kiln for lightly firing bricks or other heavy ceramic items. Because of its unique form an attempt was made to cover the feature so it can be reexamined in the future.

Round Hearth (I*a*; 154.3N-107.7W).—This feature is near the west edge of the rectangular floor. It was constructed from the sherds of a large bowl (see Fig. 11). The rim sherds were forced into the floor as a border .65 meters in diameter. Some body sherds were used as paving for the floor of the hearth. The paving is separated from the floor below by a centimeter of debris suggesting the hearth was used late in the floor's history. There were traces of gray ash in the interstices between the paving sherds.

Rectangular Hearth (I*b*; 155.8N-107.6W).—This feature was near the northwest corner of the floor. It was .80 meters by .95 meters and was hardened by a baked yellow-clay rim. It was cut about two centimeters into the floor. There were lenses of ash and carbonaceous material in it. Floor I*a* continued over it suggesting it was used early in the history of the floor.

Round Oven (I*a*, I*b*, I*c*; 152.0N-102.8W).—Immediately east of the rectangular floor and its associated features was a less compact series of floors. This area is called the *Work Floor*. On these floors was a clay oven with an inside diameter of 1.20 meters. The baked inner edge of the clay footing was preserved.

FIG. 11. Details of work area and the long oven-IB: *a.* brick debris; *b.* grinding slab fragment; *c.* rectangular hearth; *d.* adolescent human skull; *e.* long oven; *f.* round oven; *g.* large pit.

The floor was paved with small jar sherds. The oven was constructed and reconstructed on the same spot on three successive occasions.

Large Pit (I*a* or I*b* 157.0N-100W).—West of the above mentioned work floor, the edge of a large pit was investigated. This pit is perhaps more than four meters in diameter and of unknown depth. Presumably some of the debris between the floors of I*a* and I*b* was thrown from this pit.[2] The cranium of an adolescent found loose on the floor just east of the long oven may have been from a burial disturbed by this pit. The pit contains a lower gray ashy lense, and an upper dark brown silt-clay lense. Undoubtedly if the central area of the pit were investigated it would appear to be more complex.

Sloping Floor (I*b;* between 161.8 and 165.2N, 107 and 109.75W.—Northwest of the rectangular floor there is a separate very compact light brown silt-clay floor at the level of floor I*b*. To the south this floor is level at 3.50 meters above the arbitrary datum, but to the north it slopes off irregularly at about a 15 degree angle. On the level area were broken fragments of a medium-sized spouted jar, a double-rim dish, and a stone bowl. This is an unusual combination. Floor I*a* continues northward, at a level of about 3.55 meters, to the limits of the block. Thus the north edge of the site was considerably expanded between the building of floors I*b* and I*a*.

Oval Oven (I*c;* 155.0N-103.2W).—Below the less compact floor of I*b* an unusual and well-preserved oven was excavated. Its long axis is, from northeast to southwest, 1.9 meters. It is .8 meters wide. Its floor is .3 meters below the floor from which it is constructed. The inside is baked. The primary fill is a brown silt-clay with charcoal and ash. Above this is a mottled silt-clay containing fragments of the baked dome of the oven.

Other Features in the North Block.—The two complex features noted in the above stratigraphic description of the deep sounding were not sufficiently uncovered to warrant further discussion. A second oven was noted on the floor of I*c* but was not completely uncovered.

The South Block

Rectangular Structure (II ; between 104N and 111.6N, 104 and 113W).—Three walls of a rectangular structure were preserved. It was built or reconstructed on the floor of stratum II and destroyed before stratum II was sealed off by the floor of stratum III. All the construction was weathered, and individual bricks

[2]This is called Burial 1 in Appendix III.

were difficult to trace (see Fig. 12). The west wall is .93 meters thick. The footing appears to be simple mud construction. The first course of brick is composed of stretchers laid flat. Above this the second course of brick is composed of headers laid obliquely, slanting downwards to the right when viewed from the inside. These bricks average .21 by .15 meters. Given these dimensions, the first course would be six brick widths thick, and the second course would be four brick lengths wide. The south wall is .88 to .93 meters wide and similarly constructed. The bricks are, however, .18 to .20 meters long and .12 meters wide. It is possible that the first course is seven brick widths thick and the second is five brick lengths wide. Several attempts to check this possibility by tracing the bricks in plan were not successful. A single buttress was noted near the southeast corner. It is .60 meters wide and projects out .80 meters. There was not enough time to check for a similar buttress near the southwest corner. The east wall was largely destroyed by a later pit. It is .85 meters wide. The mud construction was unclear.

FIG. 12. Details of the rectangular structure-IIB: *a*. Post mold; *b*. oval hearth; *c*. large baked bricks; *d*. possible large pit; *e*. possible buttress; *f*. small pit.

Outside the wall a simple water table of baked flat bricks, averaging .26 by .18 by .11 meters, on edge, protects the wall from rain splatter. Whereas the mud construction of all three walls continued slightly below the compact floor of stratum II, these baked bricks nested on the floor and are thus an addition to the building. There is no evidence of a north wall. The southeast corner of the building was badly disturbed. The southwest corner was sufficiently investigated to reveal that building details had been obscured by a later pit.

The floor inside the building, numbered IIb, was cleaned but not penetrated. Above this are thin layers of gray ash and light brown silt. In the northwest corner of the structure there are three distinct floors in this deposit. The uppermost of these is continuous throughout the building and was numbered IIa. Floor IIb slants up markedly at its north edge. There is a possible shallow post hole .15 meters in diameter and cut .07 meters into floor IIb, at the point where the floor slants up. The debris between floor IIb and Ia at this point included a thick lense of mud construction fragments. This evidence suggests that during the time between the construction of floors IIb and IIa, this rectangular structure was open to the north, where there was a small mound of debris next to a deteriorating wall. On the lower floor Ib there is one feature: an oval hearth (108.8N, 106.7W), about .90 meters by .80 meters, bordered by two courses of brick. Both whole and fragmentary baked and unbaked plano-convex bricks were used.

The fill above Floor IIa is composed of lenses of brown silt-clay containing varying amounts of mud construction fragments and charred debris. The east-west section indicates that first some construction collapsed, then the building was burnt, then more construction debris fell in. In this higher construction debris there are two items of interest. East of the building is a cylindrical ceramic drain. This was probably fixed through the east wall to drain a flat roof. Inside the building is an alignment of at least four plano-convex bricks end to end from north to south. These probably fell from the west wall, but their function is not known.

There were no features immediately east or south of this building. Stratum II dips south of the structure indicating the site's edge, and perhaps explaining the presence of the buttress. As mentioned above, there seems to have been a mound of debris north of the building. The area west of the building was not effectively investigated. Two disturbances penetrate the debris of the rectangular structure. The large pit which destroyed the southwest corner was not investigated. Since it contains inverted conical cups, it may contain a burial. The small pit which obscures the southwest corner is about .6 meters in diameter. In its bottom are an ox scapula, other bones, and some medium-sized jar sherds.

Summary and Interpretation of the Features

Assuming Floor Ib in the north block to be contemporary with the floor of III in the south block, then the strip across the village, which is so incompletely investigated, might have looked thus: To the south, there was an unknown structure known at present only as a heap of mud construction debris under the floor of stratum II. Twenty meters to the north was a rectangular shed containing a long oven, and a rectangular hearth. East of this was an oven on a work floor. To the north, the site sloped off abruptly. The large quantity of sediment in this area may have resulted from canal cleaning. Later, the south structure fell into disrepair, the north shed was torn down, and a pit was dug in the work floor to provide fill for reconstruction.

In Ia-II times, a structure was built on the south edge of the site. This was about nine meters square with thick walls and a buttress. Such characteristics are known in contemporary buildings at Ur, and they need not indicate a two-story building. The flat roof of the building was doubtless utilized. The lower story was a living area, judging by the artifact debris and hearth on its floor. There is no way of knowing, however, whether this structure is completely revealed and, if so, how typical it is of the dwelling units on the site, without conducting more excavations. Thirty meters to the north the restored shed and long oven with a new round hearth continued to be used as before. There was as before an oven to the east. Further east, in an uninvestigated area of the site, a concentration of baked bricks was noted. These may mark the dwelling unit with which the shed and work oven were associated.

We can draw two useful points from this discussion of the features at Sakheri Sughir:

1) There is little architectural evidence for specialized activities. The unusual long oven might have been used for the firing of small quantities of brick. The other features are to this day used in Iraqi villages.

2) Domestic units were not densely packed. On the site, about 25 meters separates the two complexes at any time, regardless of how one correlates the levels of the north and south

blocks. This figure has been used in the computation of rural population given in Chapter III even though it is based on a minimum of evidence.

TECHNOLOGY

In this section, the artifacts manufactured from each different raw material are discussed. After this, possible functional categories of items are discussed.

Chipped Stone

Most of the stone is a fine to medium grain, homogenous or mottled light gray-brown flint. The stone sometimes exhibits a pitted chalky cortex or a white patination. This is not available in the nearby stony desert. Its source is unknown.

A single blade core and a core platform trimming flake were found on the surface of the site. A core side trimming flake was excavated. These few items indicate only that blades were struck from cores on the site, rather than imported.

Two complete blades and seven blade fragments were found. Three had irregular retouch suggesting use (Fig. 13b, c).

Twenty-five denticulate sickle blades are recorded. These were manufactured from small segments of blades, most of which are between 1.5 and 3.5 centimeters in length. On at least one edge there is a set of small deep notches. On 15 examples there are traces of the bitumen, which probably held the sickle blades into a wooden handle. Four examples are fixed in lumps of bitumen and in two of these the bitumen lump was molded into the basal sherds of vessels. These blades, all new or retouched, were probably dropped in the hot bitumen as the owner was preparing to fix them into a sickle handle.

A microscopic study of a surface sample of sickle blades is now being attempted. Preliminary observations suggest that the reaper pulled the sickle at an angle toward the shoulder of the arm holding the sickle. Simple examination of the sheen caused by the silica in the stems of grasses, on the excavated sample revealed the following patterns of wear:

15 had no definite sheen. They were little used (Fig. 13d, e, h).

5 had sheen on the bottom of the blade, and on top both in and between the notches. They were well used on one side (Fig. 13g).

3 had sheen on the bottom of the blade and on the top between the teeth but not in the notches. Two of these had definitely been well used, retouched, and discarded (Fig. 13f).

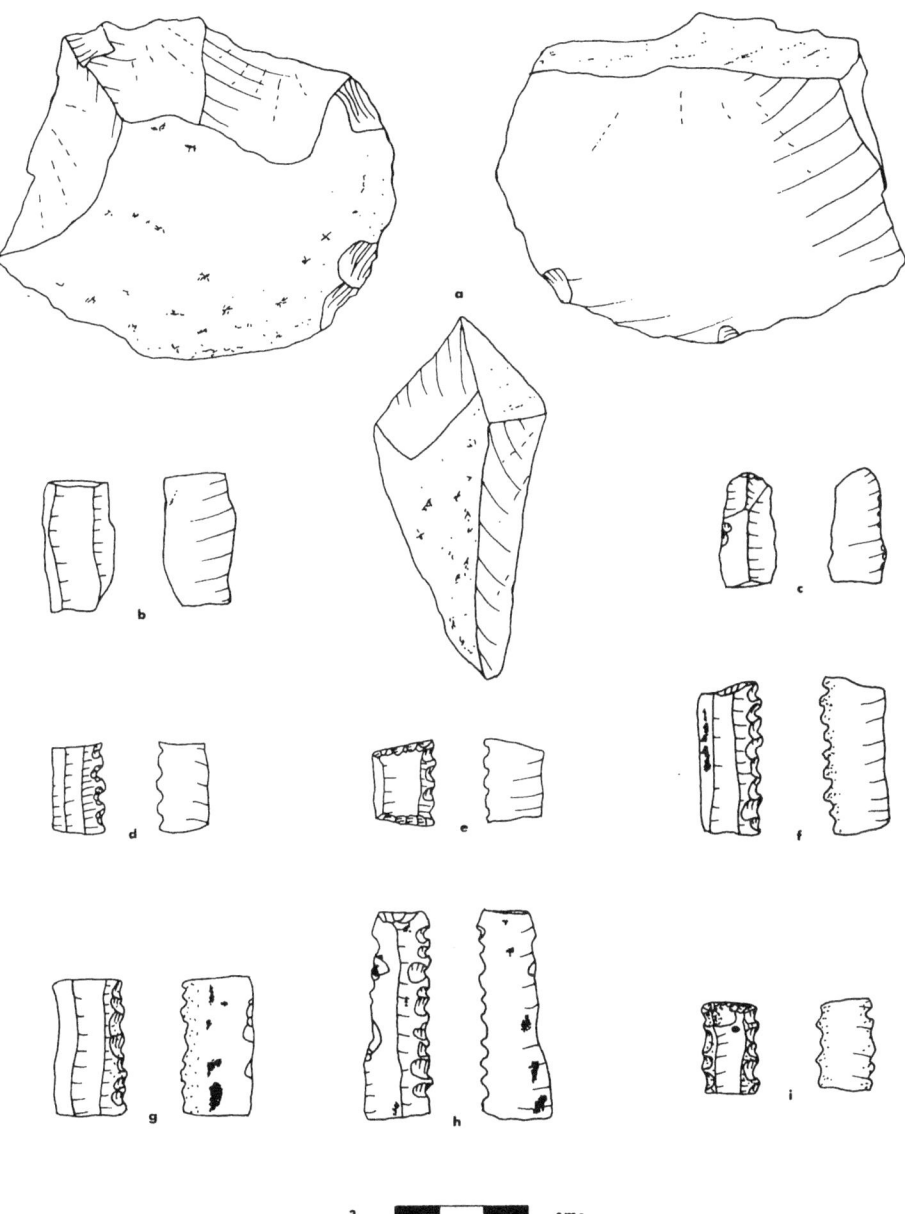

FIG. 13. Chipped stone artifacts: *a*. Chopper (00005); *b-c*. blade segments (03000, 02700); *d-e*. unused denticulate sickles (08341, 08340); *f-i*. used denticulate sickles with sheen and bitumen (00014, 07138, 03730).

1 had complete sheen on one edge and sheen only on the bottom of the other edge. This had been well used on one edge, turned over and worked on the other edge, lightly used, and retouched.

1 had complete sheen on both sides of both edges (Fig. 13*i*). This had been well used on one edge, turned over and worked on the other edge, and well used on this new edge.

In general, the sickle blades were not used until they could no longer be retouched. This suggests that stone was in good supply.

Finally, there were two heavy tools. One was a large flake of quartzite utilized as a cleaver (Fig. 13*a*), the other was a bifacially-worked chopping tool made from a pebble of poor quality flint. The latter was battered from use.

Ground Stone

Ground stone items are rare.

3 fragments of grinding slabs of igneous rock probably grano-diorites, were noted

1 battered pebble may have been a hammer

12 stone bowls are represented by rim sherds. Five were of soft coarse limestones, probably available in the stony desert to the south. One was of a coarse gypsum. Six were of harder transluscent materials perhaps marbles. These bowls are of simple form and are between 11 and 30 cm. in diameter. A small example, only 9 cm. in diameter, had a hole in its base. Presumably it did not function as a container.

A small perforated disc, concave on one side and convex on the other, probably limestone, was noted in the field but subsequently lost.

2 very small red carnelian beads were noted.

Bitumen

This was the second most common surviving raw material at Sakheri, after clay. A chemical study to learn the composition, origin, and processing techniques of this material is being conducted by Dr. Robert Marschner of the Americal Oil Company, Whiting Research Laboratories. There are four categories of bitumen items:

Plain-shaped pieces.—Round or rectangular flat pieces comprise 35 per cent of the sample. Three of the twenty-one were complete enough to measure. These ranged from 6.9 to 9.9 centimeters in length, 5.8 to 7.9 centimeters in width, and 2.0 to 3.0 centimeters in thickness. It is possible that bitumen was distributed in small solid cakes and heated when needed for use (Fig. 14*a*).

Mat-impressed pieces.—These comprise 30 per cent of the sample. At least one was a rectangular-shaped piece that happened to have been placed on a reed mat when soft. The remainder were flat broken fragments of coatings which had been poured over mats (Fig. 14b). The mats will be discussed below.

Sherd-impressed pieces.—Six per cent of the sample had cooled in the bottom of a pot.

Other impressed pieces.—Six per cent of the sample had been impressed in various unusual ways. Three had the imprints of the insides of small sticks or canes. One is a small plug with a rounded head.

Eleven are parts of three or four architectural elements. Each has the imprints of heavy canes and lashings, and one has, in addition, the imprints of mats tied to the canes by the lashing. Some of the mat-impressed pieces must be parts of such elements. It seems likely that those elements were parts of doorway or window covers, but the possibility that bitumen was in sufficient supply to coat entire reed huts cannot be rejected (Fig. 14c).

Finally there are two fragments which may be from the coating of a *gufa*, or round boat. The fragment was formed around both the finely lashed rim of the object and a coarsely lashed rib, perpendicular to the rim. To my knowledge this pattern of lashing today is used only on the gufa. There is a possibility however, that this pattern was used for large baskets in the third millennium (Fig. 14d).

Miscellaneous fragments.—These comprise the remainder of the sample.

Reed

Observations could be made on seven reed mats. Six are imprints on bitumen and one is carbonized. Both over-two-under-two and over-three-under-three weaves occur. The reed ranges from .7 to at least 2.2 centimeters in width. The carbonized example is only .65 centimeters wide but it has probably shrunk. Dr. Wilhelm van Zeist has identified this as a *Scirpus sp.*, a club rush.

Metal

A single corroded lump of relatively pure copper was found on the surface of the site.

FIG. 11. Bitumen artifacts: *a*, plain-shaped piece; *b*, mat-impressed piece; *c*, architectural element; *d*, possible boat coating.

Bone and Shell

A fish vertebra was modified by triming off the spines and enlarging the hole in its center. Presumably it was used as a bead (Unit 109). A shell of the genus *Oliva* found nearby may have had a similar decorative use (Unit 107).

Ceramic

Clay was, without doubt, the most commonly used raw material. Most baked clay items were fragments of containers. First, noncontainers will be considered.

Most of the architectural elements noted were bricks, both baked and unbaked. Most were markedly plano-convex in shape. Most were lightly straw tempered. Some were made of a relatively coarse silt-clay (Fig. 15*b*, *c*).

Fragments of cylindrical drain pipe were found as mentioned above. This is 112 centimeters in length. The two open ends are slightly constricted. The cylinder was made on a potter's wheel, and both inside and outside were subsequently evened by scraping (Fig. 15*a*).

Ten ceramic rings were found. These ranged from 6.5 to 10.0 centimeters in diameter. Most were about 8.0 centimeters in diameter, with a hole of about 2.0 centimeters. Similar rings were found in the Temple Oval at Khafage still attached to a net (Delougaz, 1940). Therefore, at least one function of these items was as fish net sinkers (Fig. 15*d*).

There is one fragment of a funnel with a hole 1.0 centimeters in diameter (Fig. 15*e*).

Now let us consider the containers. Most had rather sandy pastes and may have been deliberately tempered with sand. A few were definitely tempered with straw. Most vessels exhibited horizontal scorings or scratchings implying that they were turned, or at least finished on, a wheel. Some vessels, most commonly jars, had a light coating on their outer surface. This coating may be a slip or it may be a sludge of ferrous chloride caused by salts in the clay. Clearly there are a number of technical problems with these ceramics. A program of mineralogical analyses and firing experiments with Mesopotamian clays and ceramics has been begun, but will take a number of years to complete.

Detailed observations are available on 651 conical cup bases, 168 bowl and jar bases, 82 bowl rims, 103 jar rims, and various appendages and vessel fragments. The actual number in each

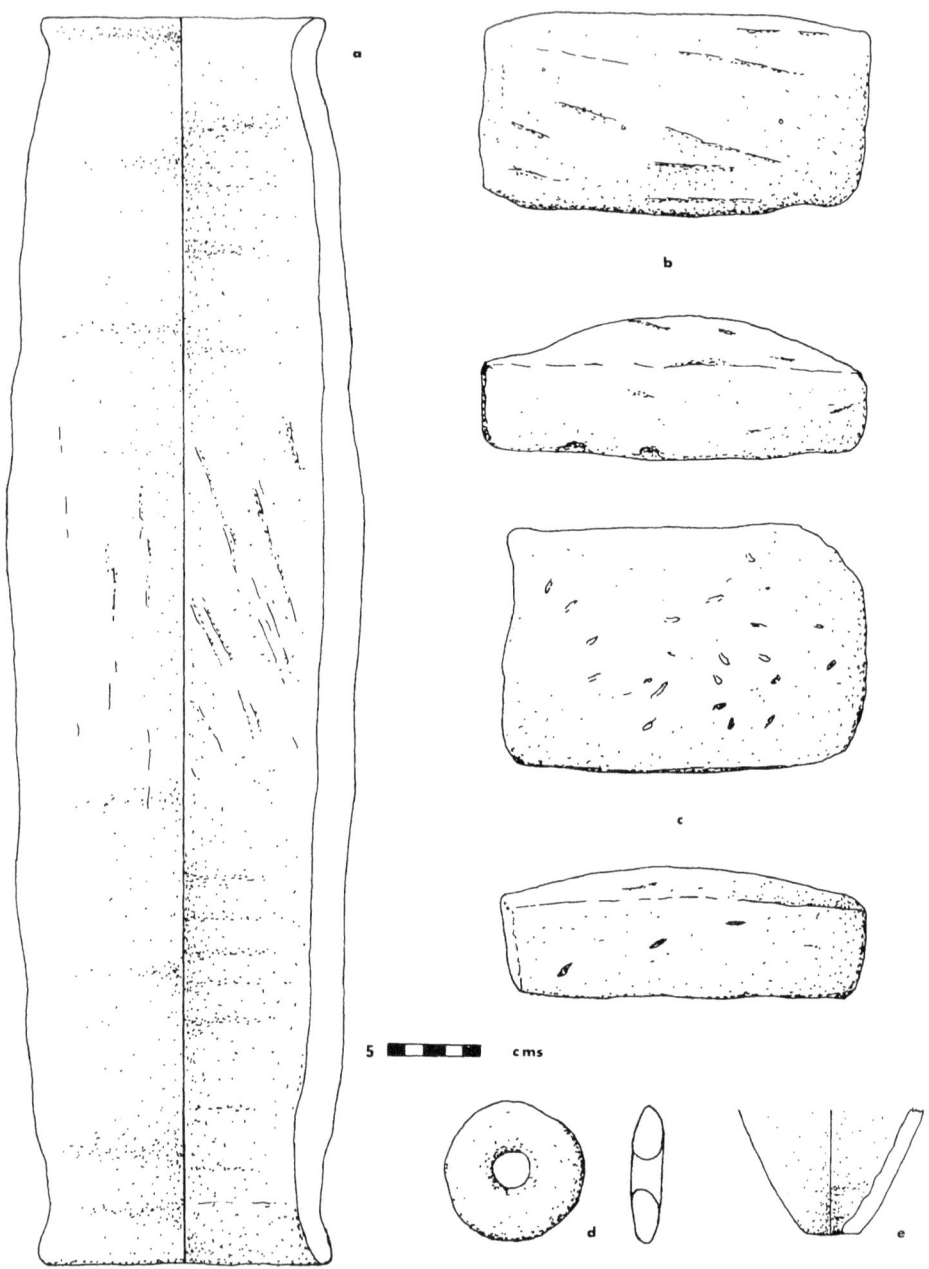

FIG. 15. Ceramic artifacts: *a*. cylindrical drain pipe (00020); *b-c*. plano-convex bricks (11600); *d*. possible net weight (06411); *e*. possible funnel (08800).

of these categories of items was higher, but some examples were too fragmentary to measure.

Conical cups.—This term is applied to small conical bowls with flat, expanded bases. Experiment suggests that these are made by placing a large lump of prepared clay on the potter's wheel and forming cup after cup from the top of the large mass. As each cup was completed, it was cut from the mass by pulling a string against its stem while the wheel was still. The cups vary in shape from a narrow form with a high solid base to a wide form with a low base (Fig. 16a-f), but in the possessions of a domestic unit at a given time there seem to have been a few preferred proportions from this possible range of variation. A simple technique for differentiating the preferred forms has been developed by Dr. Hans Nissen of the University of Chicago Oriental Institute. From the study of many conical cups from Warka, he empirically developed the set of curves shown on Figure 22. Using this chart the profile of any cup can be expressed as a single number. The range in variation in cups from a level or series of levels can be shown in a bar graph as in Figure 23.

Such variations will be discussed in the next section of this chapter.

Bowls.—This term is applied to vessels with unrestricted or only slightly restricted mouths. Conical cups are bowls, but they are dealt with separately because of their distinctive manufacturing process. The bowls dealt with here were made individually on the wheel.

Bowls seem to be rare in previously reported Early Dynastic town and cemetery ceramic complexes (Delougaz, 1952; Woolley, 1934, 1955). Therefore, it was surprising to find a substantial number of distinctive bowl forms at Sakheri Sughir. First let us consider the attributes of the vessels, then let us consider the ways in which these attributes are combined.

The form of most vessels is hemispherical in shape with sides convex in section. Some bowls have convex-sided bases but concave-sided restricted rims, few are conical in shape with straight sides. The rim of most vessels is rounded in section. In some cases it is beveled outward. Sometimes this bevel is carried to the point where there is a distinct lip or ledge on the out of the rim. In some cases there are plastic alterations of the exterior of the vessel. A plain strip, a hatched strip, an incised line, a reserve slip, or a lip spout can occur. Only a few definite bowl bases are evidenced in the sample. All are simple flat bases.

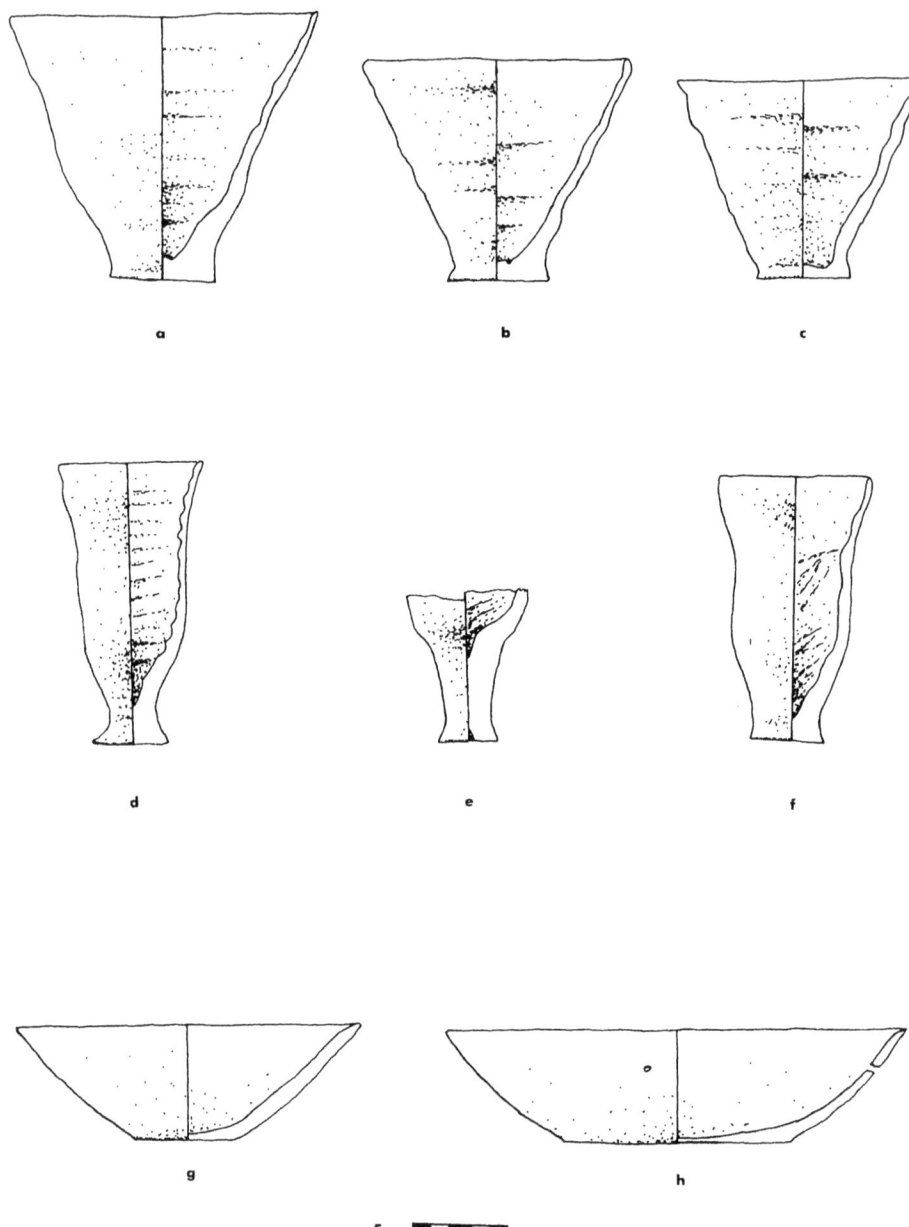

FIG. 16. Conical cups and stone bowls: *a-c*. wide cups (06800, 00017, 07610); *d-f*. narrow cups (00002, 00103, 00013); *g-h*. stone bowls (10511, 10765).

The bowls with basically hemispherical form can be arranged in a single series from simple to more complex (Fig. 17).

1) Seventy per cent are plain bowls ranging from 10 to 65 centimeters in diameter. They have thin walls and a rounded rim. Two have lip spouts. One exceptional bowl had horizontal scorings leaving the lighter clay of the vessel as reserve strips. This lighter clay is not demonstrably a slip, however the traditional term "reserved slip" will be used for this type of decoration (Fig. 16 g, h; 16a).
2) Fifteen per cent are bowls with beveled or ledge rims, ranging from 35 to about 80 centimeters in diameter. In some cases there is a slight ridge on the body below the rim. This may strengthen the vessel (Fig. 17b).
3) Five per cent are bowls with ledge rims and hatched strip bands below the rim. These range from 40 to 75 centimeters in diameter. The rim and the strip together often create a concavity of the upper body of the vessel (Fig. 17c).

There are other uncommon bowl forms which do not fall in this series:

4) Five per cent of the bowls have a hemispherical lower body but concave upper body. These have simple rounded rims. They range from 40 to 50 centimeters in diameter. One is plain, but the remainder have a broad curving line incised around the upper body (Fig. 17d).
5) Five per cent of the bowls have roughly conical forms with thick walls and straight sides. Most have plain rounded rims, but one has a beveled rim with a rough crosshatching on the lip.

In conclusion, there are at least five types of bowls. Two of these, the ledge rim bowl with hatched strip and the bowl with the curving line, are quite distinctive and should be useful in geographical or stratigraphical studies.

Jars.—This term is applied to vessels with markedly constricted mouths, and, in most cases, a roughly cylindrical neck. As in the case of bowls, the attributes of jars will be considered first, then the various combinations of attributes can be considered.

The form of the jars is of two basic types: a simpler globular form and a form with a conical, often almost cylindrical, lower body; a sharp junction; and a slightly convex, almost flat shoulder.

There are five types of rims:

1) The unmodified rim, as it is produced on the wheel, is lightly thickened and beveled (Fig. 18b). These are very rare in this assemblage of jars.
2) Pressure on the unmodified rim with a soft substance as the wheel turns will produce a rounded rim (Fig. 18a, c-e).

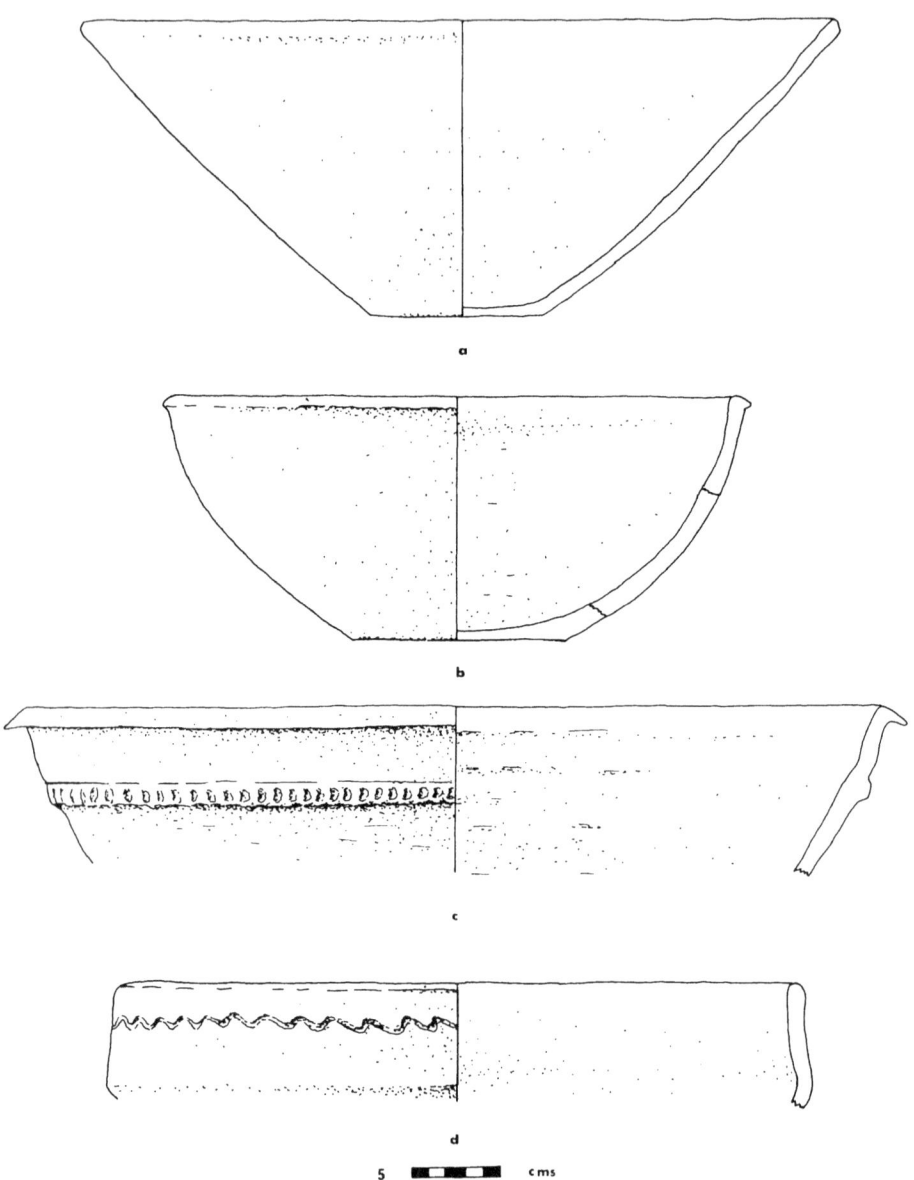

FIG. 17. Bowls: *a*. plain bowl (02201); *b*. ledge rim bowl (02202); *c*. ledge rim bowl with hatched strip band (05004); *d*. bowl with concave upper body and wavy incised line (05328).

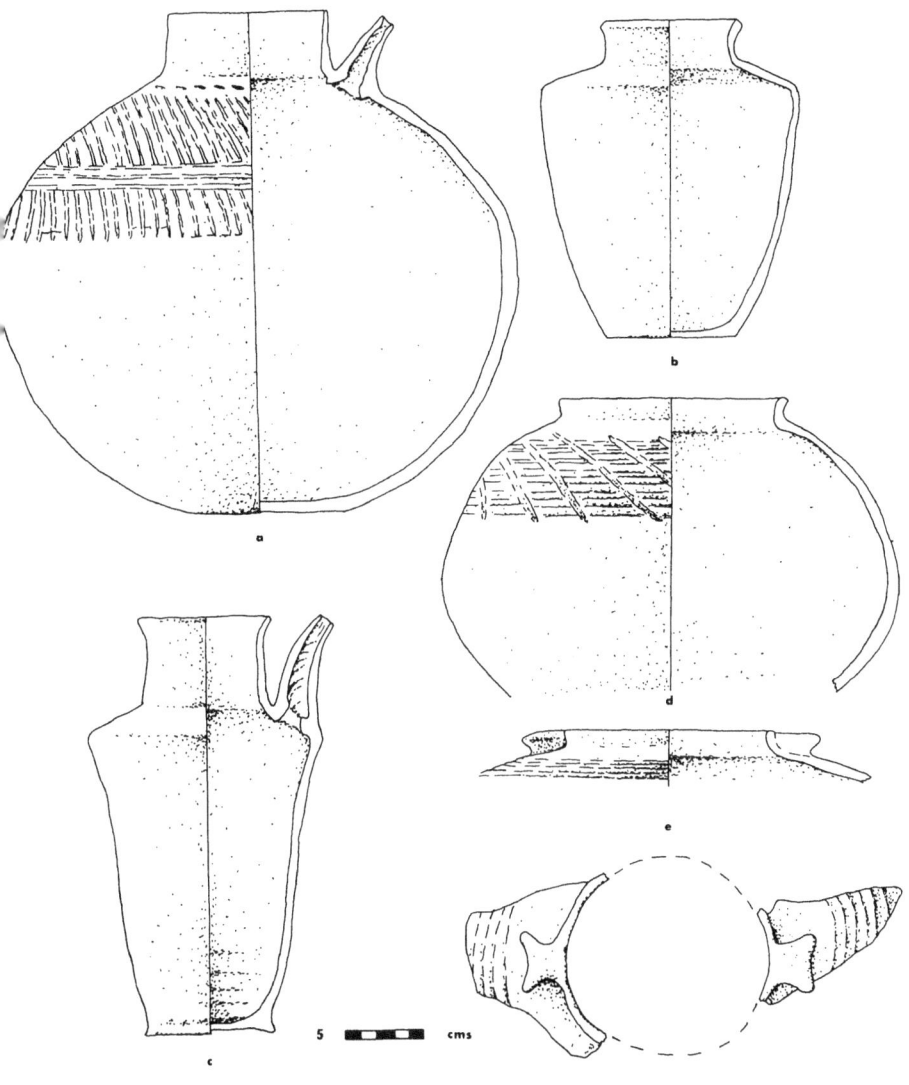

FIG. 18. Jars: *a*. high round rim-jar with spout and reserve slip decoration (00011); *b*. jar with unmodified rim (00905); *c*. high round rim-jar with spout (00010); *d*. low round rim-jar with grooved decoration (10802); *e*. same with flat lugs (07844).

Cutting with a wire loop or wire angle may be necessary to trim the three other types of rim.

3) If the rim is beveled until there is a pronounced outward overhang of the lip, a ledge rim is produced (Fig. 19a–c, e).
4) If a ledge rim is formed downward until its beveled surface is more than 40 degrees from horizontal, it is termed a band rim (Fig. 19d).
5) If a band rim is deeply grooved in the lip, a lock rim is formed. This name is used because it seems possible that a top was fitted into such a groove (Fig. 19f).

Necks are essentially cylindrical forms varying from .3 to 6.5 centimeters in height. However, neck heights distribute trimodally: Those between .3 and 2.0 centimeters in height are termed low; those between 2.0 and 3.0 centimeters are termed medium; and those between 3.0 and 6.0 centimeters are termed high.

Shoulders may be modified in a variety of ways:

1) About one-third of them are completely unmodified, but such sherds are difficult to separate from the other body sherds of jars so an exact percentage cannot be given.
2) About one-fifth have a concentric groovings around the shoulder (Fig. 18e). These markings were made while the pot was on the wheel. Once again an exact percentage cannot be given.

Three other shoulders with actual decoration could be more accurately counted:

3) One or more concentric circles of punctates set around the neck occurs on about 64 per cent of the decorated shoulders (Fig. 19b).
4) A similar circle of punctates, with reserve slip lines radiating obliquely from the neck occur on about 28 per cent of the decorated shoulders (Fig. 18a; 19d, e; 20e). In one case, concentric reserve slip circles were added.
5) Crosshatched incised plats or band with excised triangles occur on eight per cent of the decorated shoulders (Fig. 20a, b).

Bases may be of two types: the flat base is often scored; rarely is it string cut. The ring base has a pinched ring around its circumference. Often finger impressions are visible on the ring.

Finally, there are appendages which can be attached to a jar. Most common are simple straight spouts, generally between 3.0 and 6.0 centimeters long (Fig. 18a, c; 19d). There are also flat-lying concave-sided lug handles (Fig. 18e). Among the unique appendages are a crude multiple filet handle (Fig. 20g, a possible large twin loop handle, one on either side of a jar neck (Fig. 19c), a roughly rectangular upright suspension lug (Fig. 20h), and a roughly beak-shaped suspension lug (Fig. 20i).

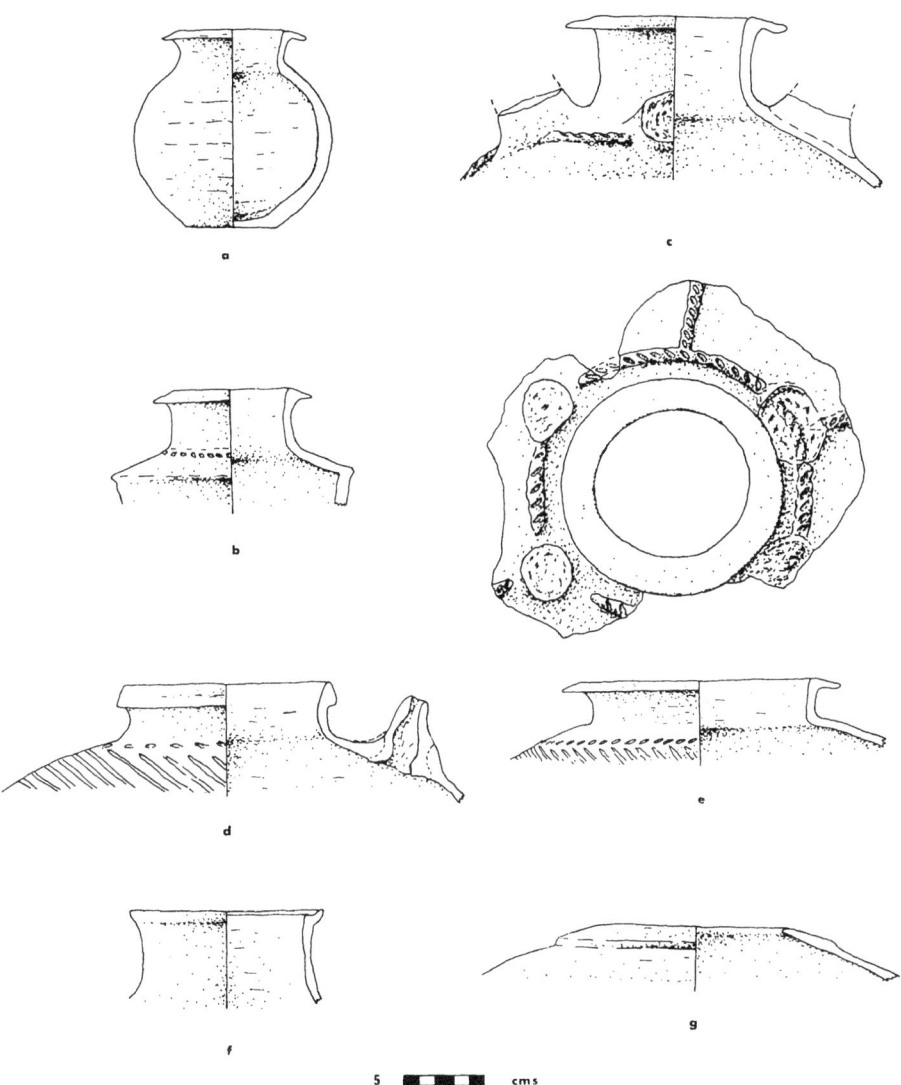

FIG. 19. Jars: *a*. ledge rim jar (00012); *b*. ledge rim jar with punctates (01622); *c*. ledge rim jar with hatch strip and unusual handles (00606); *d*. band rim jar with spout and reserve slip (00018); *e*. ledge rim jar with reserve slip (00001); *f*. lock rim jar (10600); *g*. flat rim jar (10100).

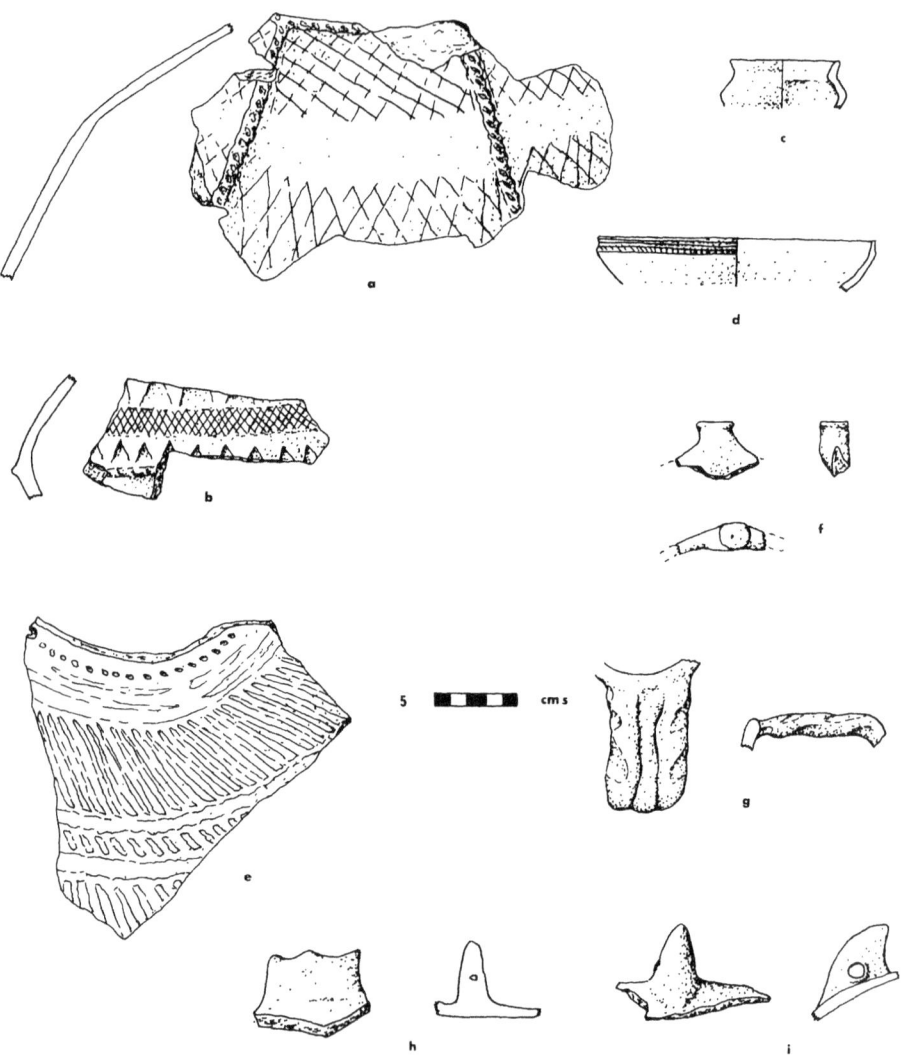

FIG. 20. Vessel fragments: *a-b*. incised jar shoulders (00801, 15625); *c-d*. unusual small vessels (00900, 07117); *e*. reserve slip jar shoulder (07300); *f*. unusual appendage (06400); *g*. strap handle (reconstructed) (10700); *h-i*. unusual appendages (08600).

Having described some of the attributes of jars, let us now consider the way these attributes are combined to form types of jars. This typology must be even more tentative than our typology of bowls, since in only a few cases are the rim, shoulder, and base of a given jar known. Six reoccurring types of jars, based primarily on rim form, are defined:

Low round-rim jars
　These usually have a globular body. Plain shoulders occur but grooving on the shoulder is more common. Two to four flat lug handles around the rim are common. Spouts are unknown. This type constitutes 24 per cent of the jars (Fig. 18 d, e).

High round-rim jars
　These usually have a conical body with flat shoulder, though globular forms occur (Fig. 18a). About half the shoulders are plain. The remainder are either punctate or reserve slip. The spouts observed on this type are relatively long. This type constitutes 30 per cent of the jars (Fig. 18a, c).

Ledge-rim jars
　These usually have a conical body with flat shoulder. Shoulder decoration is similar to the high round-rim jars. Spouts are unknown. This type constitutes 28 per cent of the jars (Fig. 19a-c, e).

Band-rim jars
　These probably have the conical body with flat shoulder. On the two reasonably well-preserved examples, there is reserve slip decoration and a relatively small spout. These constitute 14 per cent of the jars (Fig. 19).

Lock-rim jars
　In no case are any shoulder or body elements of these vessels preserved. These constitute 4 per cent of the jars (Fig. 19f).

Flat-rim jars
　These are the only jars without necks. Either ledge-rim has been formed down until it joins the body or a ledge has been cut out with a wire angle. The body of the examples seems to have been globular and the shoulders are plain. These constitute 2 per cent of the jars (Fig. 19g).

　In summary, jars are the most varied form of vessels. All five types seem relatively distinctive. Unfortunately the sample is not large enough to study the distribution of jar types within the site.
　Miniature vessels.—Six small thin-walled vessels are recorded. There are a small jar, a small bowl, and a small constricted cup (Fig. 20c, d; 21e). The latter is unparalleled, and resembles forms of the first millennium B.C., but was in a reasonable

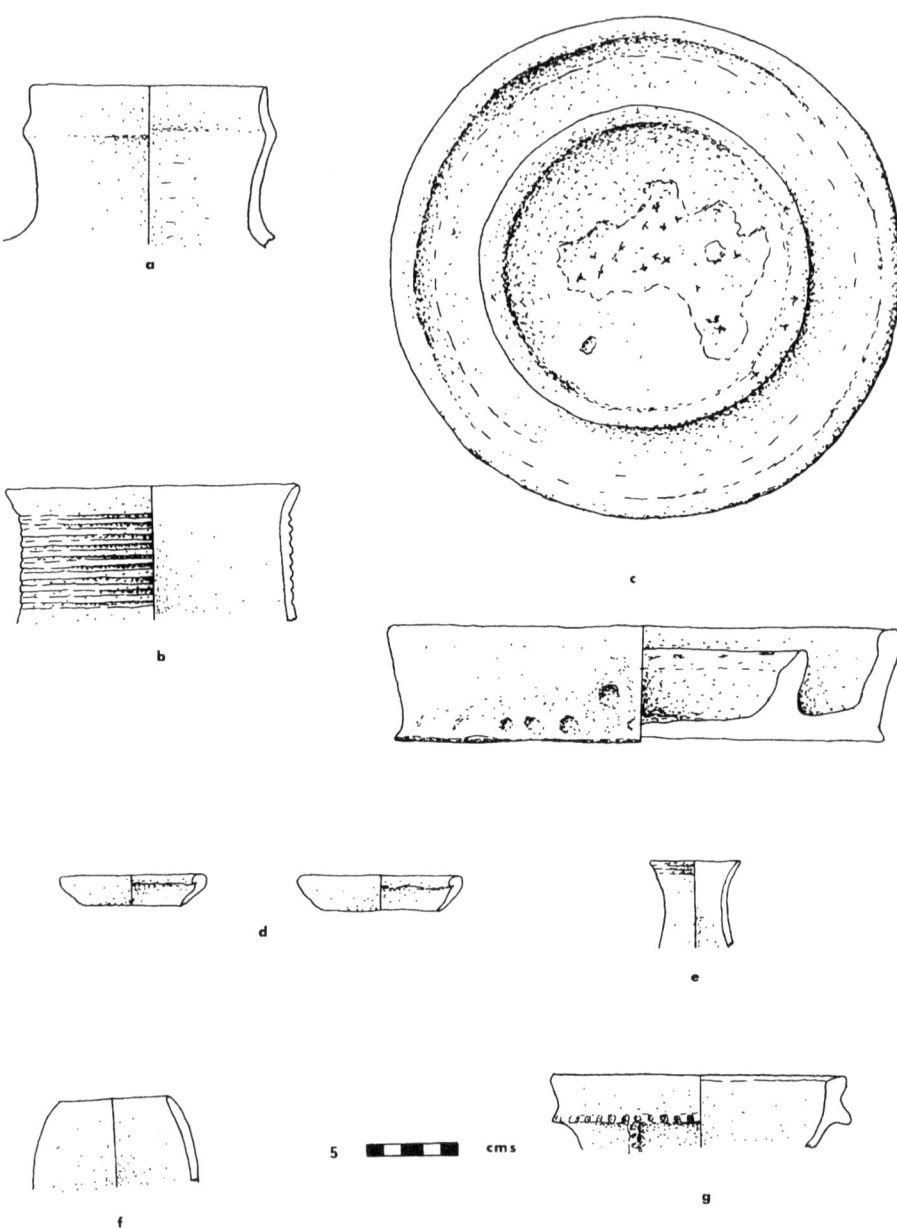

FIG. 21. Other vessels: *a-b.* unusual jars (03400, 10700); *c.* double-rim dish (00015); *d.* small rolled-rim rings (10700, 10700); *e-g.* unusual small vessels (10700, 00100, 10700).

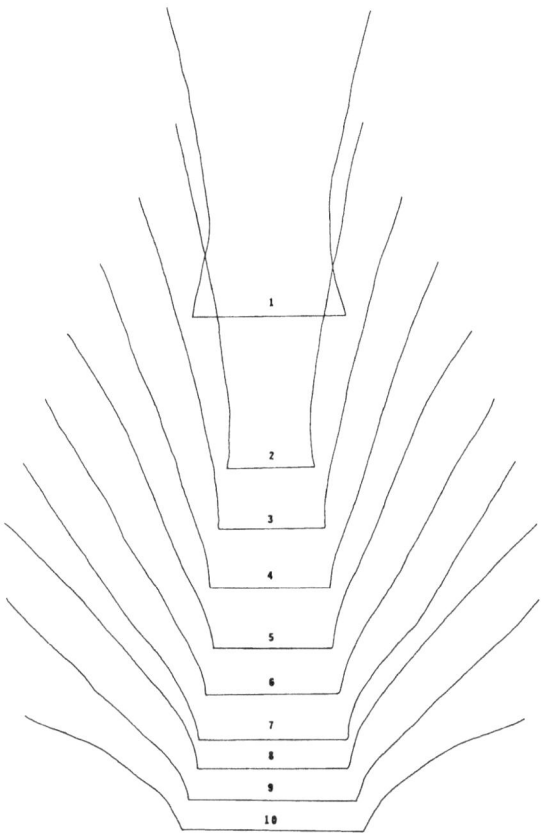

FIG. 22. Profiles of conical cups.

stratigraphic context. There are three small vessels with a very fine paste. In one case there is a simple constricted rim. In the others the rim is rolled inward and the lower break below the rim is ground to a sharp edge. The function of these three items is unknown (Fig. 21d).

Double-rim dish.—There are three examples of this strange vessel form. They are 27.0 to 30.0 centimeters in diameter with flat bases and straight or slightly flared outer rims about 6.5 centimeters high. Rising from the bottom of the vessel is another lower rim which varies from 11.5 to 18.0 centimeters in diameter and 2.5 to 5.0 centimeters in height. The outer rim is rounded but the inner rim is beveled inward. In examples from surface collections the inner rim is breached by a finger mark. The only marks of use visible on these weathered and gypsum-encrusted examples are slight pittings on the inner rim and the bottom inside of this rim. The function of these vessels is unknown (Fig. 21c).

Some unique jar forms are illustrated in Figure 21a, b, f. A unique bowl is illustrated on Figure 21g, and a unique rim appendage in Figure 20f.

A Summary of the Technology

In the above discussion artifacts were categorized by raw material. Now let us consider the significant artifact types in five categories:

1) those probably used in production
2) those probably used in or resulting from tool manufacture and repair
3) those probably involved in the storage, preparation, and serving of food and water
4) architectural elements
5) those probably used for adornment.

These are few artifacts perhaps used in production: sickle blades could be used to harvest any member of the grass family. The ceramic rings were probably net weights used in fishing. The possible fragment of gufa covering implies at least one type of boat.

There are few artifacts related to tool manufacture or repair: a battered pebble could have been used in flint working, and the few unused flakes and blades resulted from such work. The shaped pieces of bitumen were melted down in vessels for use as an adhesive, leaving sherd-impressed bitumen fragments and bitumen spilled on various things.

The overwhelming majority of the artifacts found at Sakheri Sughir are probably related to food. Choppers and used blades were probably used in butchering, leaving respectively blunt marks and cut marks on the bones. The grinding slabs were probably used in grain preparation, however, containers make up the bulk of this category. It is very difficult to infer the specific uses of types of vessels from form alone; all that can be said is that spouted vessels contained liquids and that the cups and smaller bowls were probably used in the serving of foods.

Of the architectural elements, bricks are common. Bitumen-covered reed constructions are used. Ceramic drains are rare.

Items of adornment are very rare. There are two kinds of beads, one of bone and one of carnelian.

THE DISTRIBUTION OF ARTIFACTS IN THE EXCAVATIONS

If the original random sample had been completely investigated then an adequate study of the relation of artifact types to features and to each other would have been possible. With only half of the planned sample investigated, any such study must remain tentative. The distribution of artifacts in thirty-two provenience units on the site is given in Table 14.

The first approach to a distributional analysis was to study the actual number of each type of vessel part in each provenience unit. Each type was correlated with each other type using a product-moment correlation coefficient. This approach proves to be invalid because the range of numbers of a type in all provenience units is not distributed as a "normal" or bell-shaped curve. It is an underlying assumption of the coefficient that each variable be normally distributed.

The second approach was to study the percentage of each type of vessel part in each provenience unit. These percentages are normally distributed. However, out of the 120 correlation coefficients computed, only three were greater than $\pm.50$. This is to be expected by chance alone. Chance aside, with so few high correlations, it would be impossible to factor out sets of vessel parts which are distributed in similar ways unless there were a very few such sets.

The third approach was to study the presence or absence of nine key artifact types in all of the provenience units except small features. These types were selected because they are neither ubiquitous nor rare. The types are: sickle blades, clay rings, bitumen lumps, sherd-impressed bitumen, ledge bowl rims (with and without hatch strips), concave bowl rims, high rounded jar rims, band jar rims, and stone bowl rims. Out of the 36 coefficients of association between these key types computed, only two are significant. This is to be expected by chance alone.

After these three attempts, I would conclude that there is no evidence of sets of artifacts distributed in similar or contrasting patterns in the excavated area of the site.

A fourth approach was to study the vertical and horizontal distribution of each type or group of types by itself. There are several interesting distributions though their statistical significance is difficult to assess.

One of these is horizontal. There are nine ceramic rings, probably net sinkers, in the northern block around the work area. There is only one in the southern block near the rectangular structure. Repair of nets must have been undertaken primarily in the work area.

Three are vertical distributions. The percentage of ring bases among jar and bowl bases is from 11 per cent to 14 per cent in strata I*c*, and I*b* in the north block, and stratum III in the south block. In higher and more recent stratum I*a* in the north block and II and I in the southern block, the ratios are from 27 per cent to 33 per cent. This marked increase in the relative frequency of ring bases supports a correlation of the floor of I*a* in the north block with the floor of II in the south block.

The percentage of reserve slip jar shoulders among all jar shoulders is from 21 per cent to 34 per cent in all strata in the north block and strata II and III in the south block. These are absent in the higher and more recent stratum I in the south block. This further supports the correlation suggested on depositional grounds in the first section of this chapter and supported in the above paragraph.

Finally there is the distribution of varieties of the conical cup base. Figure 23 presents the per cent of profile types amon

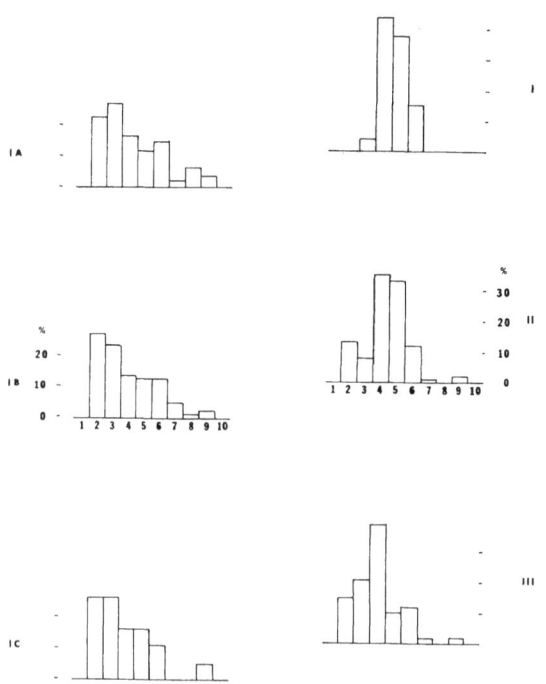

FIG. 23. Stratigraphic distribution of cup base types.

the measurable cup bases of each stratum as a bar graph. The north block is dominated by high percentages of relatively narrow types 2 and 3. The south block is dominated by high percentages of wider types 4 and 5. As deposits accumulated in the south block, types 2 and 3 decline in importance and type 5 increases in importance. This implies a general trend toward wider cups. There are two possible explanations.

1) There is a general decrease in popularity of the narrow cups in this community. My correlation of Ia in the north block with II in the south block is incorrect, and in fact, the excavated strata in the south block are all later than those in the north block. This could be tested by digging a connecting trench between the two blocks. This will certainly be an important task should excavations be continued.
2) My correlation is correct. The difference between the north and south blocks is variation in the cups of two contemporary domestic units reflecting different sources of pottery or differing participation in the shifts of fashion. It will be necessary to excavate additional domestic units on this site and a series of kiln areas on nearby towns to fully investigate this hypothesis.

In summary, the distributional study of the artifacts implies three points: (1) the various tool maintenance and food preparation activities were conducted in sufficient proximity that their debris was discarded in the same places; (2) there was some general style change in jar form and decoration during the brief period of time represented by the upper strata of the site; (3) there are interesting distributions in the varieties of conical cups, but these cannot at present be explained.

EARLY DYNASTIC GRAVES AT TELL 'UBAID

The two burials found at Sakheri Sughir were of young individuals. The nearby Early Dynastic cemetery adjacent to the rural center at Tell 'Ubaid contained a majority of adults. It is likely that some of the adults buried here were from the village of Sakheri Sughir. Furthermore, it is likely that the people buried around the rural center rather than in the cemeteries around the towns were in some way connected with rural activities regardless of where they lived. Therefore, the study of this cemetery should reveal something about the human population which labored in the countryside, and something about the way it was organized.

The cemetery was excavated by Sir Leonard Woolley in 1923 and 1924 (Hall and Woolley, 1927). Bone preservation was variable. Erosion and disturbance must have obliterated many graves. Woolley provides a description of all the features in the cemetery. With this it is possible to sort out a group of 28 definite graves probably of the period with which I am concerned. In the few cases where the description and the plan of the graves conflicted, the evidence of the plan was accepted.

Sir Arthur Keith's study of the skulls from 'Ubaid (Hall and Woolley, 1927:214-40) is directed at an assessment of the racial affinities of the population. Nevertheless one can attempt to infer something about the physical characteristics of the population from Keith's data and that provided by Dr. Mayhall and Dr. Merbs on the two individuals from Sakheri Sughir.

These people had relatively long narrow heads and prominent noses. They are thus similar to many Near Eastern populations of today. Their necks were thick and heavily muscled (Hall and Woolley, 1927:238). It is likely that the rest of the body was similarly muscular, though only one postcranial skeleton was examined. The jaws are relatively large (Hall and Woolley, 1927:237). The adults from 'Ubaid have extreme tooth wear. Keith observes only that caries are rare but that abscesses resulting from gumboils are common (Hall and Woolley, 1927:234). Without information on the location of the abscesses and their association with various age and sex categories, nothing can be inferred about their possible causes. The teeth of the young individuals from Sakheri Sughir are well preserved. They exhibit no distinctive pathologies. Adult incisors and canines were present on one individual. They are remarkably large. Finally Keith notes that at least eight of the fifteen preserved individuals were over sixty years of age. Obviously the sample is biased. Several of these aged individuals had rheumatic changes in the cervical vertebrae. In summary, there are suggestions that the population was robust and that some individuals lived an unusually long time. Little can be said about diet and disease. Large, carefully excavated samples of complete skeletons are needed.

Now let us turn to the problem of how this population was structured. The inference of social structure from burial data is based upon two related assumptions. First, that an individual's status in life is reflected in his funeral. The major archeological evidences of this funeral are the placement of the skeleton and the types and placement of other objects with the skeleton. Second is that the dimensions of variation in individual funeral ritual are homologous with the dimensions of social structure

(Brown, 1967). In order to discover these dimensions the information available on the burials is recorded on edge punch cards and each attribute of the skeletal placement and the objects is compared with all other categories in order to demonstrate nonrandom distribution or associations of attributes. Dimensions in funeral ritual are defined on the bases of these distributions and associations.[3]

Some problems with the 'Ubaid graves are their small number, their disturbed character, and cursory description. The following analysis is thus tentative indeed. Certain general points should be mentioned before the analysis is presented.

First, none of the females was found in a grave with offerings. One female is very late; the rest are from "ruined and otherwise empty graves." This raises the possibility that females were partially exhumed and further funeral rituals were held elsewhere, or that only certain parts of females were buried in the first place. In any event, only aged men are evidenced in our sample.

Second, the objects are discussed at length by Sir Leonard. Nevertheless, certain points need stress. A few of the graves are definitely of the Jemdet Nasr period, and some of the graves are definitely of the later Early Dynastic period. These have been eliminated from consideration. A majority are, however, of the earlier phase of the Early Dynastic period. In these graves the dominance of wide conical cups and the apparent scarcity of reserve slip and punctate jar shoulders suggest a date late in this earlier phase, contemporary with or more recent than stratum I in the south block at Sakheri Sughir.

Sir Leonard argues that the graves can be sorted into early, middle, and late groups (Hall and Woolley, 1927:176-78). This division is not completely convincing since his late group contains some definitely early types (Hall and Woolley, 1927: Plate IX, Type XCIII). It would be fruitless, however, to attempt to redefine these groups without a new stratigraphic sample from refuse deposits covering the entire Early Dynastic period from on the nearby towns. In Table 3 below, the attributes of the graves are tested against Sir Leonard's chronological groupings.

There is no pattern of relationship between these possible chronological groups and any of these classes of attributes which could not easily result from chance alone. It is possible, however, that the apparent increase in number of jars and cups and

---

[3] The graves utilized in this study are numbered C 5, 6, 7, 20, 28, 29, 35, 36, 37, 40, 42, 46, 49, 53, 56, 57, 60, 61, 63, 68, 70, 82, 83, 84, 89, 91 and 94.

TABLE 3

THE ATTRIBUTES OF THE 'UBAID GRAVES IN WOOLLEY'S
CHRONOLOGICAL GROUPS

	Early	Middle	Late
Head			
North	1	...	1
Northeast	1	...	...
East	...	...	...
Southeast	1	1	...
South	...	3	...
Southwest	3	1	5
West	...	2	...
Northwest	3	4	2
Face			
North	...	1	...
Northeast	2	4	2
East	1	2	1
Southeast	1	1	...
South	...	1	...
Southwest	2	1	...
West	...	1	...
Northwest	2	1	3
Items			
0-3 jars	5	9	2
4+ jars	4	2	6
0-5 cups	6	7	1
6-10 cups	3	2	4
11+ cups	...	2	3
Knife	1	1	...
Metal bowl	1	2	...
Stone bowl	4	1	1
Placement of Item Groups			
Head	4	3	...
Side	...	3	...
Foot	1	...	1
Head and side	3	2	5
Head and foot	1	...	2
Side and foot	...	2	...
All three	...	1	...
Group			
Northwest	1	2	...
Northeast	1	2	...
Center	2	4	3
Southwest	5	3	4

decrease in number of nonceramic items in the latest group is significant of a change in funeral behavior. Future research will tell. For the purposes of this study the 28 graves will be treated as a single sample.

Finally some of the objects, notably those of metal, contribute to the knowledge of the technology of the period. Two small copper axes and two copper daggers, and a number of copper vessels were found in the graves. A copper fishhook found loose in disturbed soil may be of the period under consideration. A variety of items of adornment also occurred.

Classes of the Attributes of the Graves

Completeness—Some "graves" contain no evidence of bodies. Some may be post-funeral offerings. These are not considered. Some graves lack crania and some lack post-cranial skeletons. Whether these conditions result from differential chemical action, accidental disturbance, or deliberate separation of body parts is not clear, so these attributes have not been used in this analysis.

Position—There is considerable variation in position, but information is not available in enough cases to compare this variation against that of other attribute variations. All burials are flexed to some extent. Of those illustrated 90 per cent have less than a 60 degree angle between upper and lower leg. Only 33 per cent have less than a 90 degree angle between spinal column and upper leg. Sixty per cent are flexed on the left side.

Orientation—Neither head nor face are randomly oriented.

TABLE 4

HEAD AND FACE ORIENTATION OF THE 'UBAID GRAVES

	N	NE	E	SE	S	SW	W	NW
Head	2	1	0	2	3	9	2	9
Face	1	8	4	2	1	3	1	6

Such distributions could arise by chance less than one time out of twenty. Heads tend to point southwest or northwest. Faces tend to point northwest or northeast. There are several possibilities here. One is that the bodies are aligned with some topographical irregularity. Second is that graves were placed in ordered plots, the first being oriented accidentally and the rest following it. Examination of the schematic map (Fig. 24) and Table 5 indicate this is unacceptable. Similarly oriented burials do not cluster spatially.

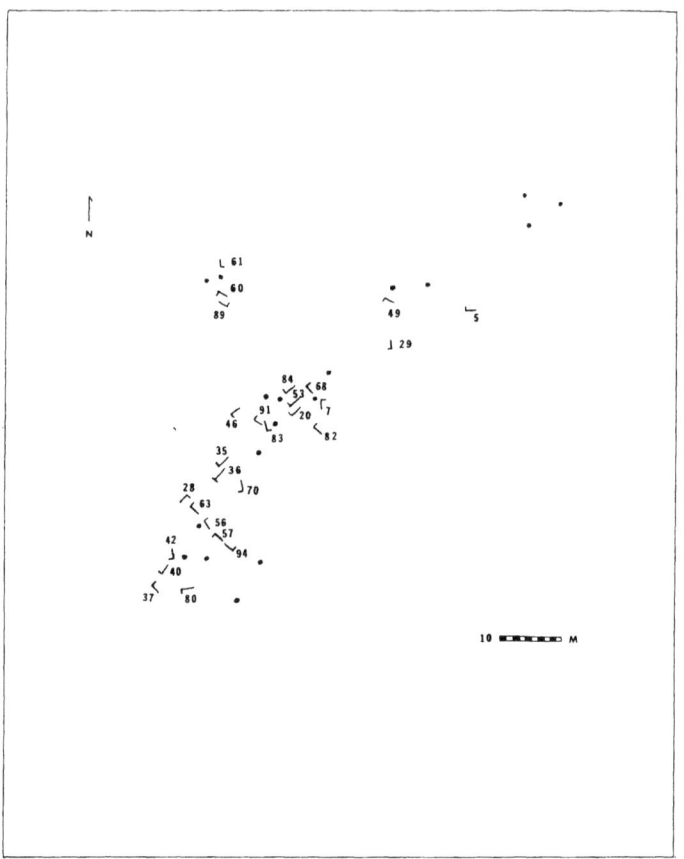

FIG. 24. Schematic plan of the 'Ubaid cemetery. The long line represents body orientation; the short line represents face orientation; the dot marks a group of pots apparently not in a grave.

Third is that the orientation is toward certain compass points. This seems unlikely since burials are oriented toward both the cardinal points and the quarter points of the compass. Fourth is that the burials are oriented toward an astronomic phenomena such as sunrise or sunset. Fifth is that the burials are oriented towards places on the earth. This hypothesis seems a possible explanation for facial orientation since 55 per cent of the burials face towards the three nearest dwelling sites, Sakher Sakheri Sughir, and Shaman. A direct test of this requires exact measurement (while the burial is being excavated) of facial orientation and assessment of movement of the cranium during decay.

TABLE 5

ORIENTATION IN THE AREAS OF THE 'UBAID CEMETERY

	N	NE	E	SE	S	SW	W	NW
Heads								
Northwest area..	...	1	1	...	...	1	...	...
Northeast area..	1	...	...	...	...	1	1	...
Center area....	...	3	2	1	...	...	...	2
Southwest area..	...	4	...	1	1	1	...	4
Faces								
Northwest area..	...	...	...	1	1	...	...	1
Northeast area..	...	...	...	...	1	...	1	1
Center area....	1	...	...	...	1	4	...	3
Southwest area..	...	1	...	1	...	5	1	4

Quantity of Objects — A variety of objects could occur in a grave. Only conical cups and small jars were common. These will be considered first. The other objects were much rarer. Some of these will be considered subsequently.

TABLE 6

THE ASSOCIATION BETWEEN JARS AND CUPS IN THE 'UBAID CEMETERY

Number of Cups	0	1-3	4-6	7-9	10+	Total
0	...	6	...	...	...	6
1-5	1	4	2	1	...	7
6-10	...	3	2	3	1	9
11-20	...	2	1	...	...	3
21+	...	1	...	...	1	2
Total	1	16	5	4	2	28

There is considerable range of variation. In general, graves with more cups have more jars. Spearman's coefficient of correlation between cups and jars is +.57. On the average, there are two cups for every jar. Cups are frequently upside down or stacked one inside the other so they were probably empty. Jars are generally right side up, and could have contained something. The containers in a grave might be thought of as a setting for a meal. such, they need not reflect the individual's status before death; they could just as well be related to something like the number of others at the funeral or the number of dead relatives of the buried individual.

If the number of containers is related to an individual's high or low status before death, we would expect the number of jars or cups to be correlated in some way with the number of items of intrinsic value. Metal and carved stone are rare as are intrinsically valuable materials which show up in a number of graves. Table 7 shows that metal and carved stone items show little association with quantity of jars or cups.

TABLE 7

THE ASSOCIATION BETWEEN VESSELS AND RARE ITEMS IN THE 'UBAID CEMETERY

	Number of Jars				Number of Cups				
	0-3	4-6	7-9	10+	0	1-5	6-10	11-20	21+
Knife	2	...	...	...	1	...	...	1	...
None	14	5	4	2	5	7	9	2	2
Metal bowl	1	...	...	1	1	1	...	...	...
None	14	5	4	1	5	6	9	3	2
Stone bowl	2	4	...	...	...	5	...	1	...
None	14	1	4	2	6	2	9	2	2

If anything, these rare items tend to occur in graves with fewer containers. Also, carved stone and metal items do not occur together in the sample. If they indicate a higher status, then such status was a sporadic phenomenon.

Thus quantity of objects indicates no more than a single status level.

Placement of Objects in the Graves—The objects tend to occur in groups. These are either at the head, the side, or the foot of the body. Table 8 illustrates the occurrence of jars and cups and other items in these locations.

TABLE 8

THE PLACEMENT OF OBJECTS IN THE 'UBAID GRAVES

Object	Position of Group		
	Head	Side	Foot
Small jar	11	15	3
Cup	14	13	7
Stone bowl	2	3	1
Miniature jar	10	2	1
Total number groups	19	15	8

There is a high frequency of miniature jars around the head. Sir Leonard notes that they often were placed near the mouth. There is a high frequency of jars and cups on the side. There is a high frequency of cups near the foot. Near the head the ratio of cups to jars seems to be random. Spearman's coefficient of correlation is -.06. Near the side the ratio of cups to jars is generally 2:1. Spearman's coefficient of correlation is +.67. Presumably it is the combination of these groups which caused the lesser correlation of gross number of cups and jars mentioned in the previous section.

Distribution of Graves in the Cemetery—Four concentrations of excavated and documented graves can be isolated. How many concentrations were left unexamined and how many had been obliterated by erosion is not clear.

We have already examined the association between head and facial orientations and those four groupings. Let us consider other such associations.

Table 9 shows the relation between the four groupings and both rare items and number of jars and cups.

TABLE 9

NUMBERS OF ITEMS IN THE AREAS OF THE 'UBAID CEMETERY

Items	Northwest	Northeast	Center	Southwest
0-3 Jars	3	3	3	6
4+ Jars	...	...	6	6
0-5 Cups	2	2	5	4
6-10 Cups	1	1	2	5
11+ Cups	...	...	2	3
Knife	...	...	1	1
Metal bowl	...	...	1	2
Stone bowl	...	...	3	3

Though it seems that the graves with more vessels are concentrated in the central and southwest groups, this distribution could result, by change alone, in more than one out of every ten samples from a cemetery with no such concentration. The distribution of rare items also implies, however, that there is a concentration of more items and of items of greater value in the south part of the investigated area (see Table 10). If so, this may result from the fact that the excavation removed the center of the cemetery, with better furnished graves, and the northern periphery, with relatively poorly furnished graves.

TABLE 10

THE PLACEMENT OF ITEMS IN GRAVES IN AREAS OF THE 'UBAID CEMETERY

Items	Northwest	Northeast	Center	Southwest
Head only	1	2	2	2
Side only	...	1	2	...
Foot only	1	...	...	1
Head and side	...	...	4	6
Head and foot	...	...	1	1
Side and foot	...	...	...	2
Head, side and foot	1	...	...	...

There is no valid statistical test for a matrix with this many blanks, however no relationships are apparent.

Dimensions of Funeral Variation —We have now considered five classes of attributes: body completness, body position, body orientation, quantity of items, and placement of items. The relation of each of these attributes to the spatial groupings of graves has been considered. Two significant dimensions of variability have been discovered: these are facial orientation and number of containers in the grave. The relation between these two dimensions is given in Table 11 below.

TABLE 11

THE ASSOCIATION BETWEEN ORIENTATION OF FACE AND NUMBER OF VESSELS

Items	N	NE	E	SE	S	SW	W	NW
0-3 Jars	1	4	4	1	1	2	1	2
4+ Jars	...	4	...	1	...	1	...	4
0-5 Cups	1	4	4	2	...	1	...	1
6-10 Cups	...	3	...	...	...	2	1	3
11+ Cups	...	1	...	...	1	...	...	2
Knife	...	1	...	1	...	...	...	...
Metal bowl	...	2	1	...	...	...	...	...
Stone bowl	...	1	1	1	...	...	...	3

Once again there are too many blanks in this matrix to test the significance of any associations. By grouping facial orientations into those facing nearby settlements (N, NE, E) and those not facing nearby settlements, and testing for the two categories of container quantity separately, it was still not possible to define any significant relationship between the two dimensions.

Summary—Of the ninety-four features reported, only twenty-eight were well-preserved graves of the general period of interest. An analysis of the reported attributes of these twenty-eight graves revealed two unrelated dimensions of variation in funeral behavior. One is that graves are nonrandomly oriented. This may have been done in order to face the body towards a particular settlement. The other is that graves contained a varying quantity of containers, not correlated in any significant way with items of preserved value. This may reflect something like the number of mourners at the funeral. These interpretations are hypotheses that I have not been able to test further.

There are two interesting points to be drawn from our considerations. First is that there is evidence for only one social class. Second is that there is no evidence of kin groups. There are no grave clusters with contrasting funeral procedures, such as can be found in the prehistoric 'Ubaid period cemetery at Ur (Woolley, 1955). This does not mean that there were no kin groups. It means only that other considerations took precedence in the preserved traces of the funeral ritual.

GENERAL SUMMARY OF THE RURAL COMMUNITY

The archeological remains of a rural village and a nearby rural cemetery have been considered. It is a reasonable assumption that the groups which left these remains were involved in rural production.

The village was an agglomeration of small domestic complexes and associated features such as ovens and hearths scattered along a small canal. It perhaps contained fifteen families. Such families probably belonged to a single social class of low rank. There is no suggestion of kin groupings larger than the extended family. Certain individuals did own personal items of presumed value such as copper axes or knives, but their rank was not otherwise differentiated. These families utilized a simple technology whose imperishable parts were made of ceramic, flint, or bitumen. Some of these tools were used in production, but most were used in food preparation. Tools were repaired or manufactured and food was prepared in such limited confines that the debris of these activities could not be statistically isolated with my limited samples of refuse. Thus there was little specialization of activities. When larger random samples at sites like Sakheri Sughir are excavated, it will be possible to estimate the rate at which materials and goods were brought from the towns to a rural domestic unit, and consumed in domestic activity and in production.

V

THE ARCHEOLOGICAL EVIDENCE OF RURAL PRODUCTION

INTRODUCTION

THE direct study of subsistence production with archeological evidence is always difficult. Fragile plant remains are seldom recovered in their true quantity, even with such methods as the flotation technique. The domestic dog and pig surely destroy animal remains. In the laboratory it is often difficult to assemble good comparative collections of modern plants and animals of the region. Finally, immense samples are necessary if an adequate study is to be done. Insufficient as the evidence is, let us consider what was produced in the vicinity of Sakheri Sughir. After this consideration of the data, the labor of production will be discussed. Finally, certain predictions about administrative structure will be made.

RURAL PRODUCTS

Wild Plants and Animals

Three genera of wild plant material are attested. Among the reeds utilized, only the club rush, *Scirpus sp.*, is tentatively identified. The one specimen had been used to make a mat. This low reed can be found in any perennially damp area. Tamarisk (*Tamarix sp.*) and poplar (*Populus sp.*) were used as a fuel, and as architectural elements. Both are trees of the river levee. They may well have been cultivated or at least protected at this time.

In the fine screen samples, where loss of fragile fish bone is minimal, fish bone constitutes 72 per cent of the total number of bones. On the other hand, fish constitutes 23 per cent of the total weight of the bones. This latter per cent is probably more indicative of the importance of fish in the meat diet of rural Early Dynastic villagers. Detailed study of the fish has been hampered by the absence of good comparative collections in North America. Three categories of fish stand out. Most common are members of the carp family (*Cyprinidae*). Today these are usually taken with nets. In addition the drum (*Otolithus sp.*) and catfish (*Silureus sp.*) occur in the collection.

A number of fresh water mussels, mostly Unionidae, were collected and eaten. Study of these has not yet been undertaken.

There are two categories of birds: a large duck and small- and medium-sized doves are identified. It is presumed that these were hunted, though the possibility of domestication cannot be rejected. If hunted, the technique is not known.

A few larger mammals were hunted. An equid of ass-size perhaps wild, a very large, probably wild pig (*Sus scrofa ferus*), and perhaps Gazelle (*Gazella subgutterosa*) are present. More specimens of the first are needed. The second is differentiated from the domestic varieties by size, and it is difficult to assess the actual number of wild individuals present. The pig is an animal of the thickets probably hunted by groups of men with spears. The Onager, wild ox, and gazelle are animals of the open plain. The hunting technique is unknown.

Domestic Plants and Animals

Only one domestic plant is definitely attested. Two grains of hulled six-row barley (*Hordeum*)[1] and two grains of barley not identifiable to variety were noted.[2] In addition, Helbaek reports a single imprint of barley on an Early Dynastic sherd from Ur, and a dominance of barley imprints in roughly contemporary deposits from nearby Warka (Helbaek, 1960). On the basis of these data, we will assume that barley was the major crop.

Certainly, however, many other domestic plants were grown. Even in the saltiest areas of the modern alluvium some wheat is grown. In addition, flax, dates, apples, plums, and grapes could be expected. One seed of knotweed (*Polygonum sp.*) was associated with the barley.[1] The seed of this ubiquitous weed was certainly edible, but this occurrence is most likely a chance inclusion in fodder or harvested barley.

The disappointing samples are entirely my own fault. The flotation techniques used are suited for temperate climates, and in arid regions special care is needed. First, since the presence and density of plant remains cannot be inferred from the type of soil, volumes of at least .05 cubic meters should be taken. The volume should always be recorded for future quantitative studies. Second, the sample should be dried in a relatively cool spot to minimize the disintegration of seeds. Third, the heavy soil residue at the bottom of the flotation tank should be

1. Identified by Dr. Van Zeist. 2. Identified by Dr. Stewart.

filtered on very fine screen to recover heavier seeds, etc. (see Struever, 1968 for a discussion of flotation techniques for temperate climates).

The distribution of individual domestic animals and their parts is given in Table 12. Domestic sheep (*Ovis aries*) and goat (*Capra hircus*) bones together outnumber cattle (*Bos taurus*) by a ratio of five to one. Sheep and goat individuals, however, outnumber cattle by a ratio of only two to one.

Since all parts of sheep and cattle occur, and since a cow provides at least four times as much meat as a sheep or goat, it is probable that the ratio of sheep meat to cow meat in the diet was roughly one to one.

Among the seventeen individual sheep-goats represented, six are definitely identifiable to species. Five are sheep and one is a goat. This ratio is to be expected in an area with such high summer temperatures. Five of the individuals were less than or near one year of age. Three were definitely old. The rest were of indeterminate or middle age. These data imply nothing about the pattern of sheep-goat husbandry.

Among the eight cattle, one is a calf. The cattle must be periodically herded with a bull for fertilization, must be milked when lactating, and must be protected from the summer sun. These strictures limit the pattern of cattle husbandry.

There are two pigs in the sample. One large animal, probably the wild form, *Sus scrofa ferus*, is represented only by a front limb. It was perhaps butchered elsewhere. One smaller immature animal, perhaps the domestic form, *S. scrofa domesticus*, is represented by cranial and forelimb fragments. It was probably butchered on the site. It is difficult to predict the requirements of domestic pigs in this area.

RURAL LABOR

Now the above information on products, the information on the traditional uses of plants, and animals presented in the area given in Chapter II, the inferences about land use given in Chapter III, and the inferences about the technology and sociology of a rural village made in Chapter IV can be drawn together.

Gathering Marsh Resources

In order to consider the organization of labor for gathering, hunting pigs, or hunting migratory water birds, we would have to

TABLE 12

PORTIONS OF DOMESTIC ANIMALS IN THE AREAS
OF SAKHERI SUGHIR

Location		Sheep-Goat	Cattle	Pig
North	0	1: Mandibular Vertebral Pelvic Distal forelimb	1: Cranial Distal hindlimb	
	IA	2: Cranial Vertebral Pelvic Distal forelimb Proximal and distal hindlimb	2: Cranial Vertebral Pelvic Proximal forelimb Distal forelimb Distal hindlimb	1: Scapular Distal forelimb
	IB	2: Cranial Mandibular Scapular Vertebral Pelvic Proximal hindlimb Distal forelimb *(Ovis)*	1: Vertebral	
	IC	1: Distal forelimb Proximal hindlimb Distal hindlimb *(Ovis)*	1: Cranial	
	II	1: Cranial *(Ovis)*		
	IIIB	1: Vertebral		
	IVB	1: Cranial Mandibular		
South	I	3: Mandibular Pelvic Distal hindlimb	1: Vertebral Scapular ?Distal hindlimb	
	II	1: Cranial *(Capra)* Mandibular Scapular Vertebral Distal hindlimb	2: Cranial Proximal forelimb Distal forelimb	1: Cranial Distal hindlimb
	III	2: Scapular Proximal forelimb Distal hindlimb *(Ovis)*	1: Cranial Distal hindlimb	
Canal		1: Vertebral Pelvic		
Total		17	8	2

EVIDENCE OF RURAL PRODUCTION

know the techniques of obtaining those items, the location of the major marsh areas, and the size and location of marsh-oriented settlements. While the first type of data is to some extent known, the latter two types are not. Until techniques for locating former marsh environments and for recognizing marsh-oriented technologies are available, this aspect of rural production cannot be further discussed.

Gathering River Resources

The major aquatic resource is fish. Fishing with hook and line or with a single net are simple activities requiring few people.

Fishing with a combined net and two or more boats is of more interest. The actions of the eight or ten men involved must be coordinated. The coordinator must decide on the basis of his prior knowledge where to fish. This is a single decision about probabilities based on his own knowledge and involving a large number of possible moves. He must also dictate the actions of his crew during the operation. These are decisions about acts based on sensory information and involving a limited number of possible moves. It is probably the physical limits of net size rather than the decision situation which determine the maximum size of a group under a coordinator.

The moving of fish to the consumer is a different problem. In the case of both single and combined net fishing, large quantities of fish can be taken. The take must be made and either delivered or preserved on a reasonable schedule or else large amounts will be wasted. At the least, this requires that one individual know how many of each kind of fishing team is operating, and that he periodically consult with the coordinator of each team in order to keep some semblance of a schedule. This administrator will therefore be making decisions about actions based on sensory information and his prior knowledge with a limited number of possible moves. It seems likely that rate of fish consumption rather than the decision situation would limit the number of fishing teams under an administrator.

Animal Husbandry

Sheep and goats may or may not require organized administration, depending on the type of herding pattern. In the Ur enclave, however, with its relatively high population density, there would have been relatively little grazing for sheep. Let us assume that a residence unit ate, on the average, three sheep or goats per year, a rate of consumption lower than the present four per year. About three thousand animals would be eaten every year. This would require a minimum of ten thousand animals. It seems likely that some winter grazing on the southern or alluvial deserts was necessary, though it is difficult to support this argument in the absence of data on the carrying capacity of the various types of grazing land available. Each flock of 40 to 100 sheep requires a shepherd. The coordinator of a group of shepherds must make decisions about the movements of flocks and the selection of campsites based on his knowledge of the area, of the weather, and of the presence of other groups. Only the last mentioned information is derived from the shepherds. Thus the coordinator of flocks has a relatively simple labor coordination problem.

Let us consider cattle. If cattle are installed with families while lactating, then all that is necessary is one individual who knows the herd and knows the families in the area. He makes a decision about an act on the basis of his prior knowledge and sensory information in which there are a number of possible moves. If, on the other hand, the cattle are always kept in a herd, and milk products are distributed, then a differentiated group of cattle and milk workers must be coordinated. The coordinator must schedule the disposition of cows and calves and must schedule the processing of milk and the distribution of milk products. This requires decision both about probabilities such as the selection of breeding stock and about acts such as the moving of products. In such cases a number of sources of information may be involved and there may be a number of possible moves. If milking institutions can be shown to exist, it is a moot point whether the decision situations or the herd size would limit the number of subordinates under a coordinator.

Plant Cultivation

Agriculture presents interesting organizational problems. There were about 5,800 people in the enclave. Eliminating the very old and young, the infirm, and the elite; perhaps 2,500 would be available for agricultural labor. There were about 6,000 arable hectares in the enclave, of which 3,000 would be cultivated in one season.

Canal and bank construction do not require large groups of workers, though they can be used. All that is necessary is someone familiar with the operation of the canal system who decides

EVIDENCE OF RURAL PRODUCTION

where such improvements must be made. Since no fewer than five small independent canal networks probably existed, there may have been a number of such individuals, each making decisions about a limited range of possible alterations in these rather small networks.

Assuming that there were about twenty kilometers of primary canals, about ten would have to be cleaned annually. This would require less labor than the 360 man-days per kilometer of the upper alluvium. Assuming 250 man-days per kilometer, the ten kilometers would require about 2,500 man-days. This would presumably be divided into separate operations for each canal network, so it would take about 500 men one day to clean each such system. The modern function of coordinators in this work is to insure attendance. Usually he is the head of some extant social group such as a lineage, and he merely passes the decision of the administrator to this group. Few decisions are required of this role. The overall administrator, however, must place the various work groups along the canal and check on their work. He is thus making decisions about acts on the basis of as many sources of information as there are groups under his direction resulting in a limited number of moves—either a group continues work or moves on to the next section of the canal. This is a relatively simple problem in labor coordination.

The allocation of land does not require large groups of laborers. Only a few surveyors are necessary to carry out the decisions of the administrator. Unfortunately there is no archeological data on the pattern of fallowing or the size of parcels of land, so it is difficult to consider the decision-making involved in land allocation. This topic will be considered in the next chapter.

Plowing and seeding require an immense input of labor and materials. If all 3,000 cultivated hectares in the Ur enclave were planted in barley, about 360,000 kilograms or 500 cubic meters of seed would be needed. Twelve thousand man-days would be required. However, at least three months are available to do this work so about forty three-man teams could do the job. Thus no large groups of laborers are necessary. The administrator of a group of plow teams would have to consider plows, seed, the team and their fodder, the upkeep of the plowman over this considerable period, and the scheduling of work. He must make decisions about acts given a large number of possible sources of information and a large number of moves. However, it is important to note that many problems of the organization of plowing, such as seed and fodder storage, allotments for workers, and plow repair, are likely to occur in the town. The rural aspect of the organization of plowing might present only the relatively simple problem of scheduling. Decision-making in the rural organization would thus be similar to that in canal construction or cleaning. Parenthetically, it is notable that the recent pattern of plowing with a single large horse or mule, rather than a team of smaller animals, has simplified these problems of labor coordination.

The allocation of water requires little group labor. Schedules are set up for each area and subarea and should they be violated the individuals who suffer water loss will complain. Someone must construct the original schedule. This schedule involves decisions that are closely interrelated with those of land allocation, and it is presumably handled at that time. Someone must satisfy water complaints but since this task involves no group labor its organization will presumably be determined by other factors such as canal distribution, frequency of disputes, and land tenure pattern.

The harvesting and division of grain requires considerable labor and coordination. If we assume each hectare requires about six man-days of harvest labor, then it would take about 1,500 people to harvest 3,000 hectares of barley in 12 days. This is well within the limits of the labor pool. Harvest of such an area would produce 2,400,000 kilograms, or 3,460 cubic meters, of barley which would have to be divided and transported. Harvest requires large groups of unskilled laborers, while division and transport require considerable coordination. In situations where land is farmed by individuals who receive the crop or part of the crop, the harvest laborers would require little coordination. In other situations a coordinator must make decisions about where to place individual laborers in the fields and what to give them in exchange for their labor. There are decisions about acts based on his own observations and resulting in a limited number of moves. Crop division requires only that the authority know the tenurial system of the field being divided. It is transport and storage that require coordination of labor. The coordinator of such an operation must know which piles of grain on the threshing floor are to go to where and what the transport schedule is. This is a point where major errors or pilfering could occur, so the amount of grain stored must be recorded and compared with land allotments. The coordinator would make decisions about acts based on his knowledge of the disposition of his transport animals or boats and the information received from the authority who divided the crop in which there would be a limited number of moves. The coordination problems presented by this situation would be further compounded because the operation is spread out between field and storehouse. A factor which cannot be assessed with archeological evidence is the proportion of the fields which were institutionally owned. If a large number were so owned at this time, then transport to the storehouse would be a major activity.

Finally, though various crucial junctures in cultivation have been discussed, the coordination of the labor of day to day upkeep of the fields has not been considered. Though each major operation such as canal-cleaning or harvest and each specialized operation such as plowing or transport require extraordinary organization, each field must be tended periodically from before seeding to harvest. Decisions about probabilities of crop success based on information about soil, water and prognostications about weather and pests, or decisions about acts such as irrigation based on unseasonal rainfall and allowing animals to graze on the young shoots must all be made by the worker in the field or by his coordinator. The sources of information would be observation of the diverse natural phenomena, and the possible combinations of moves is immense. It is possible that the organization developed to coordinate day to day fieldwork over many months will form the framework around which other special organizations can be constructed.

CONCLUSION

Where the data permits, each step in rural production has been considered in terms of the type of decision being made (i.e., is a known outcome being selected or is a probability being gambled upon?); the relative number of sources of information and the relative number of possible moves that the decision-maker can select. Factors limiting the organization of certain activities, has also been noted. My ratings of these variables are summarized in Table 13.

The table is arranged with the most complex decision situation or process at the top and least complex decision situation or process at the bottom. The theoretical considerations of Chapter I would lead to the following predictions. In general the first three activities should have a similar number of levels of decision-making and the last four should have a similar number of levels of decision-making. Specifically: (1) general cultivation, cattle husbandry, and harvest and transport should be similar;

(2) net fishing and sheep herding should be similar; (3) plowing and seeding and canal cleaning should be similar. It remains to be seen how many of these organizations are actually evidenced in the texts.

TABLE 13

ACTIVITIES AND DECISION VARIABLES

Activity	Decision	Relative Number of Sources	Relative Number of Moves	Limiting Factor
General cultivation	Probabilities and acts	Many	Many	Size of cultivated area
Cattle husbandry	Probabilities and acts	Many	Many	...
Harvest and transport	Acts	Many	Many	Length of season
Net fishing	Probabilities	Few	Many	Size of nets and boats
Sheep herding	Probabilities	Few	Many	...
Plowing and seeding	Acts	Few	Many	Size of cultivated area
Canal-cleaning	Acts	Few	Few	Size of canal system

VI

THE DOCUMENTARY EVIDENCE OF RURAL PRODUCTION

INTRODUCTION

IN economic activities writing is used to record information for later reference. The information recorded may be a description of something already done; for instance, it may be a property title or an account of stored goods. It may be a plan for future activity, such as a rate of exchange or of goods allotment. If there is no requirement for future reference to a description or plan, then there is no reason to record it. It is possible that some of the activities discussed in the previous chapter did not require written records. Even though a document may record an activity, the key words may not be known and the document may be misinterpreted. Finally, through the accidents of archeological discovery, only certain types of activity may be documented in the sample. In this chapter I will consider certain characteristics of the Ur Archaic Texts in general, the details of the activities recorded in the texts, and the structure of the organizations mentioned in the texts.

Let us consider the documentation of economic activity in Sumerian texts in general. Documents of the Third Dynasty of Ur of about 2000 B.C. have been found in numerous sites. About 16,000 economic texts are published. Many more lie unstudied in the museums of the world. The detail of these records is unbelievable: precise counts of a wide range of commodities, labor in fractions of man-days, careful dates, and unambiguous noting of the nature of each transaction and the people involved are all found in many texts. About 1600 earlier economic texts from the vicinity of ancient Lagash are published. They date from the very end of the Early Dynastic period. There are contemporary examples from Ur and Uruk. In these the date and the nature of the transaction are sometimes difficult to infer. About 180 economic texts from Fara, ancient Shurrupak, are published. They are a century or two earlier than the Lagash texts. There are contemporary examples from Adab and Abu Salabikh. They are not dated and the phrase describing the transaction is always laconic and often not in grammatical order. The Ur Archaic texts contain a very few laconic descriptive phrases. They are usually merely lists of numbers of items followed by a proper name. In many cases it is difficult to tell whether a text records collection or distribution.

Despite these problems with text format, as well as the lexical problems noted in the preface, it is possible to categorize the texts in terms of general function in the following way:

1) Exercise texts: These were discussed in Chapter III (see Fig. 25, text 225).
2) Goods deposit texts: These list large amounts of related goods such as types of grain, or types of small animals. A personal name and sometimes with a title or place name, ends this sort of text (see Fig. 25, text 185).
3) Goods allotment texts: These list a quantity and commodity in the first register, a personal name in the second register, and a quantity and name in each succeeding register unless the commodity changes, in which event the procedure is repeated. In a few cases there is a phrase indicating that items were eaten, or in part returned, supporting the interpretation of allotment texts (see Fig. 26, text 186).
4) Land survey texts: These usually brief texts give a quantity of land and a personal name or status, or a description of the block of land (see Fig. 26, text 102).
5) Land allotment texts: These usually long texts often being with the term "GAN," a surface measure. Each register notes a quantity of land and a personal name, status, or group name. This is the only category of texts on which totals are commonly recorded (see Fig. 27, text 226).
6) Personnel texts: These are lists of names each usually preceded by the number one. Additional comments, supervisors' names, and totals occur on various of these texts (see Fig. 27, text 371).

The quantities recorded on the texts use three distinct systems of numbering. One is for pure numbers, one is for volume, and one is for area. These are relatively well understood. The major problem is the size of the units or area and volume. The iku, the unit of area, was .35 hectares during the Third Dynasty of Ur. Other values are not known and in the absence of internal checks in the Ur Archaic Texts, the above value must be assumed. The unit of capacity may vary tremendously from time to time and city to city, so it is fortunate that the texts provide an internal check for Ur. Given the above assumption, then text 20, which records 54 gur of seed for 342 iku of area, and the ethnographic seed ratio noted in Chapter II, 120 kilos or 166 liters of barley per hectare, indicates a gur of about 270 kilos or 370 liters. It is unfortunate that a single text must be relied upon.

DOCUMENTARY EVIDENCE OF RURAL PRODUCTION 101

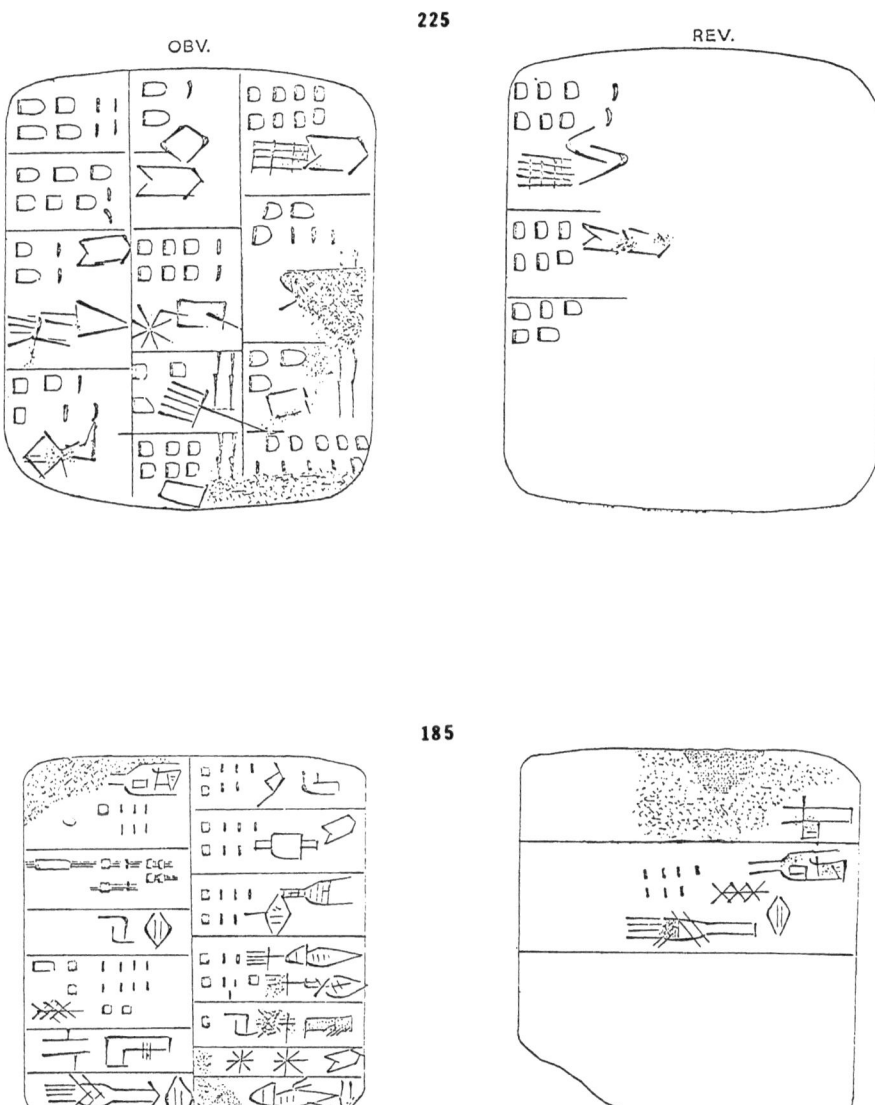

FIG. 25. An exercise text and a goods deposit text.

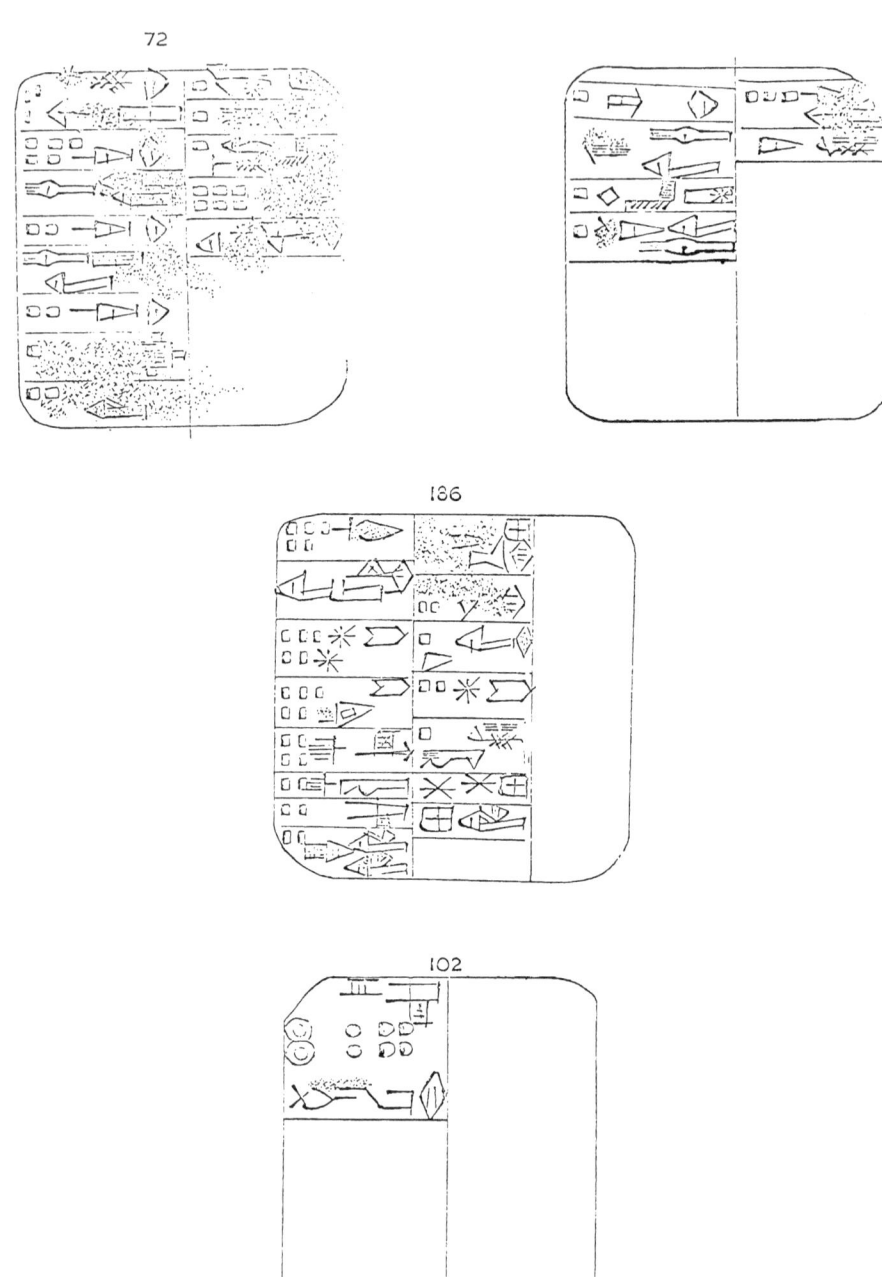

FIG. 26. Two goods allotment texts and a land survey text.

DOCUMENTARY EVIDENCE OF RURAL PRODUCTION 103

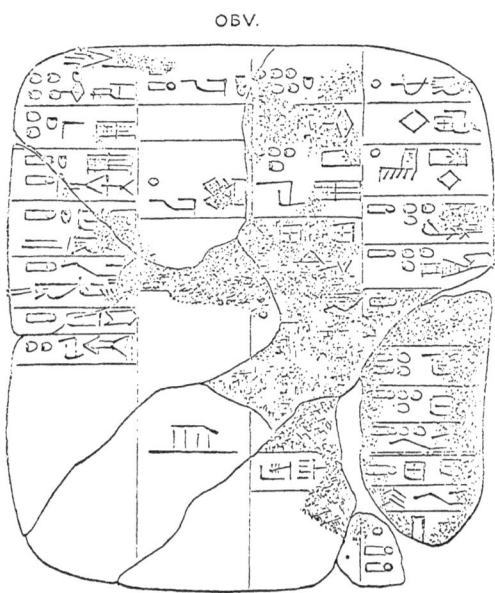

FIG. 27. A land allotment text.

Given these metric equivalents of the units of ancient Ur, then the production figures of Chapter II can be converted into Ur Archaic units: on tenanted estates with careful planning, an average of 1.2 gur per iku of barley and 1.1 gur per iku of wheat would be produced. On small farms not benefiting from large-scale planning, .9 gur per iku of barley and .7 gur per iku of wheat would be produced. Henceforth, the presentation will be in terms of gur and iku.

RURAL ACTIVITIES

Wild Resources

Reeds and reed products are referred to in five texts. In text 48 a type of reed (GI:KI) in units of eight to 140 are associated with four people. In text 25, perhaps a list of building materials, eight units of reeds (GI:GAL:GAL) are noted. In fragments 23, 138, and 235, small quantities of reed mats, some perhaps used in construction (kid.ig.sag) and others of unknown function (kid.uri$_2$), and reed baskets (pisan) are noted. In the last, these items are associated with the titles of foremen (ugula).

Wood is noted in three texts. In text 25, noted above, poles (giš ma.gíd), logs (giš tur.tur), and other possible woods are noted. In fragment 230 unknown woods are noted. In text 24, loads of poplar wood (gú.asal) are recorded. Five sets of twenty loads are noted in connection with one individual. Six sets of five loads are associated with another.

In contrast to the extensive documentation of fishing in the Lagash documents, there is only one fragment dealing with fishing from early Ur. In fragment 19, from 6 to 600 of various kinds of fish and 20 to 30 containers of fish are noted. In addition 10 to 30 of various kinds of birds including ducks (uz) are noted.

In none of these documents is the type of transaction clearly described. Almost nothing can be said about the organization of activities related to wild products.

Cultivated Resources: Animal Husbandry

A key document in the interpretation of these activities is text 16, a count of various types of sheep. On the obverse, 21 unknown animals, 36 probable rams, 16 ewes (u$_8$), 13 kids (máš), perhaps 8 fat-tail sheep (gukkal) and 6 grain-fed sheep (udu.niga) are recorded in connection with a partially obliterated phrase and the title nu.banda$_4$. On the obverse, 12 female lambs (sila$_2$.geme) and 14 male lambs (sila$_2$.nita) are recorded. Thirty per cent of the sheep are young, both males and females are present though the ratio is unclear, and a small proportion of goats are present. These are the expected characteristics of a flock as outlined in Chapter II. It is possible that this text is a flock census.

Most of the animal texts record small allotments to a number of people. The most explicit is text 186, which records two to five kids (máš) and one or two other small animals in connection with eleven names. More than 30 animals are noted. The text ends with the phrases "distribution of sheep, sheep to be eaten" (ḫal.ḫal.udu, udu.kú).

Similar documents include the following: text 3 records fourteen kids (máš) in lots of one or two in relation to twelve people. Text 47 records ten kids in lots of one to three to five people. Fragment 24 records more than twenty-four sheep (udu) in lots of one to five. Fragment 255 records single grain-flattened sheep (udu.niga) and another obscured item. Fragment 231 records more than thirty-four lambs (sila$_2$) in lots of two to four. Fragment 30 records various animals in connection with five people: more than thirty-nine rams (udu.nita) are noted in lots of five to fourteen. More than twenty-nine ewes (u$_8$) are noted in lots of two to eleven. More than two grain-fattened sheep are noted in lots of one to four. More than twenty adult animals are noted. If these are being distributed without decreasing the flock size below the annual natural increment, these can be no more than 35 per cent of the adults in the herd. There were probably more than 230 adults in the source flock or flocks. Documents comparable to these are found among the late Early Dynastic texts from Ur. In particular, Supplement 13 and Supplement 46, both consignments of many animals are comparable (Burrows, 1935). There is little reason to doubt that the above described Archaic texts are all allotments of some kind rather than collections.

Text 237 records 30 goats (uz) and some other items in relation to an individual. This resembles Supplement 39 and Supplement 42 and probably records a single consignment.

Fragment 80 records something about sheep-shearing (udu.ur$_4$).

Fragment 289 records one cow in connection with personal names. Later Supplement 45, an allotment for a feast, is similar.

In summary, these texts provide data about sheep and goat husbandry which considerably clarify the archeological data. These animals were kept in large herds, and probably were distributed by a central institution of some kind. This will be discussed subsequently.

Cultivated Resources: Agriculture

People in Agriculture

Before discussing agriculture itself something must be said about the people of the Ur area as they are revealed in the texts. This is a discussion of types of people rather than roles. The formal roles will be discussed in the next section.

Each presumed name which occurred in more than four informative contexts was placed on a card. Every mention of the name was analyzed. This limited biographic information was compared in terms of land allotment, food allotment, and offices held. Six groups can be defined, two of which are at present uninformative, and two of which can be combined.

1) Names which do not clearly refer to individuals or groups: A:PA:dug, I:ZI, šul.
2) Names which may refer to more than one individual: ^{d}Innanak, Lu.Lu, Ušum.gal, Pa.bil.ga.
3) Minor farmers: these are individuals who receive plots if six to twenty-four iku of land and small allotments of bread, beer, or animals. Seven of these have no other recorded activities: Ama.ušum.gal, Amar.Lugal, Amar^{d}Muš, Ib.mud, Lugal.ušum.gal, Ur.banda$_4$, Ur.sag. Two, in addition, handle large quantities of grain perhaps in transit to a grainary: Amar.ezen, Sal.é.ti. One utilizes some seed: Amar.ib.
4) Minor officials: These are individuals occurring on food allotment lists with small farmers, but who seldom receive land. They all appear as minor officials: Amar.u$_4$.sar, Mes:lu, Ku.li.
5) Important people: Some people receive much food, large plots of land, or large plots of land and much food together. There is much overlap of these groups. It seems likely that the differences are minor and perhaps result from the small number of biographic references in each case. Some important people were officials.
   a) Individuals allotted 36 to 216 iku of land but little food: A.geštin, Ag.Lu, Geštin, Nám, Lum.ma, Zur.zur.
   b) Individuals allotted 30 to 429 iku of land and much food: A.mer, A.ušum.gal, Ag[a], Ama.é.si, Ama.IGI+BUR, Amar.kisal, É.IGI+BUR, Kisal.si, Mes.pád.da, and Si.si.
   c) Individuals allotted little land but much food: Ama.alam, Ama.ka.dúg, Amar.É.BÍL, Amar.Lal, Amar.nab, Amar.sanga, Ma.NUNUZ+SAR, NA ŠEŠ:IB:GIŠ:TI:KALAM, Ur.sag.Nanna, Za.ma.

In summary, for purposes of this study there are two broad classes of people which I have termed minor people and important people. Clearly this rough division is neither final nor exhaustive.

Before turning to roles, a few comments must be made about personal names. The range of variation is remarkably small and sign groups often occur in more than one name. One is tempted to suggest a relation between individuals with similar names. To demonstrate this would require a comparative study of personal names in all Early Dynastic texts. Such is beyond the scope of this study.

Roles of Agriculture

The relationships between roles in specific organizations will be discussed at the end of the chapter. The following is a list of roles and some general comments on each:

1) arad and geme$_2$: In later times, these terms refer to male and female servants. In text 259, a group including many important men and women are so termed. It is difficult to conceive of these people as servants, so the designations may indicate simple male and female.
2) engar: This term distinguishes the individual who cultivates or directs cultivation of a block of land from the individual to whom the land is allotted. It is only used when there might be some confusion.
3) ugula: This term is written "PA." By itself it applies to the immediate supervisor of an activity as in ugula.gud, foreman of the oxen, or ugula.KU$_6$, foreman of the fishermen. In other cases, when the use of the term is unclear, it is written descriptively as PA.
4) Nu.banda$_4$: This term refers to an overseer of foremen in cases involving agriculture. There is a specific overseer of the palace, nu.banda$_4$.é.gal, mentioned in text 112.
5) Sanga: This term refers to an individual usually connected with large quantities of grain. The Sanga.AB is often noted. In the Fara literary texts, the term sanga frequently appears in place of dub-sar, scribe, in the colophon. It is possible that the sanga is the recorder of a storehouse in the Ur Archaic Texts.
6) PA:GIN: This term applies to an official in charge of a harvest. It is known from some later texts. In the Lagash texts he appears as an individual who directs 23 people in an unknown task (Nickolsky, 1905: Volume I, text 21, V6 and VII 1).
7) PA:SI: This term also applies to an official connected with harvests. Hallo (1957) suggests that this is a simple writing of PA:TE:SI, to be read ensi. He supports his contentions by pointing to parallel titles in the Fara texts. However, Ur Archaic fragment 35 contains the full writing PA:TE:SI:GAL, so the equivalence is unclear.

The PA:SI of Ur is mentioned in connection with quantities of bread in two documents (86 and 88), in connection with seed (177), and with the transport of large quantities of grain (222). The PA:SI of BAD x NIMGIR is mentioned in connection with large quantities of grain (188). Both are found in the slightly later Fara texts (Hallo, 1957:35). There is no evidence that the PA:SI of the Ur texts was any more than an economic administrator.

8) Sukkal: In the time of the Third Dynasty of Ur, this term denoted an imperial messenger. The term appears in the Ur Texts on a personnel list (112) and on a list of field foremen (343).

9) sag.dun$_4$: This term denotes the man who supervises the measuring and subdividing of blocks of land.
Other roles were discussed in Chapter III.

Agricultural Activity

Construction.—Construction work, especially for walls, is written, "AL x TAR" in later Sumerian. The sign appears in text 259 in an unclear context. The term is applied directly to land in fragment 196c. Al.tar fields of the official called the Uri$_2$.gal (gán. AL x TAR, uri$_2$.gal) are noted. In text 201 seed is issued for 412 iku of such land (here called gán. AL x TAR. DU.KU$_6$). In these contexts AL x TAR refers to an attribute of the field, perhaps that it has newly constructed banks and ditches on it or that it has been newly hoed. "AL" designates a hoe. These are the only texts which might possibly indicate rural construction.

Land allotment.—Fifty-eight texts and large fragments deal solely with the division of land. Twenty-two of these describe land in more than quantitative terms. These descriptions will be considered in detail below. In some of these documents the total area of the block of land is given, in others it is possible to estimate the total by substituting the average of the preserved registers for the obscured registers. In most cases the range of sizes of divisions of the total block can be estimated. Thus individual allotments are known though the total land area allotted to an individual during a given year is not known. Given these descriptions and areas it is possible to infer quite a bit about land allotment and holding.

In some cases a specific place is designated by the affix "ki." Three documents mention Ga:ki. In text 206, 286 iku are noted. One hundred thirty-eight are surveyed (sag.dun$_4$.ak) and 44 are treated in some other way (sag.me.an.ak). In fragment 208, plots of land ranging from 6 to 84 iku are allotted to individuals. In fragment 140, a 12 iku plot is allotted. Two documents mention BIR:ki. In damaged text 15, plots of 4 to 18 iku are allotted. A final figure of 253 iku BIR:ki may be a total. Fragment 79 notes 99 iku BIR:ki. Thus land from named places is surveyed and allotted in plots of varying size. It is not possible to generalize about totals and average size of plots, and no additional descriptive information is associated.

In some cases, the agricultural condition of the field may be indicated by the term "šà" which is written later as a.šà. The šà.BÍL is divided into four large blocks all designated gán.en

DOCUMENTARY EVIDENCE OF RURAL PRODUCTION   109

(see below). Three large blocks of cultivated land (gán.mu) are allotted to individuals, two of whom, Mes.pád.da and É:IGI+BUR were known as important people. A single 120 iku block is designated šà.si and not allotted. In fragment 36, a portion of šà.BIL is surveyed into plots of six to twelve iku. Since šà.si contrasts with gán.mu, it may be uncultivated land. If so, it is difficult to interpret text 185, in which the šà.si produces much grain.

In text 143, 216 iku are noted. The land is allocated in lots of nine to thirty-six iku averaging fourteen iku. Apparently all this land is called cultivated land (gán.mu). Most of it is designated gán.en.šà.x (see below). Some is designated fields not allotted (šà.ta.nu.è), and some is designated šà.RU, the meaning of which is unknown. Šà.RU may contrast with šà.BIL, though there is no way to be certain given the available documents.

In summary, the usage of the affix "šà" is unclear.

The social condition of publicly held land is indicated by a set of three terms: gán.uru$_4$, gán.kur$_6$, and gán.en. The term gán.uru$_4$ is similar to the gán.uru$_4$.lal of the Lagash archives. In these later documents the term designates land allotted to cultivators for a share of the crop (Diakanov, 1959:286). Gán.uru$_4$ is mentioned in three of the Ur Archaic documents. In text 102, a block of 400 iku gán.uru$_4$ is recorded but not allotted (šà.ma.gíd). In damaged text 104, 14 plots ranging from 8 to 22 iku and averaging 17 iku are measured (a.gíd). The sign "uru$_4$" occurs at the end of each column. This may indicate suballotment of some type of land by an important person to cultivators (engar which is written "uru$_4$") or it may indicate allotment of small blocks of uru$_4$ land.

A key document for interpretation is text 127 (Fig. 28). This test has three parts: (1) the first three registers record copper vessels (urudu.dug) and ingots of copper (ma.na.urudu) in connection with certain people; (2) the remaining registers except the last three, in which the same people are recorded with equivalent amounts of copper, and other people are recorded in connection with copper or oxen; (3) the last three registers which record a total of 304 iku of gán.uru$_4$ also designated gán.Nanna (see below), some of the oxen, and all of the copper pots. The repeated equivalent amounts allow the inferences that a copper vessel weighed 3.5 ma.na. Two or three vessels are associated with some people, one or two oxen with others. If variations in number of items are distributed unsystematically through the registers, which they seem to be, this can be taken to mean that an ox is slightly more valuable than a pot. Assuming an ox to be equivalent to 5 ma.na of copper, then the total of items would be

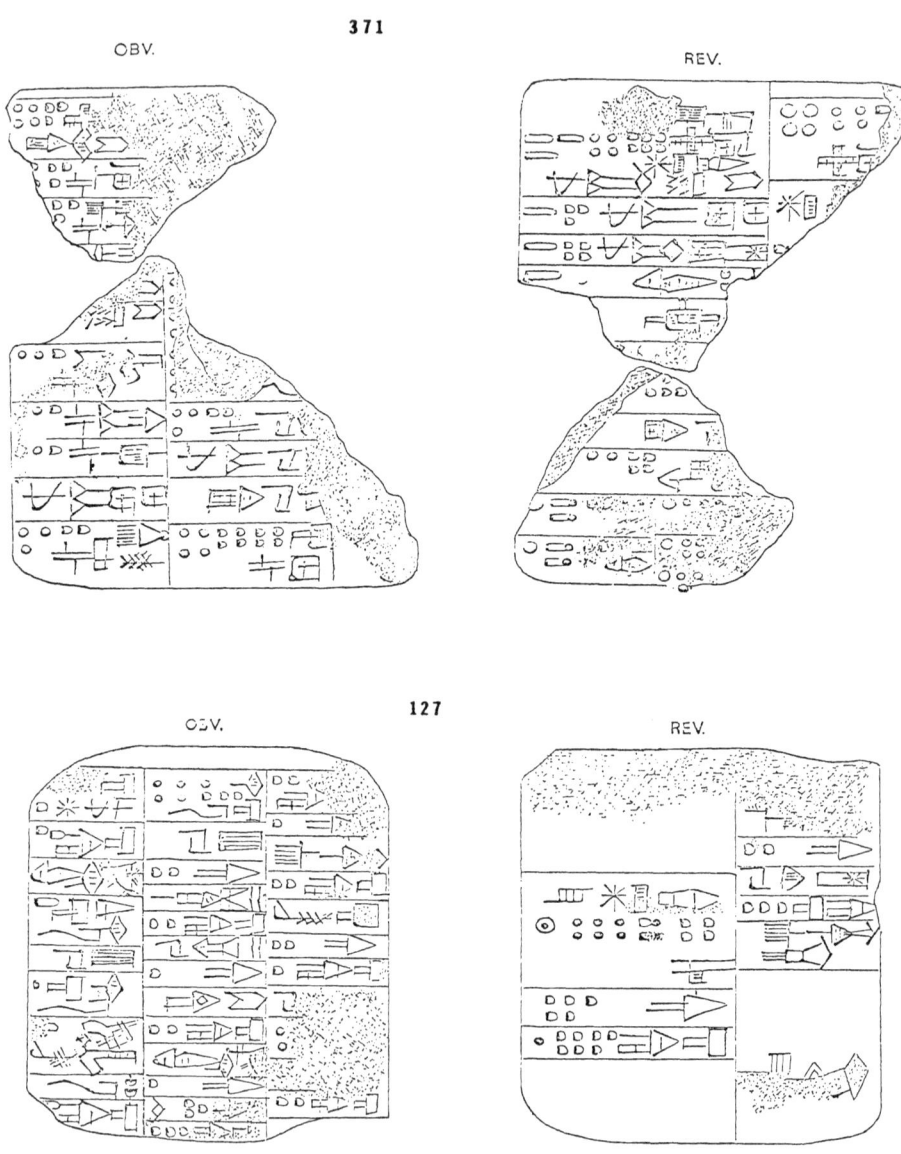

FIG. 28. A personnel text and a miscellaneous text.

DOCUMENTARY EVIDENCE OF RURAL PRODUCTION 111

equivalent to 85 ma.na of copper. Even if the total of oxen is miscopied, then the total would only be equivalent to 105 ma.na of copper at most. In the Fara texts (Deimal, 1924:30-42) land is sold for two to three ma.na for an iku. At minimum 304 iku would be worth about 600 ma.na. It does not seem likely that text 127 records a sale. The relative values involved suggest that the named individuals are paying a rent for gán.uru$_4$. In the absence of other similar texts, the interpretation is tentative.

In the Lagash documents gán.kur$_6$.ra designates land allotted to temple personnel in exchange for their services (Diakanov, 1959:286). Gán.kur$_6$ is noted or implied in four texts. In fragment 365 a total of 1070.5 iku of gán.kur$_6$ is recorded but not measured (šà.ma.gíd) and 492 iku is recorded in a damaged register. In text 163 a total of 486 iku gán.kur$_6$ is recorded and subdivided. A complex suballocation of land seems to be recorded, but there are enough damaged registers to prevent the interpretation of the procedure. In one column, several people receive 17 to 63 NIG.kur$_6$, probably food. In fragment 202, land is also mentioned in connection with NIG.kur$_6$. Allotments of 3 to 30 iku are recorded. Document 371, discussed below, records an organization perhaps involved in the cultivation of some gán.kur$_6$.

In the Lagash documents gán.nig.en.na designates unallotted land worked by temple personnel whose produce went to maintain the temple's activities (Diakanov, 1959:286). In the Ur Archaic documents, there are three dealing with gán.en. Texts 143 and 160, discussed above, record allotments of large blocks of 144 to 180 iku. Gán.en are allotted and in one case subdivided into units averaging 14 iku. In damaged text 184 the measuring (a.gíd) of 164 iku of gán.en for allotment to farmers (engar) is recorded. The land is divided into three large blocks: the first, 174 iku, is allotted to an unknown party and subdivided into small plots called open fields (gán.bar). The second, of 36 iku, is allotted to an important person, É.IGI+BUR, and the third, of 54 iku, is allotted to an important person, Geštin, and subdivided into plots called open fields (gán.bar).

In summary, gán.uru$_4$ occurs in large blocks of 300 to 400 iku and is allotted to cultivators in plots of various sizes, perhaps in exchange for goods in one case. Gán.kur$_6$ occurs in large blocks of 450 to 1100 iku and can be either allotted in smaller plots in complex ways, or worked by a large group. Gán.en occurs in large blocks of about 500 iku and is allotted to important people in blocks of 30 to 180 iku which could be suballotted to cultivators.

Perhaps related to gan.en are various parcels of land associated with important officials. In fragment 364 the Ukkin.gal receives 312 iku, and the GEME:DU$_{10}$:GÁL receives 198 iku. In the same fragment an important person without title, Mes.pád.da receives 429 iku. Though office holders usually do not use a personal name, this association supports the obvious suggestion that they were drawn from among the important people. Other official lands are recorded: fragment 361 may deal with land of the lugal. Fragment 108 recorded allotment of the land of the Ukkin.gal in plots of 3 to 21 iku averaging 11 iku. Text 82 records a subdivision of 720 iku of the Uri$_2$.gal. Important officials are clearly holding and subdividing large blocks of land of about 200 to 800 iku.

Finally, much land is designated gán.Nanna, fields of the principal god of Ur. Text 127 has been discussed. Fragment 147 notes 525 iku of gán.Nanna. Fragment 358 records the allocation of small plots of 10 to 24 iku averaging 14 iku of gán.Nanna. The absence of a term for the land of the other frequently noted diety, gán.Innana; it seems difficult to interpret this as temple land. It is more reasonable to interpret the term as meaning public land of the town of Ur. It is therefore perhaps a generic term for almost all the types of land appearing in the texts.

Plowing and Seeding.—Text 20, discussed in the introduction to this chapter, is the key to plowing and seeding. In this text one individual is given 30 gur of seed (še.numun) and 20 gur of barley to feed the oxen (še.gud.kú) for the working of 342 iku of land. Supplement 21, a later Early Dynastic text, from Ur records two gur for seed and one gur for the oxen. Similar ratios are recorded from contemporary Lagash (Deimel, 1923:1-7).

Seed is mentioned in other texts. In damaged text 177 about 52 gur are distributed to farmers. About 27 are actually used as seed, 10 are perhaps sold and 15 are returned. Each individual receives about two gur, enough to seed a plot of about 20 iku. In damaged text 201 seed is distributed in connection with 412 iku of gán.AL x TAR. Each individual receives an average of two gur. Were the entire text covered with registers, then 244 gur of seed, enough to seed about 260 iku, would have been allotted. The discrepancy is not great. It is possible that the average of two gur per individual is incorrect in this case. In any event, these texts indicate seed was not only distributed to plowmen, but also directly to minor cultivators.

Harvest.—Thirty-six tablets deal solely with grain and meal. Barley (še), various wheats (zíz, gig, gíg), flax (gu), and malt (munu$_3$) are recorded. Two otherwise unknown forms NINDA$_2$ x GIŠ+DAR and NINDA$_2$ x BAPPIR may be varieties of barley and wheat respectively, since it is difficult to interpret them as a processed grain such as a meal, a grain destined for a specific function such as a beer ingredient, or a special unit of measure for grain.

A few of these documents note very large quantities of grain apparently in connection with harvest or storage. Two refer to the field. Damaged text 73 notes 660 gur of barley and 610 gur of wheat (zíz) from the fields of Nanna. In all these amounts would require about 1100 iku of land, given the metric equivalents of the introduction to this chapter. Damaged text 185 notes at least 1866 gur of various grains from ša.BÍL. This would require about 1700 iku of land. An additional 1201 gur is recorded in association with individuals, some known as minor farmers. This may be portions of the first noted grain, or yet more grain.

Three refer to large quantities of grain in connection with officials. Fragment 222 records 460 gur of grain in connection with the PA:SI of Ur. This would require 430 iku of land. Other large lots of grain are recorded in subsequent registers but the designation of the associated person is damaged. Finally it is perhaps noted that the grain was transported (še.ig). Fragment 188 records 1982 gur of barley in connection with the PA:SI of BÀD x NIMGIR. This would require about 1700 iku of land. Fragment 162 records a variety of goods associated with the sanga.lugal, 1462 gur of barley and 1380 gur of wheat (zíz) are noted. These would require about 2400 iku of land. This is perhaps an inventory of a storehouse, since the sanga usually records beer and bread allotments from the AB, and since commodities are recorded elsewhere on the text.

The inferred units of land suggested above are in general larger than any actually noted on land texts. Thus it is possible that the method suggested earlier is wrong. A gur of 150 liters, roughly that of later Early Dynastic Lagash would bring land estimated down to a size range similar to these allotted in land texts. In any event, it is significant that the quantities of grain noted from fields and transported by officials are of roughly the same order of magnitude while the quantities of grain inventoried in a storehouse are much greater.

THE ORGANIZATION OF RURAL ACTIVITY

The general structure of four rural organizations can be inferred. These include sheep and goat husbandry, plowing and seeding, harvest and transport, and general cultivation. Before describing these let us consider briefly a town organization.

Large fragment 112 records the names of individuals and either an associated toponym or both a toponym and official. A total of 75 individuals are recorded. A number of these are designated "gú.gal.gal," a possible status term of unknown meaning. The group is apparently under the supervisor of the palace (nu.banda$_4$.é.gal). The entire list is headed EZEN : É : SUKKAL. If "EZEN" indicates a period of time and "SUKKAL" designates a messenger, this may represent appointment to a rotating messenger's role. It is unfortunate that this explicitly described organization cannot be associated with any specific rural task.

The organization for large-scale sheep and goat husbandry is not explicitly described. As noted above, a flock of about 100 adult animals under a nu.banda$_4$ is counted in text 16. In addition, a flock or flocks with more than 230 adults is implied by fragment 30. In the rural area the nu.banda$_4$ would have overseen several UGULA:UDU, to be read "sipa," who in turn would have overseen the sheep and goats. Thus the rural sheep and goat organization must have had only two levels of decision-making.

Plowing and seeding are similarly indirectly attested. In text 20, one individual is allotted seed and fodder for oxen in order to cultivate 342 iku. Plowing with a team of oxen requires several assistants. The problem is whether there is one team or more in the above case. Another seed text mentions 412 iku of land, which is of the same order of magnitude as 342 iku. Assuming the maximum rate of two iku worked per man-day and a minimum of three men per ox team then one team would take no less than two months. This is not impossible, but two teams would be easier. In the event that more than one is involved, then the individual receiving seed and team fodder for the large block is a supervisor of ox teams. Thus there are certainly two levels of decision-making in the rural plowing organization, but there may be three.

Neither is the organization for harvest and transport explicitly described. Harvest texts note as many as 1900 gur of grain handled by the PA:SI. This clearly came from a large block of land, no less than 800 iku even assuming a small 150 liter gur. Fragment 343 provides some indirect evidence of harvest. A sanga otherwise known as an important person records the allotment of some commodity to the ugula of the gán. abzu perhaps the fields of Eridu. If the tablet was of normal width-length proportions, then ten to twelve ugula were recorded. These may be under a sukkal-gal, though this is unclear. In any event these ugula were associated with a single storehouse. The rural harvest organization thus had three levels of decision-making: the workers, the ugula, and the PA:SI.

General cultivation can be approached from two directions. Fragment 371 records an organization perhaps for cultivation of the gán.kur$_6$. The entire group is called the un.šèr.ra. Fragment 368 contains the phrase "kur$_6$.šèr.ra." There were about 700 of these šèr.ra people recorded on the complete document. These were divided into 6 groups of 63 to 226 men under a nu.banda$_4$. These groups were subdivided into about 20 smaller groups of 21 to 54 men under an ugula. A total of about 1900 iku is allotted to these people. This is about 3 iku per worker or 60 per 150 per ugula or 190 to 800 iku per nu.banda$_4$. Note that in most cases the subgroup of workers plus an ugula is divisible by 11. There may thus be yet a further subdivision into groups of 11. Thus this text implies three, perhaps four, levels of decision-making in rural organization for general cultivation.

Another approach to general cultivation is through the land allotment texts. Minor cultivators usually receive 10 to 15 iku. Important people usually receive 30 to 180 iku, about the same as that directed by an ugula in the above text. Large blocks of land range from 300 to 1100 iku, about the same as that under a nu.banda in the above text. Thus the inference of three levels of decision-making, the engar, ugula, and nu.banda$_4$, is supported by these texts.

Note, however, that in the first case the ugula directs 21 to 54 men, while in this second case an ugula would direct 3 to 20 men. It is not the number of men, but the number of tasks that is significant. Fifteen men working 10 iku each is equivalent to 50 men working 3 iku. The important thing for the supervisor is not the number of people he must coordinate but the number of tasks per unit time he must coordinate.

I have emphasized the rural portions of these organizations for the following reason: the town portion, the uppermost level or levels of decision-making in each case, may be in fact one generalized town institution. The same individuals may be making decisions on the highest level about the administration of land, plowing, and sheep, as well as such things as craft, ritual, and politics. Such a generalized organization would not be structured for any one rural activity. I avoid this complex problem of the central institution or institutions partially because my textual data is inadequate and partially because my theoretical framework is too simple to explain it.

I have inferred that while rural sheep and goat husbandry has only two levels of decision-making, and rural plowing and seeding perhaps has only two, harvest and general cultivation certainly have three. On the basis of the first working hypothesis of Chapter I, I deduced in Chapter V that general cultivation and harvest would require a similar number of levels of decision-making and that sheep and goat husbandry and plowing and seeding might require a similar number of levels of hierarchy. These hypotheses are confirmed. On the basis of the second working hypothesis of Chapter I, and the difference in levels of decision-making noted above, I deduce that general cultivation and harvest should require more complex decision-making than sheep and goat husbandry. This is what was inferred in Chapter V (Table 12). Thus, unsatisfactory as the evidence and the analytical procedure may be, there is no reason to reject my hypotheses. The frame of reference of Chapter I is a potentially fruitful approach deserving of further inquiry. The hypotheses should be further tested with data from well-documented periods, such as that of the Third Dynasty of Ur, and with ethnographic data.

VII

THE RURAL ECONOMY: A SUMMARY

A GEOGRAPHICAL OVERVIEW

AT the beginning of the Early Dynastic period, Ur was a large town of about twenty hectares. It was dominated by a large central temple compound probably dedicated to the god Nanna. Small cramped dwelling units occupied portions of the town. Though there is no direct evidence until somewhat later in the period, the area around the temple was probably occupied by large public buildings such as storehouses and the houses of ranking personages. Many of the approximately 4,000 inhabitants, perhaps comprising 600 residence units, must have worked primarily as agricultural laborers. A smaller proportion were individuals of importance and their families and craft specialists and their families. The actual political and ritual organization of the town at this time are unknown.

Near Ur was a smaller town of eight hectares perhaps containing 1,600 inhabitants. In addition there were a few small rural settlements, a rural center with a shrine, and a few cemeteries. Thus in the enclave there are a set of activities performed by ascribed groups and maintaining the population. The Ur enclave conforms to the definition of an urban system given in Chapter I.

Within working distance of these settlements were perhaps 6,000 hectares of cultivable land. A branch of the ancient Euphrates flowed through this area by the towns, and various small canal systems carried the river water to the fields.

CATEGORIES OF PEOPLE

Judging from the remains of settlements, about 6,000 people, perhaps a thousand residence units, lived in and around Ur. Within this population, certain broad categories of people can be defined though these categories are by no means exhaustive since children, servants, craftsmen, and others cannot be considered with the available evidence.

Among the forty frequently mentioned and distinctively named individuals in the texts, eleven were minor farmers who were recorded as receiving small allotments of land. Because the texts were not dated it is not possible to estimate the total amount held by a small farmer in a given season. These individuals also received small amounts of commodities. There were three individuals who were not allotted significant amounts of land, but who seem to have been minor overseers and officials. These also received small amounts of commodities. There were twenty-six individuals of importance. Some received large blocks of land, some received many commodities and some received both. These differences within this group may result from the small sample of tablets. When an individual became a titled official he was usually referred to only by his title, so it is not usually possible to ascertain whether or not these important individuals are also important officials. The low ratio of minor farmers to important individuals presumably reflects a tendency for important people to be more frequently mentioned in documents, rather than the actual ratio in the population.

Since the important individuals had to allot their large holdings to small farmers of some sort if they were to cultivate them, and since little more is known of the large farmers, let us consider the small farmer, the man in the field, in more detail. In the total population of 6,000, perhaps 800 heads of residence units might be called small farmers. Perhaps the small dwellings at Ur, and most certainly the structures at Sakheri Sughir and the cemetery at 'Ubaid, are the material remains of small farmers. The cemetery provides no evidence of group-specific funeral patterns or of differences in rank. There is a possibility that burials face the various nearby settlements, perhaps the location of the homes of the deceased or of institutions with which they were affiliated in life. The dwellings in both town and country contain similar ranges of conical cups and spouted jars. Ovens and large bowls, perhaps indicative of certain types of food preparation in the home, are not reported in town dwellings. No definite indications of craft activity occur in the town dwellings. Boat, net, and sickle repair, and perhaps small-scale brick manufacture were undertaken at the rural settlement. The limited range of activities reflected in both the excavated and surface evidence from the rural site may reflect the concentration of specialized craftsmen in the town. Apparently the occupants of the rural settlements worked primarily in subsistence production. It is important to remember that these rural settlements contained, even assuming half of them were not located in the survey, about sixty

THE RURAL ECONOMY: A SUMMARY 119

residence units, contributing a small proportion to the probable total number of small farmers. On the other hand, these few people living some distance from the town must have been concerned almost entirely with rural production. They are thus better examples than town dwellers, some of whom may have performed other tasks at times other than the peak of the agricultural season.

ROLES IN RURAL PRODUCTION

Small farmers as a category of people perform a number of roles. Usually they were the engar, the cultivator per se. The ugula, the work foreman, and even the nu.banda$_4$, the overseer of foremen, were also drawn from this category.

Since the major officials are usually referred to by title only it is not possible to say from what category the role was drawn. The sanga was, at least, a storehouse recorder. The PA:SI was, at least, a harvest supervisor. The qualification is necessary because in later times these titles were associated with ritual and political roles, and it is possible that they were so associated at this time. Other titles designate unknown roles.

LAND

In the vicinity of Ur, there must have been areas of alluvial desert, marsh, river channel, trees, and cultivated fields. Only the last are directly named and described in the texts.

An unknown proportion of the land was located in named areas designated 'ki,' place. Only one such specific area is frequently mentioned, suggesting that the available land documents refer only to select portions of the Ur enclave.

A set of terms perhaps designate tenurial arrangements for public land. Gán.en, gán.kur$_6$, and gán.uru$_4$ are similar to later terms usually interpreted as indicating, respectively, land whose produce goes directly to the temple, land whose produce goes to a temple worker who cultivates or oversees it, and land a share of whose produce goes to the temple, the remainder going to a cultivator. Even substituting the neutral term "public institution" for "temple," these interpretations could not be applied to the above three terms as used in the Ur texts. In them, gán.en is allotted among specific individuals and gán.kur$_6$ is in one case farmed by organized teams. Tentatively I interpret gán.uru$_4$ as public land periodically allotted to cultivators, the produce or rent going to an institution; gán.kur$_6$ as public land either worked by teams or allotted for a share of the crop, the produce going to certain nonfarming individuals, and gán.en as public land allotted in large blocks to important individuals perhaps for support of official duties, and suballotted by them to minor farmers. Further contextual evidence is necessary.

A term which may identify the public institution in question is Gán.Nanna. This might be taken to imply that the temple of Nanna held title to various lands. However, in the absence of a comparable term "Gán.Innana" to indicate land held by the prominent temple of Innana, it is more plausible to interpret Gán.Nanna as town land.

Some land is designated as that of specific offices. Whether this is gán.en after allotment or some other kind of land is not known. The Lugal, the Ukkin.gal, and the Uri$_2$.gal are recorded as receiving or suballotting large blocks of land.

THE PRODUCTION CYCLE IN AGRICULTURE

Whether land allotments took place in late spring after harvest or in early fall before cultivation is not known. Canal cleaning probably occurred sometime during this long period.

Actual cultivation begins with plowing and seeding. Plowing was probably done by a team. There is one account of a plow team or teams. Small quantities of seed are issued to individuals, suggesting that some cultivators may seed their own plots.

Examination of the full range of land statistics shows that a basic unit was a block of 40 to 50 hectares. Those could be aggregated into larger units, or subdivided into small plots of 3 to 7 hectares for allotment to about 10 cultivators. A basic unit could be under the authority of an ugula. A large unit of several basic blocks could be under the care of a nu.banda$_4$. This complex organization is directly recorded in one special case, probably the group cultivation of gán.kur$_6$.

In the spring the crop, predominantly barley but with some wheats and other items, was harvested. Large lots of grain perhaps from 120 to 600 hectare units are connected with officials called the PA:SI and PA:GIN. A storehouse inventory recorded at an unknown time of year notes grain from perhaps 820 hectares. Thus the grain or portions of the grain from large areas is being placed in storehouses. It would seem logical to say that these were only institutionally controlled grains and that the

THE RURAL ECONOMY: A SUMMARY

cultivators and/or landholders' shares were stored in their residences. However, the evidence for this is negative: there are few grain allotment texts.

ANIMAL HUSBANDRY

Sheep and goats are directly attested. A flock of about 100 adult animals is documented. There was an institution allotting sheep from flocks totaling more than 280 animals, and the sheep butchered in the rural village could have been so obtained. There is no reason, however, to reject the possibility that residence units kept small numbers of such animals. Cattle are poorly known.

GATHERING WILD RESOURCES

These resources are a problem. Reeds, wood, fish, and fowl are all directly attested in the rural settlement. In the texts they are all accounted in quantity as part of organized activities. Did the rural inhabitants thus receive these items or did they obtain them directly? In the case of fish they probably caught their own with nets. In the case of reed mats, they probably obtained these craft products from a specialist. In other cases there is no evidence.

PRODUCTION AND CONSUMPTION IN THE RURAL ECONOMY

The 2,500 rural workers of Ur produced about 2,400,000 kilograms of grain and unknown quantities of other domestic and gathered plant and animal material. A portion of this may have been retained by the worker as a wage or share; the remainder probably went to the storehouses of important individuals and public storehouses for subsequent redistribution to noncultivators or for exchange.

Rural workers consumed the various foodstuffs produced by other rural workers; consumer goods such as ceramics, metal items, beads, and presumably cloth; technical items used in production such as flint, baskets, bitumen, and wood. Rough quantitative estimates of bitumen and ceramic consumption are possible even with the available data. The others will not be so easily measured.

The only striking fact conveyed by these paragraphs is that labor was quite specialized, and that a predominance of prepared or manufactured items rather than raw materials circulated to rural workers. Clearly the quantitative estimates needed for the construction of an input-output model of the rural economy are not available. Minimally, we would need the following: (1) detailed maps showing all forms of land use, not simply agriculture, to estimate production; (2) samples of refuse from all types of sites to estimate consumption; (3) sets of complete associated agricultural accounts so that the size and production figures of given fields can both be known, and the total holdings of individuals can be estimated. Only when such data becomes available can quantitative exchanges within the rural economy or the urban system as a whole be properly considered.

CONCLUDING NOTE

Other factors being equal, there is probably a direct relationship between the complexity of an activity and the complexity of an organization which coordinates it. Two factors not explicitly accounted for in my model are: (1) the geographic spread of the activity which may, as in the case of harvest and transport, compound the problems of coordinating relatively simple activities; and (2) a feedback from one organizational structure to another, for instance a structuring of the organization for harvest along lines similar to those for general cultivation. The relatively simple theoretical constructs of this work should be expanded to include such factors as these.

Before further research on the rural economics of early Mesopotamian urban systems is attempted, it may be more fruitful to work on other equally crucial problems. Inter-regional trade, inter-city warfare and diplomacy, and urban political organization are three of many such problems. When the key aspects of early urban systems are formalized, even in simple forms as in this monograph, then it will be possible to stimulate the development of entire networks of urban systems. When such simulations are tested and verified, then the formal explanation of the traditional phenomena of the rise of civilization and the origin of the state will be possible.

APPENDIX I

THE STATISTICS OF ARTIFACTS FROM SAKHERI SUGHIR

Introduction

This Appendix presents the total count of each category of artifact in each provenience unit and measurements of all well preserved pieces, with certain exceptions. These exceptions are conical cup bases, of which only certain exemplary samples are presented; flat bases which are remarkably nondistinctive, and very rare categories in general.

Each piece in Tables 15 to 23 is introduced by a number, the first three digits of which are its field number. There usually follows a hardness approximated on Moh's Scale and paste and surface color measurements expressed as hue, value and chroma on the Munsell Color Scale. The various measurements in centimeters and angles in degrees are explained diagrammatically in Figure 29 (page 124) and in comments on the table.

This appendix should encourage more detailed comparisons between Early Dynastic ceramic assemblages than has been usual. It should also provide data for the rapidly developing field of mathematical typology.

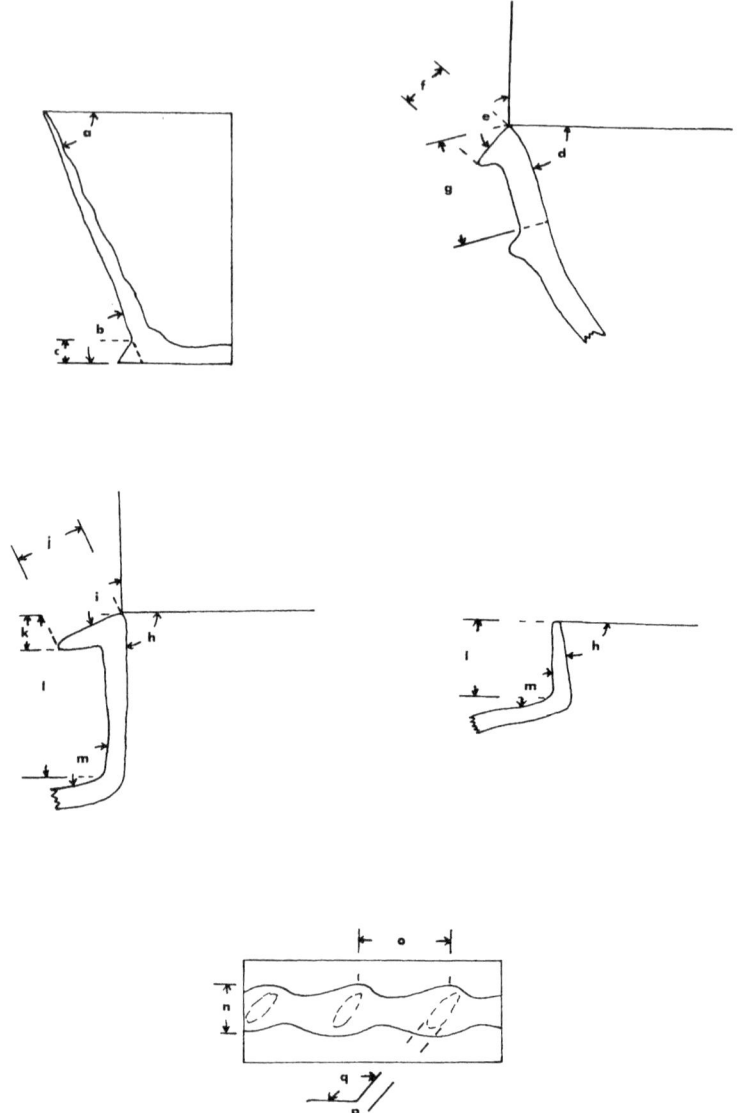

FIG. 29. Some vessel attributes: *a*. conical cup rim angle; *b*. conical cup base angle; *c*. conical cup base to constriction; *d*. bowl rim angle; *e*. bowl rim top angle; *f*. bowl rim thickness; *g*. bowl rim to band; *h*. jar rim angle; *i*. jar rim top angle; *j*. jar rim thickness; *k*. rim height; *l*. neck height; *m*. neck angle; *n*. thickness of hatched strip; *o*. period of hatched strip; *p*. thickness of gash; *q*. angle of gash.

APPENDIX I

TABLE 14
ARTIFACTS IN THE PROVENIENCE UNITS AT SAKHERI SUGHIR

North Block

Locus	Cubic Meters	Location	Stratum	Field Numbers
A		Small pit	O	001, 003
B	3.5	On rectangular floor	IA-B	002, 006, 013, 014, 015, 020, 021
C		Long oven	IA	054
D	3.3	Over work floor	IA	022, 023, 024, 025, 030, 038
E		Large pit	IA-B	012, 018, 019
F	3.4	12 meters north	IA	016, 026, 027
G	2.2	5 meters north	IA	034, 037, 045
H	0.3	2 meters north	IA	042, 043
I	1.1	8 meters south	IA	055, 066
J	1.8	On work floor	IB	031, 032, 033, 039, 040, 052, 056
K		12 meters north	IB	017
L	2.7	5 meters north	IB	035+095, 036, 046, 048
M	0.3	2 meters north	IB	044, 067
N	3.7	On work floor	IC	049, 050, 051, 053, 065
O		Oval oven	IC	060, 061
P		Deep sounding	I	010
Q		Deep sounding	II	011, 062
R		Deep sounding	III-A	063
S		Deep sounding	III-B	064, 069
T		Deep sounding	IV	074

South Block

Locus	Cubic Meters	Location	Stratum	Field Numbers
U	6.6	South of structure	I	070, 072
V	3.4	East of structure	I	077
W	1.6	South of structure	II	071, 076, 080, 098
X	2.0	East of structure	II	078, 081, 082, 083
Y	2.6	Inside structure	II-A	028, 047, 097, 099, 103
Z	1.7	Inside structure—center	II-B	087, 100
AA	1.1	Inside structure—southeast	II-B	088, 101, 102, 109, 112
BB	4.4	Inside structure—southwest	II-B	105, 106, 107, 110, 111
CC		Small pit—southwest corner	I	108
DD	2.6	East of structure	III	084, 085, 081

Canal Sounding

Locus	Cubic Meters	Location	Stratum	Field Numbers
EE	2.4		Upper	089, 090
FF	2.4		Lower	113, 114

TABLE 14—Continued

Locus	Stone						Bitumen			Ceramic
	Battered Pebble	Unusual Flakes & Blades	Used Blades	Dent. Blades	Chop.	Slab Frag.	Sherd Imp. Bit.	Mat Imp. Bit.	Bit. Lump	Ceramic Rings
A	...	...	2	...	...	...	...	...	...	...
B	...	...	...	1	...	...	1	...	1	3
C	...	...	...	...	...	...	...	...	...	...
D	...	...	...	1	...	1	...	...	1	...
E	...	...	...	...	...	...	...	...	...	...
F	...	...	1	1	...	...	1	...	...	...
G	...	...	...	2	1	...	...	...	...	...
H	...	...	...	...	...	...	...	...	...	...
I	...	...	...	...	...	...	...	...	...	...
J	...	...	...	...	...	...	...	...	...	2
K	...	...	...	...	...	...	...	...	...	...
L	1	...	...	...	...	...	...	1	...	...
M	...	...	...	5	...	...	1	...	3	...
N	...	...	...	1	...	...	1	...	1	3
O	...	...	...	...	...	...	...	...	...	...
P	...	...	...	1	...	...	...	...	...	...
Q	...	...	...	2	...	...	...	...	...	...
R	...	...	1	...	...	...	...	...	1	...
S	...	...	...	...	...	...	...	...	...	1
T	...	...	...	...	...	...	...	...	...	...
U	...	...	...	...	...	...	...	...	1	...
V	...	...	...	...	...	...	...	...	...	...
W	...	1	...	1	...	...	...	...	...	...
X	...	...	1	4	...	...	...	1	3	...
Y	...	1	...	...	...	...	1	...	...	...
Z	...	...	...	...	...	2	...	...	...	...
AA	...	...	...	...	...	1	...	1	1	...
BB	...	1	...	2	...	...	...	7	5	1
CC	...	...	...	...	...	...	...	...	...	...
DD	...	...	...	2	...	...	...	...	2	...
EE	...	...	...	...	...	...	...	...	...	...
FF	...	...	...	...	...	...	...	...	...	...

APPENDIX I

TABLE 14—Continued

Locus	Narrow Cup Base	Wide Cup Base	Bowl	Low Jar	High Jar	Collar Jar	Plain	Hatch Strip	Reserve Slip	Punctate	Grove	Flat Base	Ring Base
A	...	...	...	...	...	...	...	...	...	...	...	...	...
B	6	8	4	2	1	1	2	4	4	1	1	2	3
C	...	...	...	...	...	...	...	...	...	...	...	...	...
D	15	22	4	1	2	5	4	2	3	4	2	7	3
E	...	...	...	...	...	...	...	...	...	...	...	...	...
F	11	9	7	2	1	2	5	1	2	1	4	15	1
G	1	7	3	0	0	0	3	1	3	1	2	7	1
H	16	3	3	0	0	0	0	1	2	2	3	4	1
I	2	4	0	0	0	2	2	0	2	3	1	5	2
J	7	14	2	3	2	2	6	1	5	0	3	1	1
K	1	2	0	0	0	1	0	0	1	0	0	1	0
L	1	9	1	2	0	1	5	0	3	1	1	7	2
M	11	12	0	0	0	1	1	1	2	4	2	0	1
N	13	9	9	7	2	4	3	1	2	1	2	12	1
O	1	2	0	0	0	0	0	0	0	0	0	1	0
P	1	1	0	0	0	0	0	1	0	1	0	0	0
Q	3	2	2	1	0	2	2	1	0	0	0	4	0
R	0	3	0	0	0	0	1	0	0	0	0	0	0
S	7	9	1	2	3	0	0	0	1	0	1	0	0
T	17	9	3	1	1	1	0	0	3	0	0	2	0
U	1	11	11	3	2	2	5	0	0	2	1	5	2
V	1	20	0	4	1	2	4	0	0	0	6	5	0
W	3	22	1	1	2	1	6	1	3	2	5	2	1
X	8	79	3	9	5	10	21	4	3	2	14	8	3
Y	29	19	0	5	0	0	3	1	3	3	0	0	1
Z	4	8	3	0	0	0	2	0	3	0	1	1	0
AA	8	29	3	1	1	2	1	0	2	0	0	3	2
BB	16	49	6	6	8	3	9	1	6	2	12	7	3
CC	0	2	0	1	2	0	0	0	0	0	2	0	0
DD	11	29	2	0	0	3	3	2	3	1	0	8	1
EE	2	9	2	0	0	1	0	1	0	0	0	2	0
FF	2	15	5	0	1	1	1	0	0	0	0	44	1

TABLE 15
CONICAL CUP BASES

Work Area IA

Number	Hardness	Paste Color		Surface Color		Profile Type	Base Diam.	Base Angle	Body Thick.	Cons. Diam.	Base to Constrict
		Hue	Value/Chroma	Hue	Value/Chroma						
00201	1.5	10.0	5.5/4.0	7.5	6.5/4.0	2	3.39	75	.49	2.74	1.84
00202	1.5	5.0	5.5/4.0	7.5	7.0/4.0	4	3.85	70	.66	3.43	1.80
00203	1.5	7.5	6.5/4.0	7.5	6.5/4.0	2	3.77	80	.69	3.41	2.42
00204	1.5	7.5	5.5/4.0	10.0	7.0/2.0	8	6.37	60	1.08	6.00	.95
00205	1.5	7.5	5.5/4.0	7.5	7.5/4.0	7	5.80	55	1.11	5.68	.47
00206	3.5	5.0	7.5/3.0	2.5	8.0/2.0	5	6.00	65	.78	5.98	.63
00601	1.5	10.0	5.5/4.0	10.0	6.5/4.0	2	2.93	85	.81	2.91	2.20
00607	2.5	10.0	5.5/3.0	10.0	5.5/3.0	5	6.00	65	.87	5.98	.65
02001	2.5	7.5	5.0/4.0	5.0	5.0/4.0	3	2.95	75	.60	2.81	.82
02002	2.5	7.5	5.5/4.0	7.5	7.0/4.0	6	4.39	60	.74	4.41	.46
02003	3.5	7.5	6.0/4.0	7.5	5.0/4.0	3	3.80	80	.91	3.39	1.03
02004	3.5	5.0	6.0/6.0	7.5	7.5/4.0	6	4.97	70	.60	4.90	.57
02005	0.5	7.5	7.5/4.0	10.0	7.5/4.0	3	2.93	80	...	2.75	1.20
02213	2.5	7.5	6.0/4.0	7.5	6.0/4.0	4	3.40	75	.60	2.70	1.00
02215	3.5	5.0	4.0/4.0	5.0	5.5/4.0	2	3.85	80	...	3.40	.68
02501	2.5	10.0	6.0/4.0	5.0	5.5/4.0	3	3.50	70	.90	2.89	1.05
02503	2.5	2.5Y	5.0/2.0	2.5	5.5/2.0	3	3.61	70	.99	3.31	.91
03802	3.5	5.0	6.0/4.0	5.0	5.5/3.0	6	5.50	60	.69	5.55	.63
04201	2.5	10.0	6.0/4.0	10.0	7.0/4.0	3	2.89	70	.62	2.45	1.59
04202	2.5	10.0	6.5/4.0	5.0	7.5/3.0	8	4.43	60	.50	4.36	.74
04203	2.5	7.5	6.0/5.0	10.0	7.0/2.5	2	3.03	80	.48	2.67	1.41
04204	2.5	7.5	5.5/5.0	7.5	6.5/4.0	2	2.95	85	.59	2.48	1.00
04205	2.5	10.0	5.5/4.0	10.0	6.0/4.0	3	3.27	75	.80	3.41	.81
04206	2.5	10.0	5.5/3.0	7.5	6.0/4.0	2	3.14	80	.89	3.14	1.05
04207	1.5	7.5	5.5/4.0	7.5	5.5/4.0	3	3.13	75	.81	2.96	1.10
04208	1.5	5.0	5.0/4.0	5.0	6.0/4.0	4	3.55	70	...	3.18	.63
04209	1.5	10.0	5.5/3.5	10.0	6.0/4.0	7	4.90	65	.72	4.77	.54
04210	1.5	10.0	6.0/4.0	10.0	6.0/3.5	5	4.99	70	...	4.90	.68
01201	2.5	5.0	6.0/6.0	7.5	7.0/4.0	3	3.02	80	.50	2.82	.72
01202	3.5	5.0	7.0/5.0	5.0	5.0/4.0	4	3.11	85	.61	2.78	.91
01204	2.5	10.0	6.0/4.0	10.0	7.0/6.0	6	6.60	55	.77	6.40	.71
01205	2.5	7.5	7.0/4.0	2.5	8.0/2.0	7	4.20	55	.76	3.90	.73
01801	2.5	10.0	5.5/3.0	10.0	7.0/2.0	4	3.40	65	.76	3.20	1.56
01802	2.5	10.0	7.0/4.0	2.5	8.0/3.0	6	5.50	70	.64	5.20	.61
01901	2.5	7.5	5.5/4.0	5.0	6.0/4.0	3	3.19	75	.80	2.95	.52
Work Area IB											
03901	3.5	7.5	7.0/4.0	5.0	5.0/3.0	2	3.50	80	.70	3.09	1.20
03902	2.5	10.0	6.0/4.0	10.0	5.5/3.0	3	3.40	70	.70	2.71	1.30
03903	2.5	10.0	6.0/4.0	10.0	5.5/3.0	9	5.23	60	.90	5.11	.60
03904	3.5	10.0	6.0/4.0	10.0	7.5/2.0	3	3.70	75	.60	.30	1.30
03905	2.0	7.5	6.0/4.0	10.0	7.0/3.0	2	3.60	75	.79	3.28	1.70
03907	3.5	2.5Y	5.0/2.0	2.5Y	5.0/2.0	4	3.44	70	.65	3.12	1.60
03908	3.5	5.0	5.5/4.0	5.0	5.5/3.0	2	3.50	70	.71	2.86	1.60
03909	3.5	7.5	6.0/4.0	7.5	5.0/4.0	2	3.70	75	.72	3.09	1.55
03911	2.5	10.0	7.0/4.0	10.0	8.0/2.0	6	5.00	60	.66	4.80	.70
04003	1.5	5.0	5.5/5.0	5.0	5.5/4.0	3	3.89	80	.82	3.34	1.79
04301	1.5	5.0	5.0/4.0	5.0	5.0/4.0	2	3.02	80	.48	2.45	1.64
04302	1.5	7.5	5.5/4.0	7.5	6.0/4.0	2	2.71	75	.59	2.52	.77
04303	1.5	7.5	5.5/4.0	10.0	6.5/4.0	2	3.20	75	.40	2.67	1.10
04304	2.5	7.5	5.0/5.0	10.0	7.5/3.0	4	3.12	75	.57	2.94	1.18
04305	2.5	5.0	5.0/4.0	7.5	7.5/4.0	3	4.14	75	.62	3.15	1.37
04306	1.5	7.5	5.5/4.0	10.0	6.5/3.0	2	3.38	80	.86	3.06	.91
04307	1.5	10.0	6.5/4.0	7.5	6.5/4.0	6	5.14	70	.58	5.30	.57

APPENDIX I

TABLE 15—Continued

Number	Hardness	Paste Color Hue	Paste Color Value/Chroma	Surface Color Hue	Surface Color Value/Chroma	Profile Type	Base Diam.	Base Angle	Body Thick.	Cons. Diam.	Base to Constrict
04308	2.5	10.0	4.5/4.0	10.0	7.0/2.5	2	3.23	80	.91	2.60	1.14
04310	1.5	7.5	5.5/4.0	10.0	6.5/3.0	3	2.84	70	.51	2.70	1.68
04311	2.5	5.0	7.5/3.0	2.5	8.0/3.0	3	4.03	85	.60	3.48	1.22
04312	2.5	10.0	6.0/4.0	5.0	5.0/4.0	7	5.00	65	.49	4.87	.92
04401	2.5	5.0	6.5/6.0	10.0	7.5/3.0	2	3.09	85	.44	2.83	1.36
04402	2.5	7.5	6.0/4.0	2.5	8.0/3.0	2	3.44	80	.37	2.39	1.46
04403	2.5	7.5	6.5/5.0	7.5	7.5/4.0	2	3.07	85	.47	2.67	1.18
04404	2.5	7.5	6.0/4.0	7.5	6.5/4.0	2	3.39	85	.53	2.58	1.49
04405	2.5	7.5	4.0/5.0	10.0	6.5/3.0	3	3.18	75	.47	2.60	.89
04406	2.5	7.5	5.5/4.0	10.0	8.0/4.0	2	3.49	80	.51	2.90	.64
04407	1.5	7.5	5.5/4.0	10.0	6.5/3.0	2	3.37	80	.75	2.90	.80
04408	2.5	5.0	6.0/6.0	10.0	8.0/3.0	2	3.28	75	.69	2.76	.56
04414	2.5	7.5	6.5/4.0	7.5	7.5/4.0	5	5.12	65	.70	4.90	.89
04415	3.5	7.5	5.5/4.0	7.5	6.0/4.0	6	5.67	65	.55	5.30	.92
04416	2.5	7.5	6.0/4.0	10.0	6.0/4.0	7	5.05	70	.58	4.66	.55
05201	2.5	5.0	5.5/6.0	7.5	7.5/4.0	2	3.10	80	.55	2.69	1.36
05202	1.5	5.0	5.5/5.0	7.5	6.5/4.0	4	2.99	75	.51	2.67	1.27
05203	1.5	5.0	5.5/4.0	10.0	6.0/3.5	2	2.91	80	.94	2.75	1.30
05204	2.5	10.0	5.0/3.5	7.5	6.5/4.0	3	3.17	80	.63	3.19	1.39
05205	2.5	10.0	6.5/4.0	10.0	7.5/4.0	5	5.28	65	.76	5.72	.76
05206	2.5	7.5	5.0/4.0	10.0	6.5/4.0	6	4.62	65	.68	4.73	.74
05207	2.5	7.5	5.5/4.0	7.5	5.0/4.0	7	5.03	60	.86	5.02	.67
05208	2.5	7.5	5.0/4.0	10.0	6.5/4.0	8	4.87	55	.85	4.70	.70
05601	2.5	7.5	4.5/4.0	10.0	6.5/4.0	3	3.47	80	.52	3.11	1.63
05602	1.5	5.0	5.0/4.0	5.0	6.5/4.0	3	3.99	85	.51	3.22	1.56
05605	2.5	10.0	6.0/4.0	7.5	5.0/4.0	3	3.65	80	.75	3.04	1.48
05609	2.5	7.5	6.0/4.0	7.5	5.0/4.0	3	3.65	70	1.12	3.22	1.60
05612	2.5	10.0	5.5/4.0	10.0	5.0/2.0	3	3.72	70	.89	3.02	1.55
05613	2.5	10.0	6.0/4.0	10.0	7.5/3.0	3	3.70	75	.90	3.02	1.60
Outside Structure II											
07101	2.5	5.0	5.5/6.0	7.5	7.5/4.0	5	4.26	70	.50	3.98	.51
07102	2.5	10.0	6.0/5.0	10.0	7.5/3.5	5	4.95	65	.48	4.50	.73
07103	2.5	10.0	6.5/4.0	10.0	6.5/4.0	5	4.80	80	.64	4.41	.76
07104	2.5	10.0	5.5/3.0	7.5	5.5/4.0	4	4.62	80	.42	4.40	.57
07105	2.5	10.0	5.5/4.0	7.5	6.5/4.0	4	5.28	75	.71	4.80	.50
07106	2.5	7.5	6.5/5.0	10.0	7.5/3.5	5	4.72	70	.79	4.55	.52
07107	2.5	7.5	6.0/4.0	7.5	6.5/4.0	3	3.12	70	.60	2.68	.80
07108	3.5	5.0	5.0/4.0	5.0	6.0/4.0	5	4.35	70	.95	4.20	.50
07109	2.5	7.5	5.0/4.0	7.5	6.5/4.0	4	4.80	70	.90	4.80	.40
07801	2.5	5.0	5.5/6.0	7.5	7.5/4.0	5	5.14	75	.61	4.67	.94
07802	2.5	7.5	6.0/4.0	10.0	7.5/3.5	4	5.66	75	.64	4.85	.67
07803	3.5	5 Y	6.0/4.0	5 Y	7.0/3.0	5	5.58	70	.51	5.08	.80
07804	2.5	5.0	6.0/4.0	7.5	8.0/4.0	4	4.85	75	.64	4.65	1.05
07805	1.5	7.5	6.0/4.0	7.5	6.0/4.0	4	5.30	80	.75	4.79	1.00
07806	1.5	5.0	5.5/4.0	7.5	6.0/4.0	4	4.92	70	.60	4.68	.50
07807	2.5	10.0	5.0/4.0	10.0	6.0/4.0	2	4.00	80	.68	3.20	1.38
07808	2.5	7.5	5.5/4.0	7.5	5.0/4.0	2	4.12	80	.61	3.35	.99
07809	3.5	5.0	6.0/4.0	5.0	6.0/4.0	5	5.45	70	.70	5.18	.98
07810	3.5	7.5	5.5/4.0	7.5	5.0/4.0	4	4.68	70	.70	4.68	.85
07811	2.5	10.0	6.0/4.0	0.0	7.0/3.0	4	5.05	70	.62	4.09	.60
07812	2.5	8.0	5.0/4.0	5.0	5.0/4.0	4	5.30	70	.55	5.01	.70
07813	3.5	8 Y	7.0/3.0	5 Y	8.0/3.0	4	4.91	70	.82	4.65	.80
07814	3.5	5 Y	5.0/2.0	5.0	5.0/4.0	4	5.00	70	.80	4.80	.80
07815	2.5	10.0	7.0/3.0	10.0	7.0/3.0	4	5.18	70	.70	5.00	.80
07816	3.5	7.5	6.0/4.0	7.5	6.0/4.0	4	5.15	70	.80	4.62	.95

RURAL PRODUCTION IN MESOPOTAMIA

TABLE 15—Continued

Number	Hard-ness	Paste Color Hue	Paste Color Value/Chroma	Surface Color Hue	Surface Color Value/Chroma	Profile Type	Base Diam.	Base Angle	Body Thick.	Cons. Diam.	Base to Con-strict
07818	2.5	7.5	5.0/4.0	7.5	6.0/4.0	5	5.08	70	.65	4.90	.55
07819	2.5	5.0	5.5/4.0	5.0	5.0/4.0	4	4.80	60	.59	4.78	.80
07821	3.5	5.0	5.0/4.0	5.0	5.0/4.0	5	4.26	70	.46	4.75	.90
07823	2.5	7.5	5.0/4.0	7.5	6.0/4.0	4	5.45	70	.62	4.90	.48
07824	2.5	7.5	7.0/4.0	10.0	8.0/3.0	5	4.82	70	.68	4.60	.55
07825	2.5	5.0	5.0/4.0	7.5	6.0/4.0	4	4.60	70	.56	4.36	.60
07826	2.5	10.0	6.0/4.0	7.5	5.0/4.0	4	4.58	70	.78	4.25	1.10
07827	2.5	10.0	6.0/4.0	10.0	6.0/4.0	5	5.72	70	.58	5.46	.75
07829	2.5	5.0	5.5/6.0	5.0	6.5/6.0	5	4.80	70	.62	4.68	.48
07830	2.5	10.0	6.0/4.0	10.0	7.5/3.0	4	5.60	80	.90	5.45	.71
08101	3.5	7.5	5.5/5.0	10.0	8.0/3.0	4	4.66	70	.66	4.66	...
08102	2.5	7.5	6.0/4.0	10.0	6.0/4.0	4	7.13	70	1.19	7.00	.82
08213	2.5	5.0	5.0/4.0	5.0	6.0/4.0	5	4.80	70	.52	4.52	.70
08214	2.5	10.0	6.0/4.0	10.0	6.0/4.0	4	5.05	70	.52	4.60	.70
08215	3.5	7.5	5.0/4.0	5.0	5.0/4.0	5	5.18	70	.80	4.80	.90
08216	2.5	7.5	6.0/4.0	7.5	6.0/4.0	5	5.20	70	.50	5.00	1.05
08217	2.5	7.5	6.0/4.0	7.5	5.0/4.0	5	5.00	70	.68	4.92	.68
08218	2.5	5.0	5.0/4.0	7.5	6.0/4.0	5	5.08	70	.68	5.00	.50
08219	2.5	5.0	5.0/4.0	5.0	5.0/4.0	6	5.02	60	.70	4.36	.70
08220	2.5	7.5	5.0/4.0	7.5	6.0/4.0	3	3.95	70	.64	2.92	1.55
08221	2.5	5.0	5.0/4.0	5.0	6.0/4.0	3	4.02	80	.45	3.00	1.70
08222	3.5	7.5	5.0/4.0	10.0	6.0/4.0	4	5.00	70	.62	4.70	.60
08223	2.5	5.0	6.0/6.0	5.0	6.0/4.0	4	5.22	70	.55	4.90	.60
08224	1.5	7.5	5.5/4.0	10.0	7.0/3.0	5	5.32	70	.52	4.82	.50
08225	2.5	7.5	5.5/4.0	7.5	6.5/4.0	5	5.02	75	.50	4.95	.61
08226	2.5	10.0	7.5/3.0	10.0	6.5/3.0	3	3.40	80	.55	3.20	1.17
08227	2.5	7.5	5.5/4.0	7.5	6.5/4.0	3	4.24	80	.66	3.50	1.48
08228	2.5	7.5	5.5/4.0	10.0	6.0/4.0	5	4.91	75	.67	4.74	.55
08229	1.5	7.5	5.5/4.0	7.5	6.5/4.0	4	5.25	75	.80	5.03	.61
08231	2.5	10.0	5.0/3.5	10.0	7.5/3.0	2	3.70	75	.80	3.26	1.48
08232	2.5	5.0	6.0/6.0	10.0	7.5/3.5	5	4.80	70	.54	4.49	.78
08233	2.5	10.0	5.0/3.5	10.0	6.5/4.0	4	5.48	74	.53	5.15	.71
08234	2.5	5.0	5.5/6.0	5.0	5.5/4.0	5	5.55	70	.75	5.24	.73
08235	2.5	10.0	5.0/4.0	7.5	6.0/4.0	5	4.90	70	.66	4.71	.68
08236	2.5	10.0	6.0/4.0	10.0	7.5/3.0	4	5.67	80	.58	5.32	.67
08238	2.5	7.5	5.5/4.0	10.0	6.5/4.0	4	5.40	70	.81	5.13	.45
08239	2.5	5.0	6.5/6.0	10.0	8.0/3.5	4	5.03	75	.81	4.61	.62
08243	2.5	10.0	6.0/4.0	7.5	6.0/4.0	5	4.65	60	.75	4.61	.38
08301	2.5	5.0	5.0/4.0	5.0	5.0/4.0	4	4.60	70	.58	4.50	1.10
08302	3.5	5.0	5.0/4.0	5.0	6.0/4.0	5	4.98	70	.50	4.80	.85
08303	2.5	10.0	6.0/4.0	7.5	6.0/4.0	5	5.02	70	.85	4.55	.85
08304	1.5	10.0	6.0/4.0	10.0	7.0/3.0	4	5.58	75	.70	4.98	.55
08305	2.5	7.5	6.0/4.0	7.5	5.0/4.0	6	5.28	60	.70	4.85	.90
08307	2.5	7.5	5.0/4.0	5.0	5.0/4.0	4	5.32	75	.75	5.20	.80
08310	2.5	7.5	5.0/4.0	10.0	6.0/4.0	2	3.80	80	1.08	2.55	1.70
08311	2.5	10.0	6.0/4.0	10.0	6.0/4.0	4	5.00	70	.82	4.85	.65
Inside Structure IB											
08801	2.5	7.5	6.0/4.0	10.0	8.0/3.0	5	5.10	70	.58	4.65	.65
08802	2.5	10.0	7.0/4.0	7.5	6.5/4.0	5	5.05	65	.55	5.05	.65
08803	2.5	7.5	6.0/4.0	5.0	5.0/4.0	2	3.35	80	.75	2.90	2.05
08804	2.5	7.5	5.0/4.0	10.0	6.0/4.0	4	5.55	70	.50	5.02	.55
08805	2.5	10.0	5.0/3.0	10.0	7.0/3.0	5	4.95	70	.60	4.05	.62
08806	2.5	5.0	5.0/4.0	5.0	6.0/4.0	2	3.05	75	.80	2.69	1.00
08807	2.5	7.5	5.0/5.0	7.5	5.0/4.0	6	5.00	75	.58	4.65	.78
08808	2.5	7.5	5.0/4.0	7.5	6.0/4.0	4	5.22	75	.70	4.80	.70

APPENDIX I 131

TABLE 15—Continued

Number	Hardness	Paste Color Hue	Paste Color Value/Chroma	Surface Color Hue	Surface Color Value/Chroma	Profile Type	Base Diam.	Base Angle	Body Thick.	Cons. Diam.	Base to Constrict
08809	2.5	7.5	5.5/4.0	7.5	5.0/4.0	4	5.60	75	.89	5.36	.60
08810	2.5	7.5	5.5/4.0	7.5	6.5/4.0	2	4.10	80	.86	3.34	1.25
08811	3.5	7.5	3.5/4.0	10.0	7.5/3.5	5	4.94	65	.65	4.71	.43
08812	2.5	7.5	5.0/5.0	7.5	6.5/4.0	4	5.31	75	.81	5.29	.41
10001	2.5	7.5	5.0/4.0	7.5	6.0/4.0	5	4.80	70	.60	4.55	.75
10002	1.5	10.0	6.0/3.0	10.0	7.0/3.0	5	5.20	70	.78	4.95	.60
10003	2.5	10.0	6.0/4.0	10.0	7.0/4.0	4	5.80	80	1.10	5.38	.40
10103	2.5	5.0	5.0/4.0	5.0	6.0/4.0	4	4.72	70	.58	4.42	.90
10104	2.5	7.5	5.5/4.0	10.0	7.0/3.0	4	5.40	70	.50	4.92	.85
10105	1.5	10.0	6.0/4.0	7.5	6.0/4.0	5	5.40	70	.50	4.78	.80
10106	2.5	10.0	6.0/4.0	10.0	6.0/3.0	4	5.45	75	.68	5.06	.60
10108	2.5	10.0	5.0/3.0	10.0	7.0/4.0	5	4.92	60	.56	4.70	.70
10113	2.5	5.0	6.0/6.0	7.5	6.5/4.0	4	5.40	70	.73	5.04	.66
10115	2.5	7.5	5.5/4.0	10.0	7.5/3.0	4	4.40	75	.64	4.27	.51
10203	2.5	2.5Y	6.0/3.0	5 Y	7.5/3.0	6	5.16	65	.50	5.00	.58
10204	1.5	10.0	6.0/4.0	10.0	6.0/4.0	4	4.84	70	.73	5.21	.49
10205	2.5	7.5	5.0/5.0	10.0	6.5/4.0	5	5.29	68	.65	5.15	.44
10206	2.5	7.5	5.5/4.0	7.5	6.0/3.0	5	5.36	70	.79	5.14	.70
10208	2.5	7.5	5.0/4.0	7.5	5.0/4.0	5	7.91	80	.90	7.81	.54
10209	2.5	10.0	6.0/4.0	10.0	5.5/4.0	3	3.42	75	.80	3.24	1.06
10502	2.5	10.0	6.0/4.0	10.0	7.0/3.0	4	5.05	70	.38	4.86	.60
10503	2.5	10.0	6.0/3.0	10.0	6.0/4.0	5	5.20	65	.55	4.92	.95
10504	2.5	7.5	6.0/4.0	7.5	6.0/4.0	4	5.02	70	.64	4.88	.50
10505	2.5	5.0	6.0/6.0	10.0	8.0/3.0	5	4.70	68	.58	4.38	.60
10506	2.5	10.0	7.0/3.0	10.0	7.0/3.0	5	5.60	68	.70	5.40	.55
10507	2.5	7.5	5.0/4.0	7.5	6.0/4.0	5	5.42	65	.78	4.98	.69
10601	1.5	7.5	5.0/4.0	7.5	6.0/4.0	5	5.80	68	.72	5.40	.90
10602	3.5	5 Y	6.0/3.0	5 Y	7.0/3.0	5	5.65	60	.48	5.12	1.30
10603	2.5	10.0	6.0/4.0	7.5	6.0/4.0	6	5.10	65	.60	4.82	.72
10604	2.5	2.5Y	7.0/2.0	10.0	8.0/3.0	4	6.35	70	.55	5.60	1.02
10605	2.5	7.5	6.0/4.0	7.5	5.0/4.0	4	5.65	70	.55	5.50	1.10
10606	2.5	7.5	5.5/4.0	7.5	6.5/4.0	5	5.64	65	.72	5.20	.68
10607	2.5	7.5	5.0/4.0	7.5	6.0/4.0	5	4.91	72	.59	4.67	.66
10608	2.5	7.5	5.5/4.0	10.0	7.5/3.0	3	5.70	80	.90	5.39	.65
10609	1.5	7.5	5.0/4.0	10.0	6.5/4.0	4	4.61	75	.76	4.23	.73
10610	2.5	7.5	5.0/4.0	7.5	5.0/4.0	2	3.73	85	.80	3.19	1.06
10701	3.5	2.5Y	7.0/4.0	5 Y	7.0/3.0	6	4.18	65	.49	4.12	.52
10702	1.5	5.0	5.0/4.0	5.0	6.0/4.0	2	3.70	85	.48	3.70	.70
10703	2.5	10.0	6.0/4.0	10.0	8.0/3.0	4	5.70	70	.50	5.48	1.40
10704	2.5	10.0	6.0/4.0	10.0	7.0/3.0	4	5.20	70	.59	5.00	1.10
10706	1.5	7.5	5.0/4.0	7.5	6.0/4.0	3	4.35	75	.80	3.42	1.40
10707	2.5	10.0	7.0/4.0	10.0	7.0/4.0	4	5.40	70	.50	5.12	.50
10708	2.5	7.5	6.0/4.0	7.5	7.0/4.0	4	5.32	70	.68	5.18	.42
10709	2.5	7.5	7.0/4.0	10.0	7.0/3.0	4	5.42	68	.62	5.20	.80
10710	1.5	7.5	6.0/4.0	7.5	6.0/4.0	5	5.80	68	.55	5.50	.40
10711	2.5	10.0	6.0/4.0	7.5	6.0/4.0	4	5.98	70	.50	5.70	.60
10712	3.5	5 Y	6.0/4.0	5 Y	7.0/4.0	5	6.70	70	.58	6.25	1.22
10714	1.5	10.0	6.0/4.0	7.5	6.0/4.0	5	5.95	65	.98	5.68	.75
10716	1.5	10.0	7.0/3.0	10.0	8.0/3.0	4	5.40	70	.70	5.30	.68
10717	1.5	5.0	5.0/4.0	5.0	6.0/4.0	5	5.80	65	.66	5.34	.70
10718	2.5	7.5	5.5/4.0	7.5	6.0/4.0	2	4.10	80	.60	3.20	1.60
10719	2.5	7.5	6.5/4.0	7.5	6.5/4.0	4	5.05	70	.70	4.68	.60
10720	2.5	10.0	6.0/4.0	5.0	5.0/4.0	4	4.50	70	.72	4.50	.60
10721	1.5	7.5	5.0/4.0	7.5	6.0/4.0	2	3.50	80	.90	2.48	1.20
10722	1.5	7.5	5.0/4.0	7.5	6.0/4.0	4	5.55	70	.80	5.36	.70
10723	1.5	7.5	6.0/5.0	7.5	6.5/4.0	2	2.80	74	.76	2.65	1.27

TABLE 15—Continued

Number	Hardness	Paste Color Hue	Paste Color Value/Chroma	Surface Color Hue	Surface Color Value/Chroma	Profile Type	Base Diam.	Base Angle	Body Thick.	Cons. Diam.	Base to Constrict
10724	2.5	10.0	6.5/4.0	10.0	6.0/4.0	2	2.67	75	.58	2.40	1.18
10725	2.5	7.5	5.5/4.0	10.0	6.5/3.5	2	3.90	82	.67	2.90	1.48
10727	2.5	7.5	6.5/4.0	10.0	7.0/3.5	3	3.10	73	.76	2.49	1.42
10729	2.5	7.5	5.0/4.0	10.0	6.5/3.0	2	3.18	78	.92	2.65	1.85
10730	1.5	7.5	5.5/4.0	7.5	6.5/4.0	3	3.51	82	.88	2.93	1.59
10733	2.5	5.0	5.5/6.0	5.0	6.5/6.0	5	5.99	65	.60	5.09	.95
10734	1.5	7.5	5.5/6.0	7.5	6.5/4.0	5	5.45	70	1.12	5.21	1.04
10735	2.5	5.0	6.0/5.0	10.0	7.5/2.5	6	4.60	60	.68	4.45	.75
10736	2.5	10.0	6.0/4.0	10.0	6.0/3.5	4	5.04	75	.63	4.61	.85
10737	2.5	5.0	5.5/6.0	7.5	6.0/4.0	4	3.20	75	.64	4.87	.81
10740	1.5	7.5	6.5/4.0	10.0	7.5/3.5	4	4.91	70	.87	4.65	.59
10901	2.5	5.0	6.0/6.0	5.0	7.0/5.0	6	5.00	55	.96	4.55	.69
10902	2.5	10.0	7.0/3.0	10.0	8.0/3.0	5	5.20	75	.94	4.60	.68
10903	2.5	10.0	6.0/6.0	7.5	7.0/4.0	4	5.20	70	.72	5.15	.68
10904	2.5	2.5Y	8.0/4.0	10.0	8.0/3.0	5	5.25	65	.75	4.89	.59
11101	2.5	7.5	7.0/4.0	5.0	6.5/5.0	4	4.93	77	1.01	4.88	.55
Outside Structure III											
08401	2.5	10.0	6.0/4.0	7.5	6.0/4.0	4	4.60	70	.45	4.95	.75
08402	2.5	10.0	5.0/4.0	10.0	5.0/4.0	5	5.30	60	.50	4.92	.75
08403	2.5	7.5	6.0/4.0	10.0	7.0/3.0	4	5.45	70	.80	5.39	.60
08404	2.5	7.5	6.0/4.0	7.5	6.0/4.0	4	5.60	70	.70	5.46	.65
08405	2.5	10.0	6.0/4.0	10.0	7.0/3.0	3	3.70	75	—	3.22	1.00
08406	1.5	10.0	6.0/3.0	7.5	6.0/4.0	4	5.30	70	—	5.05	.70
08407	2.5	5.0	5.0/4.0	7.5	7.0/4.0	2	3.95	82	.80	3.20	1.60
08408	1.5	7.5	5.0/4.0	7.5	6.0/4.0	3	3.85	78	—	3.35	1.35
08409	2.5	10.0	6.0/4.0	7.5	5.0/4.0	3	3.96	80	—	2.92	1.65
08410	1.5	10.0	6.0/4.0	5.0	5.0/4.0	2	4.10	75	—	2.90	1.90
08411	2.5	10.0	6.0/4.0	10.0	6.0/4.0	4	5.32	75	.88	5.20	.80
08412	2.5	7.5	6.0/4.0	7.5	6.0/4.0	4	5.40	78	—	4.70	.65
08416	2.5	10.0	6.0/4.0	10.0	6.5/4.0	3	4.41	70	.80	4.41	.63
08607	2.5	7.5	5.5/6.0	5.0	5.5/4.0	5	5.09	70	—	4.95	.64
08608	2.5	5.0	5.0/4.0	10.0	6.0/3.0	4	4.74	63	.58	4.82	.55
08609	3.5	7.5	5.0/5.0	10.0	6.5/4.0	5	4.67	68	.51	4.49	.40
08612	2.5	10.0	6.0/5.0	10.0	7.5/3.0	4	5.40	65	.76	5.06	.56
08613	2.5	10.0	6.0/4.0	10.0	7.5/3.0	3	5.78	75	.72	5.55	.92
08614	2.5	7.5	5.0/5.0	10.0	6.0/3.5	4	5.49	75	—	5.24	.63
08615	2.5	10.0	5.0/2.5	10.0	7.5/2.5	3	3.50	75	—	3.44	.56
08616	2.5	10.0	5.0/5.0	10.0	6.0/4.0	4	5.00	72	—	4.55	.62
08617	2.5	10.0	6.0/4.0	7.5	6.0/4.0	2	3.85	82	—	3.18	.62
08618	1.5	7.5	5.0/4.0	10.0	7.0/3.0	4	4.80	70	1.02	4.58	.82
08619	1.5	10.0	6.0/4.0	7.5	6.0/4.0	2	3.65	85	—	2.85	1.02
08622	2.5	7.5	5.0/4.0	7.5	6.0/4.0	6	5.10	60	—	4.90	.50
08623	2.5	7.5	5.0/4.0	7.5	6.0/4.0	4	4.79	70	—	4.62	.55
08624	2.5	7.5	5.0/4.0	7.5	6.0/4.0	2	3.45	80	—	2.75	1.45
08626	2.5	7.5	5.5/4.0	10.0	6.5/3.5	3	3.33	72	.52	2.32	1.39
08627	2.5	7.5	5.0/4.0	7.5	5.0/3.0	2	3.05	83	—	2.83	1.16

NOTE: Munsell hue is in the YR (Yellow-Red) range unless noted as Y (Yellow). All angles are to the nearest 5 degrees.

APPENDIX I

TABLE 16
BOWL RIMS
Simple Bowls

Number	Hard-ness	Paste Color Hue	Paste Color Value/Chroma	Surface Color Hue	Surface Color Value/Chroma	Rim Diameter	Rim Angle	Body Thickness
00003	1.5	7.5	6.0/4.0	2.5Y	8.0/3.0	26	55	.80
00904	2.5	7.5	6.0/4.0	10.0	7.5/2.0	10	75	.58
01111	2.5	10.0	6.0/4.0	10.0	7.5/2.5	36	65	.74
01803	2.5	7.5	5.5/4.0	7.5	6.5/7.0	18	60	.82
01903	3.5	10.0	6.0/4.0	10.0	7.0/2.0	13	65	.60
02011	1.5	10.0	6.5/3.0	10.0	7.5/3.0	24	60	.81
02013	1.5	10.0	6.0/4.0	10.0	7.5/3.0	22	65	.52
02605	1.5	10.0	6.0/4.0	10.0	8.0/2.0	18	65	.59
02807	3.5	10.0	5.0/3.5	10.0	6.0/1.0	36	80	.73
02809	3.5	7.5	5.5/4.0	10.0	7.5/3.5	12	75	.60
03006	3.5	10.0	5.0/3.0	10.0	6.5/4.0	30	60	1.03
03513	1.5	10.0	5.0/4.0	7.5	8.5/4.0	22	80	.70
03801	2.5	7.5	5.5/4.0	5.0	4.5/6.0	34	60	.92
03917	2.5	2.5Y	7.0/3.0	5.0Y	7.5/3.0	18	95	.44
03918	3.5	7.5	4.5/4.0	7.5	8.5/2.0	28	75	.90
04219	2.5	7.5	6.5/4.0	10.0	8.0/3.0	28	75	1.17
04424	2.5	5.0	6.0/5.0	10.0	8.0/2.5	22	55	1.06
05009	2.5	7.5	6.0/5.0	10.0	7.5/3.0	26	55	.73
05010	2.5	5.0	5.0/5.0	7.5	6.5/4.0	38	60	.96
05011	2.5	7.5	5.0/4.0	10.0	8.0/4.0	40	55	.88
05102	2.5	10.0	5.5/4.0	10.0	8.0/3.0	32	65	1.24
05103	2.5	10.0	5.0/4.0	10.0	6.0/4.0	40	55	.93
05325	1.5	7.5	5.0/4.0	7.5	6.0/2.5	30	65	.89
05326	2.5	7.5	7.5/4.0	10.0	8.0/3.5	32	50	.90
05327	1.5	7.5	5.5/4.0	10.0	7.5/3.0	44	55	1.00
05624	2.5	7.5	5.5/6.0	10.0	7.5/3.0	46	60	.96
05801	2.5	7.5	5.5/4.0	10.0	7.5/3.0	35	55	.85
07114	1.5	7.5	5.5/4.0	7.5	5.5/4.0	16	65	1.54
07117	1.5	5.0	5.5/6.0	10.0	7.0/4.0	14	55	.66
07240	2.5	5.0	5.5/5.0	5.0	5.5/6.0	16	70	.70
07409	2.5	10.0	6.5/4.0	2.5	8.0/3.0	52	65	.95
08322	2.5	10.0	5.0/4.0	10.0	7.5/4.0	28	55	1.63
08419	2.5	10.0	6.5/4.0	7.5	6.5/4.0	28	65	1.19
08820	2.5	10.0	6.0/3.0	5.0	7.5/3.0	32	50	1.29
10007	2.5	10.0	5.0/4.0	7.5	6.0/4.0	53	50	1.27
10304	2.5	5.0	8.5/4.0	10.0	8.0/2.5	40	60	1.26
10622	2.5	2.5Y	4.0/2.0	2.5Y	3.5/0.0	12	70	.61
10768	2.5	5.0	5.5/6.0	10.0	7.5/3.0	44	75	1.52
10769	2.5	10.0	6.0/4.0	10.0	8.0/2.5	44	60	.94

Simple Bowls with Thickened Rims

Number	Hard-ness	Paste Color Hue	Paste Color Value/Chroma	Surface Color Hue	Surface Color Value/Chroma	Rim Diam.	Rim Angle	Body Thick.	Rim Thick.	Rim Top Angle
00212	2.5	10.0	6.0/4.0	10.0	8.0/2.5	44	85	.81	1.00	
01624	1.5	7.5	5.5/4.0	7.5	6.5/4.0	39	55	.96	1.12	
02201	2.5	7.5	5.5/4.0	10.0	7.0/3.5	36	45	1.01	.99	
02212	2.5	10.0	6.0/4.0	10.0	7.0/3.0	16	75	.34	.78	
02508	2.5	7.5	6.5/4.0	7.5	6.5/4.0	55	95	1.35	1.18	
02509	2.5	7.5	6.0/5.0	10.0	7.0/3.5	32	70	.82	.90	
01112	2.5	7.5	5.5/4.0	10.0	7.0/3.5	26	60	.81	.65	
02706	1.5	7.5	4.5/4.0	7.5	6.5/4.0	34	50	1.03	1.14	
02707	1.5	7.5	5.5/4.0	7.5	7.0/4.0	54	65	1.20	1.24	
03409	2.5	7.5	5.5/4.0	7.5	5.5/4.0	44	70	1.10	1.69	

TABLE 16—Continued

Number	Hard-ness	Paste Color		Surface Color		Rim Diam.	Rim Angle	Body Thick.	Rim Thick.	Rim Top Angle
		Hue	Value/Chroma	Hue	Value/Chroma					
04601	2.5	5.0	5.5/6.0	10.0	6.5/3.0	52	50	1.70	1.76	
05614	3.5	7.5	5.0/5.0	7.5	6.5/4.0	40	70	1.83	1.41	
07241	2.5	5.0	5.5/5.0	7.5	6.5/4.0	46	50	1.03	2.00	
07242	2.5	7.5	5.5/4.0	10.0	8.0/3.5	50	65	1.60	2.04	
07243	2.5	7.5	5.5/4.0	7.5	6.5/4.0	65	60	2.30	2.20	
07608	2.5	5.0	5.5/6.0	10.0	7.5/4.0	40	60	2.11	1.30	
08210	2.5	10.0	5.5/4.0	10.0	7.0/3.0	40	50	1.34	1.19	
10613	2.5	7.5	5.0/6.0	7.5	6.5/4.0	48	90	1.41	1.68	
11104	2.5	7.5	6.5/5.0	7.5	6.5/5.0	62	55	1.64	1.95	
11403	1.5	7.5	5.5/4.0	10.0	7.5/4.0	28	65	.79	.83	
Ledge Rim Bowls										
00213	2.5	10.0	6.5/4.0	7.5	7.5/4.0	48	90	.71	1.72	105
00602	2.5	5.0	5.0/4.0	10.0	6.5/3.0	40	75	1.00	2.07	115
02202	2.5	7.5	5.5/4.0	5.0	5.5/4.0	36	65	.93	1.37	110
03104	2.5	10.0	6.0/4.0	10.0	6.5/3.0	75	75	1.94	3.47	120
04316	1.5	7.5	6.5/4.0	2.5Y	8.0/2.0	36	60	1.02	1.10	125
08430	2.5	10.0	6.0/4.0	7.5	5.5/4.0	44	60	1.50	1.74	120
09001	2.5	7.5	6.0/4.0	10.0	7.5/3.0	36	55	1.04	1.37	110
10509	1.5	7.5	5.5/4.0	7.5	5.5/4.0	80+	80	1.98	5.20	110
10510	2.5	5.0	5.5/6.0	10.0	7.5/3.0	51	75	1.48	3.52	110
10754	2.5	2.5Y	7.0/2.0	2.5Y	6.5/2.0	58	80	1.57	5.51	105
11404	2.5	7.5	5.0/4.0	10.0	7.5/3.0	48	75	1.31	1.10	110
Ledge Rim Bowls with Band										
00603	2.5	2.5	7.0/3.0	10.0	7.5/3.0	43	85	1.36	1.79	100
00019	1.5	10.0	5.5/4.0	7.5	6.5/4.0	74	70	1.86	4.53	120
06004	2.5	7.5	5.0/5.0	2.5Y	6.0/3.0	52	65	1.04	2.25	130
06510	2.5	7.5	5.5/4.0	10.0	7.5/3.0	51	75	1.32	2.18	120
00006	2.5	10.0	5.5/4.0	10.0	7.5/3.0	63	65	1.92	3.83	110
Concave-Sided Bowls										
03203	2.5	10.0	6.0/4.0	2.5Y	7.5/3.0	14	100	.48		
03919*	2.5	7.5	5.5/6.0	7.5	6.5/4.0	46	85	.90		
05328*	2.5	7.5	5.5/4.0	10.0	7.5/3.5	46	75	1.18		
10008*	2.5	10.0	6.0/4.0	10.0	8.0/3.5	40	80	1.00		
10201*	2.5	7.5	5.5/4.0	7.5	5.5/4.0	50	70	1.27		
Heavy Conical Bowls with Chaff Temper										
08821	1.5	5.0	5.5/6.0	10.0	7.5/3.0	50	70	2.06		
08903	2.5	10.0	6.0/4.0	10.0	7.0/2.0	80	90	3.12		

*Incised wavy line below rim.

APPENDIX I 135

TABLE 17
JAR RIMS
Round Rim Jars

Number	Hardness	Paste Color Hue	Paste Color Value/Chroma	Surface Color Hue	Surface Color Value/Chroma	Rim Diam.	Neck Height	Neck Thickness	Rim Angle	Shoulder Thickness	Neck Angle	Rim Thickness
01620	1.5	7.5	6.5/4.0	10.0	5.0/3.0	12	5.43	.52	95	.90	110	.52
02007	1.5	10.0	6.5/4.0	2.5Y	7.5/2.0	10	4.16	.52	80	.66	105	.41
02516	2.5	10.0	6.0/4.0	10.0	7.0/3.0	10	4.50	.71	95	.80	110	.56
01105	1.5	7.5	8.5/4.0	10.0	6.0/4.0	18	.90	.60	105	.87	125	.76
02708	2.5	7.5	4.5/4.0	7.5	6.5/4.0	12	1.55	.99	95	.91	110	1.05
02805	5.5	10.0	5.0/2.0	10.0	3.0/2.0	13	2.04	.47	95	.64	105	.55
02810	3.5	7.5	5.5/6.0	10.0	7.5/3.0	10	1.51	.93	80	1.06	140	.93
03410	2.5	5.0	5.0/5.0	10.0	7.5/3.5	12	.46	.67	60	.55	90	.77
04502	1.5	7.5	5.0/4.0	7.5	6.0/4.0	9	2.31	.55	60	.73	85	.47
05007	1.5	10.0	6.0/4.0	10.0	7.5/3.0	12	2.43	.64	65	.59	120	.79
15107	1.5	5.0	5.0/5.0	10.0	6.0/4.0	10	1.48	.68	65	.41	110	.67
05322	2.5	7.5	6.0/4.0	7.5	7.5/3.0	12	2.48	.91	65	1.07	115	.95
05323	1.5	7.5	5.5/4.0	10.0	7.5/3.0	14	1.01	.64	80	.77	115	.82
05324	1.5	7.5	5.0/4.0	7.5	6.5/4.0	10	.86	.57	50	.46	135	.60
05507	2.5	5.0	6.0/6.0	10.0	7.5/3.0	12	4.19	.50	65	.66	120	.44
05508	2.5	7.5	5.0/4.0	7.5	7.0/5.0	10	2.20	.50	95	.95	110	.50
05628	2.5	5.0	5.5/6.0	10.0	7.5/3.0	12	1.36	.67	70	.67	130	.79
05803	2.5	7.5	6.5/4.0	7.5	8.0/3.5	10	5.00	.53	90	.70	85	.56
06408	1.5	10.0	5.0/4.0	7.5	6.5/4.0	11	2.76	.67	45	.75	130	.57
06903	2.5	10.0	4.0/3.5	7.5	6.5/4.0	11	.79	.58	90	.73	110	.66
07112	2.5	7.5	6.5/7.0	10.0	6.5/4.0	11	4.10	.56	65	.70	110	.45
07234	2.5	5.0	6.5/6.0	10.0	7.5/3.0	14	1.51	.49	75	.71	105	.45
07235	2.5	7.5	5.0/4.0	7.5	7.5/4.0	13	1.51	.67	85	.83	105	.90
07412	2.5	5.0	5.0/8.0	10.0	7.5/5.0	8	.73	.43	45	.43	115	.39
07601	2.5	7.5	5.0/4.0	7.5	6.5/4.0	10	2.15	.82	100	.95	125	.61
07723	2.5	7.5	5.5/4.0	7.5	6.0/4.0	12	1.50	.60	85	.73	115	.69
07724	2.5	5.0	5.5/6.0	10.0	7.0/3.0	12	.79	.95	80	.72	115	.80
07725	2.5	7.5	6.0/4.0	10.0	7.0/3.5	12	1.58	.46	55	.72	100	.53
07726	2.5	7.5	5.0/5.0	10.0	7.5/3.0	12	1.74	.73	85	.86	115	.68
07727	3.5	10.0	5.5/4.0	10.0	6.0/4.0	10	2.40	.50	80	1.00	100	.39
07844	2.5	7.5	5.5/4.0	10.0	7.5/4.0	12	1.27	.49	80	.94	115	.75
07845	2.5	7.5	6.5/4.0	2.5Y	8.0/3.0	12	1.38	.58	85	.92	115	.66
08205	2.5	5.0	4.5/4.0	7.5	7.5/2.0	12	2.40	.70	55	.87	75	.78
08206	2.5	10.0	5.5/4.0	10.0	7.0/3.5	16	1.18	.48	100	.81	135	.66

TABLE 17—Continued

Number	Hardness	Paste Color Hue	Paste Color Value/Chroma	Surface Color Hue	Surface Color Value/Chroma	Rim Diam.	Neck Height	Neck Thickness	Rim Angle	Shoulder Thickness	Neck Angle	Rim Thickness
08207	2.5	5.0	6.0/6.0	10.0	7.0/3.0	11	4.38	.64	80	.70	115	.46
08208	2.5	7.5	5.0/4.0	7.5	6.5/4.0	12	3.57	.60	100	.95	135	.46
08318	3.5	5.0	5.5/4.0	10.0	7.5/3.0	9	5.18	.60	40	.90	115	.50
08319	1.5	7.5	5.0/4.0	5.0	6.5/6.0	10	1.10	.55	80	.72	115	.66
08819	2.5	10.0	4.0/1.5	10.0	6.0/3.0	10	4.23	.63	80	.76	140	.51
09903	2.5	10.0	5.5/4.0	10.0	6.0/4.0	11	2.93	.68	65	.71	130	.67
10614	1.5	7.5	5.0/4.0	7.5	6.0/4.0	12	1.15	.78	100	.62	100	.68
10615	2.5	7.5	5.5/4.0	7.5	8.0/2.5	12	1.42	.52	75	.63	115	.54
10616	2.5	7.5	5.0/5.0	10.0	7.5/3.0	12	.53	.44	80	.70	105	.55
10795	2.5	10.0	6.0/4.0	10.0	7.5/3.0	10	4.79	.45	75	.60	125	.41
10752	2.5	7.5	5.0/3.0	10.0	7.5/3.0	8	1.49	.59	50	.72	95	.60
10753	2.5	7.5	5.0/4.0	7.5	5.5/4.0	12	1.10	.83	80	1.00	95	1.13
10802	2.5	7.5	5.0/4.0	10.0	6.5/3.5	10	1.30	.62	75	.78	110	.65
11301	2.5	10.0	5.0/4.0	10.0	8.0/3.5	12	3.65	.59	85	.84	80	.65
00010	3.5	10.0	6.0/4.0	2.5Y	8.0/3.0	14	6.06	.52	65	1.50	120	.46
00011	2.5	7.5	5.5/4.0	2.5Y	7.5/2.0	9	4.09	.59	100	1.35	125	.48
01207	4.5	10.0	4.0/2.0	10.0	8.0/3.0	11	.85	.67	85	.75	125	.65
01905	5.5	5.0Y	6.0/4.0	2.5Y	7.5/2.0	13	2.20	.55	65	.71	120	.46
04901	4.5	2.5Y	7.0/2.0	2.5Y	8.0/3.0	16	1.15	.92	60	.80	125	.87

Ledge Rim Jars

Number	Hardness	Paste Color Hue	Paste Color Value/Chroma	Surface Color Hue	Surface Color Value/Chroma	Rim Diam.	Rim Ht.	Rim Thick.	Rim Top Angle	Neck Thick.	Rim Angle	Neck Height	Neck Angle	Shoulder Thickness
00012	3.5	5.0	5.0/7.0	10.0	7.5/3.5	9	.73	1.35	100	.60	80	2.31	125	.75
00001	2.5	10.0	6.5/3.0	5.0Y	7.5/3.0	20	.86	2.30	105	.67	80	2.74	110	.89
00606	2.5	5.0	6.0/6.0	10.0	7.5/3.0	14	.82	2.41	105	.79	85	6.35	135	.84
00901	2.5	10.0	6.0/3.0	5.0Y	7.0/3.0	18	.68	1.87	110	.79	75	4.10	...	...
00905	2.5	7.5	5.5/4.0	5.0	4.0/6.0	8	.91	.65	110	.46	90	2.30	...	...
01622	1.5	10.0	6.5/4.0	2.5Y	8.0/2.0	11	.65	.46	125	.45	85	3.58	95	.73
01623	1.5	5.0	5.0/6.0	5.0	6.5/4.0	20	1.45	1.88	110	.77	80	3.30	...	...
01703	1.5	5.0	5.0/6.0	5.0	6.0/6.0	12	.89	1.52	110	.41	75	...	...	...
02210	2.5	7.5	5.0/4.0	10.0	7.0/3.0	12	.73	1.01	100	.95	65	.30	115	.80
02515	1.5	10.0	6.0/4.0	10.0	7.5/2.5	12	1.15	1.95	105	.61	75	1.80	110	...
02517	1.5	7.5	6.0/4.0	10.0	7.0/3.5	10	1.02	.96	90	...	70	1.02	90	.67

APPENDIX I 137

TABLE 17—Continued

ID												
02709	1.5	5.0	5.5/5.0	5.0	6.5/4.0	14	1.85	110	.52	75	...	...
04425	2.5	10.0	6.0/4.0	10.0	7.5/4.0	14	2.15	110	.69	70	3.81	...
04603	2.5	5.0	5.5/5.0	10.0	7.5/3.0	22	2.70	115	.86	70	3.01	.99
05212	2.5	5.0	6.0/6.0	10.0	7.5/3.0	13	.74	115	.63	80	6.08	.76
05509	2.5	7.5	5.0/7.0	10.0	8.0/3.5	14	.84	105	.45	85	...	...
06509	1.5	5.0	5.5/5.0	7.5	6.5/4.0	10	.67	100	.55	55	1.55	.67
06605	2.5	5.0	6.0/6.0	7.5	8.0/4.0	16	.84	100	.64	80	...	...
06606	3.5	5.0	3.0/1.0	5.0	6.0/2.5	17	1.29	105	.84	100	...	...
06607	2.5	5.0	6.0/4.0	10.0	8.0/3.0	14	.75	110	.79	80	2.48	.80
06608	2.5	10.0	6.5/3.0	10.0	8.0/2.5	12	.83	110	.47	80	4.71	...
07237	1.5	7.5	5.5/4.0	10.0	7.5/3.5	15	1.91	120	.88	65	...	...
07411	1.5	10.0	6.5/4.0	7.5	7.5/3.0	8	1.14	110	.74	65	...	...
07605	2.5	5.0	5.0/4.0	5.0	5.0/4.0	15	.82	110	.55	60	4.07	...
07728	2.5	10.0	4.0/3.0	10.0	8.0/3.0	10	1.42	110	.70	70	4.17	.92
07729	1.5	10.0	5.0/4.0	7.5	5.5/4.0	14	2.17	120	.99	75	3.71	.95
07841	2.5	7.5	5.0/4.0	7.5	7.5/4.0	20	1.40	125	.66	55	4.10	...
07843	3.5	7.5	5.5/4.0	10.0	7.5/3.0	18	2.03	110	.96	95	...	...
08204	3.5	10.0	6.0/3.0	5.0Y	7.5/3.0	22	1.61	120	.68	90	...	...
08317	2.5	7.5	5.0/4.0	7.5	6.5/3.0	11	1.08	105	.67	65	3.29	.77
08429	2.5	10.0	6.0/4.0	2.5Y	8.0/3.0	17	.85	120	.80	75	...	...
08817	3.5	10.0	7.0/4.0	2.5Y	8.0/4.0	14	1.60	105	.75	75	3.64	...
10617	2.5	5.0	5.0/5.0	7.5	6.5/4.0	26	1.40	120	1.04	65	...	1.10
11201	2.5	5.0	7.0/4.0	10.0	8.0/4.0	9	.56	105	.54	80	2.41	...
Band Rim Jars												
00018	2.5	5.0	5.5/5.0	10.0	7.0/2.5	13	1.70	155	1.00	65	3.40	1.13
00111	3.5	5.0	7.0/6.0	7.5	8.0/3.0	11	1.34	155	.56	85	...	...
00306	3.5	10.0	5.0/3.0	7.5	6.0/4.0	9	1.78	165	.44	75	2.75	.98
01004	1.5	7.5	5.5/4.0	10.0	7.5/3.0	19	1.40	145	.80	50	...	...
02006	2.5	7.5	6.0/4.0	7.5	7.5/3.0	12	1.49	145	.49	90	3.88	.60
02710	1.5	10.0	7.5/4.0	7.5	7.5/3.0	10	1.53	145	.42	80	2.67	.63
05320	2.5	7.5	5.5/4.0	7.5	6.5/4.0	12	1.54	135	.71	70	...	...
05321	1.5	7.5	5.0/4.0	7.5	7.5/4.0	10	1.11	140	.70	75	...	.78
05623	2.5	5.0	5.5/4.0	10.0	6.5/4.0	12	1.67	145	.64	75	4.13	...
07842	2.5	5.0	5.5/4.0	5.0	8.0/3.5	13	1.93	150	.64	70	...	...
08201	2.5	7.5	5.0/4.0	10.0	5.0/4.0	12	1.67	165	.50	65	...	1.25
08202	3.5	10.0	6.5/3.0	5.0Y	7.5/3.0	10	2.00	155	.60	82	4.96	...
08203	2.5	7.5	6.0/5.0	10.0	7.5/3.0	11	2.12	155	.55	75	4.15	...
08315	2.5	10.0	6.5/4.0	10.0	7.5/3.5	12	1.75	165	.59	65	...	...
08316	2.5	10.0	6.0/4.0	10.0	8.0/3.5	10	2.25	165	.53	70	...	...
08818	2.5	10.0	6.5/3.0	2.5Y	8.0/3.0	12	3.23	165	.67	80	...	...

TABLE 18
JAR SHOULDERS

Punctate

Number	Hardness	Paste Color Hue	Paste Color Value/Chroma	Surface Color Hue	Surface Color Value/Chroma	Thick.	Period Gash	Length Gash	Width Gash
01004	1.5	7.5	5.5/4.0	10.0	7.5/3.0	.98	1.20	.76	.14
01620	1.5	7.5	6.5/4.0	10.0	5.0/3.5	.90	.45	.50	.15
01622	1.5	7.5	6.0/4.0	2.5Y	8.0/2.0	.73	.67	.52	.48
02012	2.5	10.0	6.0/4.0	5.0Y	7.0/3.0	.94	1.32	.62	.25
02606	1.5	10.0	6.0/4.0	2.5Y	8.0/2.0	.93	.70	.57	.13
02607	1.5	10.0	6.5/4.0	10.0	7.5/3.0	1.01	.77	.63	.17
02705	1.5	10.0	6.0/4.0	7.5	7.5/3.0	.83	.61	.44	.20
02804	4.5	10.0	4.0/2.5	10.0	6.0/2.5	.61	.61	.84	.27
03920	2.5	7.5	5.5/4.0	10.0	6.5/4.0	.63	1.50	.75	.26
04215	3.5	2.5Y	6.5/2.0	2.5Y	7.5/2.0	.76	1.51	.69	.20
04216	1.5	7.5	4.0/4.0	10.0	7.0/3.0	.80	.91	.67	.15
04317	2.5	7.5	6.0/4.0	5.0Y	7.5/3.0	.68	.48	.79	.35
04417	2.5	7.5	5.5/5.0	2.5Y	8.0/3.0	.91	.53	.67	.19
04419	1.5	7.5	6.0/4.0	7.5	6.5/4.0	1.03	2.38	2.10	.28
04420	2.5	7.5	6.0/4.0	2.5Y	8.0/3.0	.71	1.30	.73	.46
04603	2.5	5.0	5.5/6.0	10.0	7.5/3.0	.81	2.19	1.03	.18
04704	3.5	10.0	4.5/4.0	10.0	6.5/4.0	.93	1.00	.54	.19
05330	1.5	5.0	5.5/6.0	10.0	7.5/3.5	.71	.45	.72	.15
15510	2.5	7.5	5.5/6.0	10.0	7.5/3.0	1.05	1.08	.73	.28
05511	2.5	7.5	5.5/4.0	10.0	7.5/3.0	1.14	1.01	.68	.26
05804	2.5	10.0	6.0/4.0	10.0	7.5/3.0	.93	1.39	.67	.19
06607[1]	2.5	7.5	6.0/4.0	10.0	8.0/3.0	.80	1.40	.91	.11
07003	2.5	7.5	5.5/4.0	7.5	6.5/4.0	.93	1.31	1.20	.25
07115	2.5	10.0	7.5/3.0	10.0	7.5/3.0	.64	.67	.48	.14
07238	3.5	5.0Y	6.0/4.0	5.0Y	7.5/3.0	.57	.52	.61	.17
07239	2.5	10.0	6.0/4.0	5.0Y	7.5/3.0	.77	1.37	.77	.22
07606	2.5	5.0	5.5/6.0	7.5	6.5/4.0	.80	1.43	.76	.37
07842	2.5	5.0	5.5/4.0	10.0	8.0/3.0	.78	1.80	.65	.21
07843	3.5	7.5	5.5/4.0	10.0	7.5/3.0	.95	2.19	.54	.35
07841	2.5	7.5	5.0/4.0	7.5	7.5/4.0	.92	1.08	.85	.17
08211	2.5	5.0	5.5/6.0	10.0	7.5/3.5	.84	1.95	.65	.20
08602	3.5	10.0	6.0/4.0	10.0	7.5/3.5	.70	1.44	.95	.23
09803[2]	2.5	7.5	4.5/4.0	7.5	5.5/4.0	.72	.62	.66	.15
10617	2.5	5.0	5.0/5.0	7.5	6.5/4.0	1.17	.58	.65	.18
10618	2.5	7.5	6.0/4.0	10.0	7.5/2.5	.80	1.00	.69	.35
10619	2.5	7.5	6.0/5.0	10.0	7.5/3.0	.90	1.32	.70	.17
10766	2.5	10.0	6.0/3.0	2.5Y	7.5/4.0	.79	.70	.71	.25

Punctate with Reserve Slip

Number	Hardness	Paste Color Hue	Paste Color Value/Chroma	Surface Color Hue	Surface Color Value/Chroma	Thick.	Period Gash	Length Gash	Width Gash	Width Reserve Line
00001	2.5	10.0	6.5/3.0	5.0Y	7.5/3.0	.79	1.01	.83	.25	.33
00011	2.5	7.5	5.5/4.0	2.5Y	7.5/2.0	1.35	1.97	.78	.17	.34
00018	2.5	5.0	5.5/5.0	10.0	7.0/2.5	.90	1.89	1.20	.27	.55
00211	2.5	5.0Y	7.5/3.0	5.0Y	8.0/3.5	.67	1.01	.53	.18	.50
02513	3.5	5.0	5.5/6.0	10.0	7.0/3.5	.80	.70	.45	.24	.61
03007	3.5	10.0	5.5/4.0	2.5Y	7.5/3.0	.89	.84	.64	.24	.37
04418	2.5	10.0	5.0/3.0	2.5Y	7.5/2.0	1.18	.95	.51	.21	.63
04705[1]	2.5	10.0	5.0/4.0	7.5	6.5/4.0	.90	1.19	.94	.20	.60
05622	2.5	10.0	7.0/4.0	10.0	7.5/5.0	.89	.75	.87	.30	.36
05803	2.5	7.5	6.5/4.0	10.0	8.0/3.5	.67	1.76	.65	.31	.43
07410	2.5	5.0Y	6.0/4.0	5.0Y	7.5/3.0	.85	1.70	.75	.19	.25
07602	2.5	10.0	6.0/3.0	2.5Y	6.5/3.0	.97	.95	.51	.17	.34
08321	2.5	7.5	5.0/6.0	10.0	7.5/3.0	.50	1.24	.77	.21	.73
08702[3]	2.5	7.5	5.0/6.0	10.0	8.0/2.5	.96	...	...	...	.81
09902	2.5	7.5	5.5/5.0	10.0	7.0/4.0	1.05	1.03	.63	.17	.33
10767	3.5	7.5	6.0/5.0	10.0	7.0/3.5	.95	1.80	1.05	.23	.45

[1]Arc-shaped punctate. [2]Concentric incised lines parallel to punctates. [3]Gashes very irregular, reserve slip lines are concentric rather than oblique.

APPENDIX I

TABLE 19
HATCHED STRIP DECORATION

Number	Hard-ness	Paste Color		Surface Color		Thick. Strip	Median Period Gash	Median Width Gash	Angle Gash	Thick. Sherd
		Hue	Value/Chroma	Hue	Value/Chroma					
00006	2.5	10.0	5.5/4.0	10.0	7.5/3.0	1.90	2.34	.87	105	1.95
00209	2.5	5.0Y	7.5/3.0	2.5Y	7.5/4.0	.51	.62	.23	95	.81
00210	2.5	10.0	7.0/2.5	2.5Y	7.5/2.0	.67	.81	.29	90	.59
00302	...	7.5	7.0/6.0	2.5Y	8.0/4.0	1.00	1.20	.29	130	.60
00603	2.5	7.5	7.0/3.0	10.0	7.5/3.0	.91	1.03	.49	115	1.36
00604	2.5	5.0	5.0/5.0	10.0	6.5/3.0	1.07	.54	.19	55	1.03
00605[1]	2.5	7.5	6.0/4.0	10.0	7.5/3.0	.71	.49	.11	110	.80
00606[2]	2.5	5.0	6.0/6.0	10.0	7.5/3.0	1.04	.68	.30	130	.76
00801	2.5	7.5	5.5/4.0	10.0	6.5/3.5	.89	.96	.42	65	.64
01005	1.5	7.5	5.5/4.0	5.0	6.0/4.0	.95	1.14	.23	55	.81
01006	2.5	7.5	5.5/4.0	10.0	6.0/4.0	.80	1.27	.30	90	1.37
02009	2.5	10.0	7.5/3.0	2.5Y	8.0/2.0	.67	.53	.20	90	.62
01106	1.5	7.5	5.0/4.0	7.5	5.5/4.0	.91	1.02	.30	65	.82
02608	1.5	10.0	6.0/4.0	2.5Y	8.0/3.0	.78	1.18	.49	90	.57
02703[3]	1.5	7.5	6.5/4.0	10.0	7.5/3.5	1.84	2.27	.27	...	1.05
02803	3.5	10.0	5.0/3.5	10.0	8.0/3.5	.71	.55	.32	75	.73
03924	2.5	5.0	5.5/5.0	7.5	8.0/3.0	.79	.63	.17	70	.64
04217	2.5	10.0	6.0/3.5	10.0	7.5/3.0	.75	.80	.20	65	.74
04421	2.5	7.5	5.5/4.0	10.0	6.5/2.5	.79	.57	.22	75	1.07
05004	2.5	7.5	5.0/5.0	2.5Y	8.0/3.0	1.17	.66	.33	70	1.14
05213[1]	3.5	2.5Y	5.5/2.0	5.0Y	7.5/3.0	1.02	.45	.13	...	.87
05329	2.5	7.5	6.0/5.0	10.0	8.0/3.0	.90	.96	.39	90	.64
05625	2.5	10.0	6.0/4.0	10.0	7.5/3.0	.75	.46	.08	115	.86
05702	2.5	7.5	6.0/5.0	10.0	8.0/3.5	.79	.90	.40	90	.69
05802	2.5	7.5	6.0/4.0	10.0	8.0/3.5	.82	.95	.32	105	.67
06510	2.5	7.5	5.5/4.0	10.0	7.5/3.0	.77	1.21	.45	55	1.33
07116	2.5	10.0	6.0/4.0	10.0	7.5/3.0	.89	.73	.23	60	.54
07246	2.5	5.0	5.5/5.0	10.0	6.5/4.0	2.67	2.36	2.78	90	1.84
07247	2.5	5.0	5.0/5.0	10.0	7.5/3.0	2.13	2.89	1.85	90	1.47
08323	2.5	10.0	5.0/3.5	7.5	7.5/3.0	.80	1.13	.46	90	1.18
08324	2.5	7.5	6.0/4.0	10.0	7.5/3.0	.80	1.20	.50	80	.50
08420	1.5	7.5	4.5/4.0	7.5	5.5/4.0	.95	.70	.30	100	1.51
08421	2.5	10.0	6.0/3.0	10.0	7.0/2.5	.85	.80	.35	110	.91
08422[2]	2.5	5.0	5.5/6.0	10.0	7.0/3.5	.92	1.13	.25	120	1.04
08701	2.5	5.0	5.5/6.0	10.0	7.5/3.0	.93	.61	.18	120	1.05
10620	2.5	7.5	5.0/4.0	5.0	6.0/5.0	.71	.63	.22	105	.79

[1] Arc-shaped handle.
[2] Vertically oriented.
[3] Round punctates, not gash, true "cable ornament."

TABLE 20
JAR SPOUTS

Number	Hardness	Paste Color		Surface Color		Rim Diam.	Base Diam.	Length	Hole Diam.
		Hue	Value/Chroma	Hue	Value/Chroma				
00010	3.5	10.0	6.0/4.0	2.5Y	8.0/3.0	1.25	3.63	6.54	.89
00011	2.5	7.5	5.5/4.0	2.5Y	7.5/2.0	1.61	3.88	4.24	1.00
00018	2.5	5.0	5.5/5.0	10.0	7.0/2.5	.84	4.59	4.10	1.11
00214	3.5	10.0	6.0/3.5	10.0	7.5/3.0	1.79	...	5.50	1.13
00216	1.5	10.0	6.0/3.5	10.0	7.5/3.0	1.80	4.12	4.47	1.23
03501	2.5	10.0	6.5/4.0	5.0Y	7.5/3.0	1.56	3.21	4.29	.89
03502	2.5	5.0	5.5/6.0	10.0	8.0/3.5	1.58	3.89	7.62	1.17
03922	1.5	5.0	5.5/6.0	10.0	7.5/3.0	1.93	4.21	5.33	1.29
04218	2.5	10.0	6.0/4.0	10.0	8.0/2.5	.50	3.50	4.48	1.08
04503	3.5	10.0	6.0/4.0	2.5Y	8.0/3.0	1.41	3.97	3.80	.93
05008	2.5	5.0	5.5/5.0	5.0	5.0/4.0	1.71	3.07	2.45	1.18
05336	2.5	5.0Y	6.0/4.0	5.0Y	6.0/3.5	1.65	2.79	4.11	1.32
07249	2.5	5.0	6.0/6.0	10.0	8.0/3.5	1.67	3.46	5.25	1.10
07861	3.5	10.0	6.0/3.0	10.0	7.0/3.0	1.48	3.64	4.17	.83
07862	2.5	10.0	6.0/4.0	10.0	7.5/3.0	1.40	3.48	4.32	.83
07842	2.5	5.0	5.5/6.0	10.0	7.5/2.5	1.21	2.74	3.35	.67
08208	2.5	7.5	5.0/4.0	7.5	6.5/4.0	1.78	4.24	4.62	1.11
08209	3.5	5.0Y	6.0/4.0	5.0Y	6.5/3.0	.54	3.79	5.00	1.03
10511	2.5	5.0	5.0/5.0	10.0	7.5/3.0	1.41	4.37	5.60	1.06
10621	2.5	10.0	6.5/4.0	10.0	7.5/3.0	2.06	5.06	3.79	.89
10622	2.5	5.0	5.5/4.0	10.0	7.0/3.5	1.70	4.05	4.77	.90
10755	3.5	5.0Y	6.0/4.0	5.0Y	7.5/3.0	1.81	4.37	4.57	1.06
10756	2.5	10.0	6.0/4.0	10.0	7.5/4.0	1.87	3.77	5.49	1.00
10758	2.5	10.0	6.0/4.0	10.0	8.0/3.0	1.45	3.74	4.40	.89
10803	2.5	10.0	6.5/4.0	10.0	7.5/3.0	1.63	4.09	4.27	1.10

TABLE 21
CERAMIC RINGS

Number	Hardness	Paste Color		Surface Color		Maximum Diameter	Thickness
		Hue	Value/Chroma	Hue	Value/Chroma		
00612	2.5	10.0	5.5/4.0	10.0	5.5/4.0	9.0	2.5
01501	1.5	10.0	5.0/4.0	10.0	6.0/2.5	10.0	2.2
02008	1.5	5.0	5.0/6.0	7.5	6.0/4.0	3.0	2.1
05106	1.5	10.0	5.5/4.0	7.5	5.5/4.0	10.0	3.3
05210	1.5	7.5	5.0/4.0	7.5	6.0/4.0	8.0	2.2
05331	1.5	7.5	4.5/4.0	10.0	6.0/3.0	8.0	1.8
05332	1.5	7.5	6.0/4.0	10.0	7.5/3.0	8.0	2.1
05624	1.5	10.0	5.0/3.0	7.5	6.0/4.0	8.0	2.0
06411	2.5	5.0	4.5/4.0	7.5	6.5/4.0	7.5	1.8
10763	2.5	5.0	5.0/4.0	10.0	6.5/4.0	6.5	2.1

APPENDIX I

TABLE 22
STONE BOWLS

Number	Stone Type				Color
	Rim Diameter	Body Thickness	Grain	Acid Reaction	
03411[1]	14	.97	Fine	Strong	Pale yellow
03514	20	.91	Fine	Weak	Light gray
03515	11	.98	Coarse	None	Pale yellow
03516	16	1.20	Fine	Strong	Pale yellow
04426	30	1.83	Coarse	Strong	Light gray
05513	24	1.97	Coarse	Strong	Light gray
06102[2]	21	1.13	Coarse	Strong	Light gray
07607[2]	26	.76	Fine	Weak	(Burned)
08300	9	1.35	Fine	Weak	Light gray
10511	18	1.12	Fine	Weak	Pink
10764	11	1.31	Fine	Weak	Light gray
10765	24	1.13	Fine	Weak	Pale yellow

[1] The stone with strong reactions to hydrochloric acid is calcite. The stone with none is gypsum.
[2] Small fossils in the stone.

TABLE 23
DENTICULATE BLADE SEGMENTS

Number	Length	Width	Thickness	Length Notch	Depth Notch	Period[1] Notch	Blade Sheen	Notch Sheen	Bitumen
02022[2]	3.02	1.48	.34	.32	.18	.54	...	...	X
08323	3.44	1.41	.32	.39	.16	.47	X	...	X
08524[3]	2.39	1.34	.43	.17	.11	.37	...	...	X
08524[3]	1.96	1.31	.20	.21	.11	.45	...	...	X
01025	1.91	1.31	.75	.27	.14	.41	...	...	...
01126[4]	2.31	1.35	.41	.25	.17	.43	...	...	...
01127[4]	1.81	1.51	.37	.18	.13	.38	...	...	...
02228	2.85	1.46	.32	.21	.15	.41	X	X	X
02729	2.54	1.57	.27	.31	.19	.53	...	...	X
03730 A[5]	2.13	1.29	.28	.37	.12	.35	X	...	...
03730 B	...	...	...	.35	.11	.48	X	X	...
04431[6]	3.21	1.32	.44	.21	.17	.36	X	X	X
04432[6]	2.48	1.10	.35	.30	.16	.47	X	X	...
04433	3.19	1.17	.35	.24	.12	.44	...	...	X
04434	1.86	1.34	.39	.24	.14	.34	...	...	X
04435	1.82	1.19	.43	.24	.13	.30	...	...	X
04436	2.37	1.81	.30	.27	.21	.45	...	...	...
05337 A[5]	2.23	1.31	.33	.30	.11	.47	X	X	...
05337 B	...	...	...	.20	.09	.36	X	X	...
07138	4.77	1.61	.41	.21	.17	.46	...	...	X
08239	2.14	1.31	.29	.18	.13	.41	X	...	...
08340	1.94	1.43	.25	.14	.11	.45	...	...	...
08341	2.08	1.18	.23	.25	.18	.48	...	...	X
10742	2.78	1.16	.39	.31	.17	.60	X	X	X
10743	3.19	1.64	.29	.28	.14	.46	X	X	X
10770	1.97	1.41	.38	.29	.10	.46	...	...	...
00014	3.66	1.50	.35	.28	.15	.41	X	...	X

[1] Average distance from maximum depth to maximum depth.
[2] In bitumen fragment attached to a sherd.
[3] From same core, in bitumen, attached to sherd.
[4] From same core.
[5] Blade notched on two sides.
[6] From same core.

APPENDIX II

FAUNAL REMAINS FROM SAKHERI SUGHIR

by

Sandor Bökönyi and *Kent V. Flannery*

Introduction

The animal bones from the excavations were studied by Kent V. Flannery and Miss Jane Wheeler at the Smithsonian Office of Anthropology in December, 1966. They were further studied by Sandor Bökönyi of the Hungarian National Museum in February, 1967. Both parties gave a series of notes to Henry Wright. This report is an editing of these various notes.

Samples

There were two categories of bone samples. Some are samples recovered from debris loosened with a small pick. Others are samples recovered with a fine screen with a one millimeter mesh. These two methods result in remarkable differences.

TABLE 1

A COMPARISON OF TWO RECOVERY PROCEDURES

	Identifiable Non-fish	Identifiable Fish
Unscreened	140	64
Screened	54	251

A screened sample provides more complete information on the bone preserved in the site. The twenty-three screened samples contained 596 mammal bones of all types weighing 454 grams and 1305 fish bones of all types weighing 139.1 grams. Now let us consider the identifiable material alone.

Ovis and *Capra*

One hundred seventy-six bones may be either domestic sheep or goat. Of these 136 are accepted by all investigators, of these sixteen may be sheep, of which four are accepted by all, and three may be goat, of which one is accepted by all. The horn core of this specimen indicates that the goats had twisted horns. One right proximal metacarpal of a sheep exhibits the blunt depression of a chopper blow. Otherwise, butchering marks are not evident. Bökönyi notes that four vertebral and scapular fragments may be gazelle. The following measurements were made by Flannery and Wheeler.

TABLE 2

SHEEP METAPODIA FROM SAKHERI SUGHIR
(In Millimeters)

Provenience	Diameter Small (Outer) Spool	Diameter Large (Inner) Spool
051	10.0	15.3
084	9.7	14.9
084	10.3	15.4

Thirty bones of cattle are accepted by all. Only one specimen, the distal end of a humerus, is beyond the range of variation of early domestic cattle measurements. This could be either a wild aurochs or a large domestic bull. Until larger samples of Mesopotamian cattle have been measured, it is wisest to consider the entire sample as *Bos taurus*. No butchering marks are notable, but three of the four second phalanges in the sample are partially burnt.

The following measurements were made by Flannery and Wheeler:

TABLE 3

CATTLE FROM SAKHERI SUGHIR
(In Millimeters)

Provenience	Skeletal Part	Length	Breadth	Width
066	First phalanx	65.2	30.2	...
103	Humerus, distal end	...	93.7	...
108	First phalanx	69.1	35.5	...
108	First phalanx	69.3	36.0	...
108	Second phalanx	45.4	35.1	...
108	Glenoid fossa sespus	...	52.0	73.5

Equus

Two specimens may be from equids. One distal end of a radius and ulna corresponds closely with that of *Equus hemionus*.

APPENDIX II

Sus

Seven possible pig bones are present of which six were accepted by all investigators. Some represent a small individual probably *Sus scrofa domesticus*. The others represent a larger individual perhaps *Sus scrofa ferus*. Its scapula exhibits sharp cut marks such as result from butchering with flint blade or flake.

Canis

Twenty-seven probable canid bones are present. Bökönyi took special notes on these and states that there are two forms of dog: (1) a small one with a broad brain case resembling the *Canis familiaris palustris* of Europe, (2) a larger one about the size of a setter. It is not possible to say whether or not these forms represent two distinct breeds or two extremes in a wide range of variation.

Herpestes

A calcaneus and phalanx of a small mongoose probably *Herpestes auropunctatus* were found on the Rectangular Floor (IA-B) in provenience unit 014. Such bones could have been transported to the site in a pelt. The mongoose favors cultivated areas.

Nesokia

The maxilla and a possible incisor of *Nesokia indica*, the bandicoot rat, were found in units 019, the Large Pit (IA) and 049, the Work Floor (IB-C), respectively. This crop pest prefers to burrow in moist soils such as canal banks. Neither these specimens nor the ones noted above would have been recovered without the use of screens.

Aves

There are six bird bones representing three individuals. In unit 003, the Small Pit (0), was the ulna of a large dove, resembling the genus *Columba*. In unit 012, the Large Pit (IA-B) was the femur of a small dove resembling the genus *Streptopelia*. In unit 015, over the Rectangular Floor (0-IB) there were four fragments and a carpometacarpus perhaps from a duck larger than a mallard. Were more detailed identifications possible and were more known about the habits of these birds, they would be quite useful in reconstructing the former environment of Sakheri Sughir.

Pisces

Hundreds of potentially identifiable fish bones were recovered. As a result of the lack of comparative collections for Tigris-Euphrates fish, only a few have been identified as to family or genus. The carp family is dominant, but drum and catfish occur.

Conclusion

The faunal collections from Sakheri Sughir indicate the importance of fish in the diet, the preponderance of sheep among the caprines, and the relative importance of cattle. The following table was prepared by Flannery and Wheeler.

TABLE 4

COMMON IDENTIFIED FAUNAL REMAINS
AT SAKHERI SUGHIR

North Block

Small Pit (Stratum 0) - 001, 003
 Ovis/Capra .. 1 premolar
  2 lower incisors
  1 tooth fragment
  1 axis
  4 vertebral fragments
  1 intermediate carpal
 Bos .... 1 sesamoid
  1 occipital condyle fragment
 Pisces ..... 1 Otolithus
  2 Cyprinidae (dorsal spine, phalangeal arch)
 Mollusca ... 9 valves

On Rectangular Floor (Stratum IA-B) 002, 006, 013, 014, 015, 020, 021
 Ovis/Capra .. 1 cheek tooth
  1 mandible fragment
  1 occiput fragment
  2 cranial fragments
  2 vertebra fragments
  1 atlas
  1 proximal end femur, unfused
 Bos ...... 3 vertebra fragments
  1 distal end of humerus
 Pisces .... 1 *Silureus* (spine)
 Mollusca ... 12 valves

Over Work Floor (IA) 022, 023, 025, 030, 038
 Ovis/Capra .. 3 incisors
  5 cheek teeth
  1 atlas
  1 vertebral fragment
  1 acetabulum
  1 patella
  1 right second phalanx
 Bos ...... 1 cervical vertebra fragment
  1 vertebra fragment, unfused

APPENDIX II

TABLE 4—Continued

                1 calcanum, unfused
                1 proximal metacarpal
                1 third phalanx
Canis . . . . . 1 distal end, radius
Pisces . . . . 2 Otolithus (1 jaw, 1 otolith)
Mollusca . . . 2 valves

Large Pit (IA-B) 012, 018, 019
  Ovis/Capra. . 6 teeth fragments
                1 accessory carpal
  Bos . . . . . . 1 sacrum
  Sus . . . . 1 scapula
                1 metacarpal
  Canis? . . . . 1 accessory carpal
  Pisces . . . . 2 Otolithus (1 jaw, 1 otolith)
                7 Cyprinidae (dorsal spines)
  Mollusca . . . 12 valves

Twelve Meters North (IA) 016, 026, 027
  Ovis/Capra. . 1 third molar
                1 fragment of astragalus
  Equus . . . . . 1 distal end of radius and ulna
  Canis? . . . . 1 fragment of carpal

Five Meters North (IA) 034, 037, 045
  Ovis/Capra. . 2 teeth fragments
  Bos . . . . . . 1 vertebra fragment
                1 rib fragment
  Mollusca . . . 8 valves

Two Meters North (IA) 042
  Canis? . . . . 1 distal end phalanx
  Pisces . . . . 2 Cyprinidae (dorsal spines)
  Mollusca . . . 7 valves

Eight Meters South (IA) 055, 066
  Ovis/Capra. . 1 cheek tooth
  Bos . . . . . . 1 horn core fragment
                1 tarsal
                1 first phalanx
  Sus . . . . . . 1 ulna fragment
  Pisces . . . . 1 Cyprinidae (pharyngeal arch)
                1 Silureus (spine)

On Work Floor (IB) 031, 032, 033, 039, 040, 052, 056
  Ovis/Capra. . 3 mandible fragments (1 with P_4 deciduous, M_2 erupting)
                5 cheek teeth
                1 cranial arch (Ovis)
                1 axis
                2 scapulae fragments
                1 vertebra fragment
                1 petrous (Ovis?)
                2 innominate fragments
                1 metapodial fragment
                1 ulna fragment
                1 accessory carpal
                1 first phalanx
                1 articulated first and second phalanx
                1 third phalanx (Ovis)
  Bos . . . . . . 1 vertebra fragment
  Pisces . . . . 1 Silureus (spine)
  Mollusca . . . 9 valves

Five Meters North (IB) 035 + 095, 036, 046
  Mollusca . . . 1 valve

Two Meters North (IB) 044, 067
  Ovis/Capra. . 1 distal femur, unfused
  Canis . . . . . 1 upper first molar
  Mollusca . . . 3 valves

On Work Floor (IC) 049, 050, 051, 053, 065
  Ovis/Capra. . 1 proximal radius
                1 metapodial condyle (Ovis)

TABLE 4—Continued

Ovis/Capra —continued
    1 distal end femur, unfused
    1 calcaneum
Bos . . . . . . 1 cheek tooth
Reptilia . . . 3 fragments turtle carapace
Pisces . . . . 4 Cyprinidae (3 dorsal spine, 1 pharyngeal arch)
    2 *Otolithus* (jaws)
    1 *Silureus* (spine)
Mollusca . . . 10 valves

Oval Oven (IC) 060, 061
Mollusca . . . 3 valves

Deep Sounding (I) 010
Ovis/Capra. . 1 radius (unfused)

Deep Sounding (II) 011, 062
Ovis/Capra. . 1 cranial fragment (*Ovis*)
Pisces . . . . 2 Cyprinidae (dorsal spines)
Mollusca . . . 1 valve

Deep Sounding (III B) 069
Ovis/Capra. . 1 vertebra fragment

Deep Sounding (IV) 074
Ovis/Capra. . 1 mandible (P_3 deciduous, worn; M_1, new)
    2 cheek teeth, mature animal

South Block

South of Structure (I) 070, 072
Ovis/Capra. . 2 third molars from 2 individuals
    3 cheek teeth fragments
    2 mandible fragments from two individuals
    1 metapodial, unfused
    1 ascending ramus fragment
Mollusca . . . 2 valves

East of Structure (I) 077
Bos? . . . . . 1 atlas fragment

South of Structure (II) 071, 076, 080, 098
Ovis/Capra. . 1 mandible fragment
    1 vertebra fragment?
Canis . . . . . 1 incisor
    1 mandible with P_2, P_3
Mollusca . . . 1 valve

East of Structure (II) 078, 081, 082, 083
Ovis/Capra. . 1 horn core fragment (*Capra*)
    1 occipital
    1 mandible fragment (P_2, P_3, M_1, M_2)
    1 tooth fragment
    1 scapula
Pisces . . . . 1 Cyprinidae (dorsal spine)
Mollusca . . . 3 valves

Inside Structure (IIA) 028, 047, 103
Ovis/Capra. . 1 cheek tooth
Bos . . . . . . 1 fragment humerus, distal condyle

Inside Structure—Center (IIB) 087, 100
Ovis/Capra. . 1 mandible (large adult P_1, P_2, P_3, M_1)

Inside Structure—Southeast (IIB) 088, 101, 109
Canis . . . . . 1 distal end tibia
Pisces . . . . 4 Cyprinidae (dorsal spines)
Mollusca . . . 11 valves

APPENDIX II

TABLE 4—Continued

Inside Structure—Southwest (IIB)
105, 106, 107, 110, 111
- *Ovis/Capra* . . 1 incisor
  - 4 cheek teeth
  - 1 cranial fragment
  - 1 distal end tibia
  - 1 right proximal metacarpal
- *Canis* . . . . . 2 fragments innominate
  - 1 carpal—tarsal, unfused
  - 3 phalanges
- *Sus* . . . . . . 1 frontal
  - 2 carpals, unfused
- *Pisces* . . . . 4 Cyprinidae (dorsal spines)
- *Mollusca* . . . 7 valves

Small Pit—Southwest Corner 108
- *Bos* . . . . . . 1 scapula
  - 1 left first phalanx
  - 1 articulated right first and second phalanges
  - 2 other right second phalanges

East of Structure (III) 084, 085, 086
- *Ovis/Capra* . . 1 scapular fragment
  - 1 very large proximal humerus
  - 1 distal metapodial
  - 1 distal tibia, just fused
- *Bos* . . . . . . 1 occipital condyle
  - 1 proximal metatarsal

Canal Excavation

Lower Canal 113, 114
- *Ovis/Capra* . . 3 vertebral fragments
  - 2 rib fragments
  - 1 innominate fragment

Definitive statements on the varieties of sheep, cows, pigs, and dogs present would require a sample at least ten times larger than the present one. Further sampling should make careful use of special recovery techniques such as screening and washing.

APPENDIX III

THE DENTITION OF TWO HUMAN BURIALS FROM SAKHERI SUGHIR

John Mayhall, D.D.S.

Materials and Methods

In total, parts of two individuals' dentitions were studied, including thirty-two permanent teeth, thirteen deciduous teeth, and portions of the palate of one individual, as well as a small portion of a mandible from another burial.

The teeth included maxillary Pm^2's (2), M^1's (2), and M^3's (2) of Burial One, and a complete complement of permanent teeth with the exception of the mandibular right central incisor, the mandibular left second molar, and all of the third molars of Burial Two. The latter burial also revealed 13 deciduous teeth which included all of the canines, molars, and the lower right central incisor.

These teeth were in excellent condition with a remarkable resistance to breakage. All of the teeth showed some evidence of the leaching of the soil pigments by bluish tinge present in them. The available material was measured using a sliding caliper accurate to 0.05 of a millimeter. Also radiographs of the larger pieces of the bony portions were obtained and studied.

Results

Because of the small number of individuals represented in this sample it is impossible to draw any definite conclusions regarding the physical characteristics of the population that these burials represent. On the other hand, with such a good representation of the dentitions of these two individuals it is possible to present a rather complete description of the dentition. The measurements of these teeth, along with comparative data from other populations, can be noted on my Tables 1 through 8.

General Description of Teeth

From Tables 1 through 4 it can be observed that the anterior teeth of the permanent dentition are larger than those of the other populations found in the same area. The posterior teeth do not follow the same pattern as the anteriors. The premolars and molars are generally the same dimensions as those of the other comparative populations.

These teeth exhibit none of the characteristics that are usually attributed to a Mongoloid dentition. The unerupted teeth show extreme wrinkling, but this is soon worn away after eruption into occlusion. It is interesting to note the rapidity of wear of those teeth that were in occlusion. In the older individual (Burial 1) the wear has proceeded through the enamel into the dentin on the cusp tips of the maxillary first molars. This individual's age is estimated to be fifteen years. The age estimate was made by examining the degree of formation of the third molars and the second premolars.

The age of the other burial (Burial 2) is estimated to be nine years, in view of the degree of root formation evidenced by most of the permanent teeth as well as the degree of root resorption of the deciduous teeth.

Permanent Incisors

The available incisors are from Burial 2. All four of the maxillary incisors exhibit a lack of shovel-shaped appearance. There is only a slight development of the lingual marginal ridges and the cingulum. The mamelons are still visible on the incisal edge of these incisors which would be expected due to the relatively recent eruption of these teeth. The roots are not completely formed, having about one-third of their length remaining to be formed. The root canals are of normal size for a child in this stage of development.

The maxillary incisors present an unusual root formation. The root just above the cemento-enamel junction curves toward the lingual. This curve continues to approximately the middle one-third of the root where the curve is reversed. While the apical portion of the root is not formed it is possible to note that this curve would probably continue, thus giving the root a crescent-shaped appearance when viewed from the proximal aspect. If we accept the theory that root formation is a reflection of the environment of the surrounding jaw, then it can be hypothesized that this individual probably exhibited a procumbancy of the anterior teeth.

All of the incisors (maxillary and mandibular) exhibit a small pit in the enamel on the incisal edge, usually between the mamelons, but in the mandibular incisors it is on the central and highest mamelon. This pit does not appear to extend into the dentin.

The mandibular incisors also show little or no wear. As in the maxillary incisors little cingulum development is noted, and there is no evidence of a shovel-shaped appearance. The apices of these teeth are not completely formed.

Permanent Canines

Burial 2 has all four canines present. As in the incisor series a small pit is noted on the incisal surface. The maxillary canines also show a pitting of the enamel in the cingulum area. The cingulum on the maxillary canines is relatively well developed and the lingual ridges appear strong. There are deep fissures between these marginal ridges and the body of the canines. The mandibular canines do not show the lingual ridge development present in the maxillary canines. The mandibular canines also show a large developmental enamel defect in the cervical one-third of the crown. The root development has proceeded to approximately seven millimeters from the lingual cemento-enamel junction. These teeth had not erupted at the time of death as evidenced by the one canine (maxillary) which was found in a small fragment of the mandible.

Permanent Premolars

One is immediately impressed by the deep fissures of the occlusal surfaces of these teeth. The teeth in this series from Burial 2 show the same type of pit on the buccal cusp tip that was found on the incisal edge of the anterior teeth. The premolars from this individual are unworn as evidenced by the presence of the deciduous teeth that are the precursors of the premolars.

Burial 1 exhibits two maxillary second premolars which show normal occlusal wear and dilacerated roots. The apical one-third of these roots are sharply dilacerated toward the distal.

None of the premolars exhibit any unusual morphologic characteristics.

Permanent Molars (Maxillary)

The maxillary molars from Burial 2 exhibit four cusps in a rhomboidal configuration. The first molars from this burial exhibit development of all the cusps with a full expression of the hypocone. The second molars exhibit a reduced hypocone and, to a lesser extent, a reduced metacone. The first molars also display an expression of the Carabelli's cusp similar to that shown in plaque P12 of Dahlberg's classification. The second molars exhibit small pits indicating a slight expression of the Carabelli's cusp. The first molars of Burial 1 show only an extremely small pit in the region of development of the Carabelli's cusp.

The wear exhibited by the first molars is somewhat accelerated in respect to the age of the individual at the time of burial. All of the other teeth in the molar series are unworn. These teeth also show deep occlusal fissures as well as pitting of the enamel on this surface. Only one of the molars (M-1) shows any evidence of calculus.

The third molars of Burial 1 show extreme variation in the cuspal pattern. One has four cusps with the hypocone and metacone somewhat reduced, while the other exhibits only two large cusps and a small metacone. The hypocone of this last specimen is absent. Both third molars are unerupted and evidence no root formation.

Permanent Molars (Mandibular)

The first molars of Burial 2 exhibit a dryopithecoid pattern, while the second molars have a +4 pattern. None of the cusps on the molars appear to be suppressed. These teeth show no indications of a protostylid formation. As in the maxillary molars, these teeth exhibit deep occlusal fissures as well as pitting of the enamel. There is a slight extension of the enamel into the bifurcation of these teeth, but not to the extent described by Pedersen in the East Greenland Eskimo.

The buccal grooves of the first molars are deep with slight pits at their termination in the middle one-third of the crown.

Deciduous Dentition

All of the deciduous teeth are extremely worn, thus preventing any analysis of cusp size and configuration. The maxillary and mandibular canines show a curvature of the root toward the labial in the apical one-half.

Pathology

No evidence of caries is noted in either the permanent or deciduous dentitions. The small fragments of bone exhibit no evidence of periapical pathology. No evidence of periodontal pathology is noted.

Discussion and Conclusions

The permanent anterior teeth of these two burials are very large when compared with other populations which inhabited the same general area. We notice the same trend in the deciduous teeth, large anterior teeth (poorly represented in the burials) and "normal"-sized posterior teeth.

Also interesting to note is the Carabelli's cusp expression. The Jarmo material showed only small cusps in two individuals studied, while Dahlberg describes the Natufian material as having well-developed cusps. Carbonell found only slight expression of this trait in the Kish population she studied. Burial 2 shows a cusp development on the first molars and pits on the second molars. Burial 1 exhibits only a pit in the area of the usual Carabelli's cusp development.

There are no indications of the typical Mongoloid characteristics of shovel-shaped incisors. This compares favorably with the Jarmo and Kish populations.

Unfortunately, the individuals were young at the time of death, making it impossible to speculate as to their diet from wear patterns on the occlusal surfaces of the teeth. These two individuals were too young to expect to find any evidences of periodontal disease or any other debilitating diseases that would be evidenced in the dentition or its bony supports.

It can be hypothesized that the one individual with permanent anterior teeth present probably represented a procumbancy of the anteriors, while the other individual appears to have had relatively "normal" dental appearance in profile. This latter aspect is hypothesized from the sockets present in the two portions of the palate examined.

TABLE 1

COMPARATIVE MESIODISTAL CROWN DIAMETERS OF
PERMANENT MAXILLARY TEETH

(In Millimeters)

	Burial 1	Burial 2	Jarmo	Natufian	Kish
I^1	...	9.76	8.8	8.92	8.48
I^2	...	7.82	6.7	6.67	6.58
C	...	8.33	8.3	7.72	7.31
Pm^1	...	7.37	7.5	7.01	6.56
Pm^2	6.43	7.23	7.8	6.85	6.69
M^1	10.55	10.93	10.8	10.87	10.49
M^2	...	9.92	10.2	10.52	9.65
M^3	9.05	...	8.4	9.34	8.51

TABLE 2

COMPARATIVE BUCCOLINGUAL CROWN DIAMETERS OF
PERMANENT MAXILLARY TEETH

(In Millimeters)

	Burial 1	Burial 2	Jarmo	Natufian	Kish
I^1	...	7.43	6.6	7.26	7.04
I^2	...	6.38	6.0	6.82	6.12
C	...	8.39	8.4	8.61	7.96
Pm^1	...	9.18	9.5	9.44	8.60
Pm^2	9.27	9.45	9.8	9.53	8.64
M^1	11.52	12.00	11.4	12.30	10.80
M^2	...	11.94	11.4	12.14	10.74
M^3	10.75	...	10.7	11.30	10.46

TABLE 3

COMPARATIVE MESIODISTAL CROWN DIAMETERS OF
PERMANENT MANDIBULAR TEETH

(In Millimeters)

	Burial 2	Jarmo	Natufian	Kish
I_1	5.88	5.3	5.37	5.25
I_2	6.23	6.0	5.95	5.74
C	7.47	7.1	7.03	6.47
Pm_1	7.70	8.0	7.06	6.68
Pm_2	7.70	8.3	7.18	6.85
M_1	12.17	11.4	11.52	10.65
M_2	11.20	11.0	11.05	10.17
M_3	...	11.1	10.90	10.14

APPENDIX III

TABLE 4
COMPARATIVE BUCCOLINGUAL CROWN DIAMETERS OF PERMANENT MANDIBULAR TEETH
(In Millimeters)

	Burial 2	Jarmo	Natufian	Kish
I_1	6.38	5.8	6.21	5.65
I_2	6.53	6.1	6.61	5.95
C	8.88	7.7	7.91	7.27
Pm_1	7.73	7.4	7.82	7.39
Pm_2	8.30	8.6	8.24	7.81
M_1	10.55	10.5	10.76	10.19
M_2	10.00	10.1	10.62	9.72
M_3	...	10.8	10.40	9.43

TABLE 5
COMPARATIVE MESIODISTAL CROWN DIAMETERS OF DECIDUOUS MAXILLARY TEETH
(In Millimeters)

	Burial 2	Jarmo	American Whites
dc	7.28	6.8	6.88
dm_1	7.54	7.6	6.84
dm_2	8.94	9.7	8.87

TABLE 6
COMPARATIVE BUCCOLINGUAL CROWN DIAMETERS OF DECIDUOUS MAXILLARY TEETH
(In Millimeters)

	Burial 2	Jarmo	American Whites
dc	6.58	6.1	...
dm^1	8.88	9.0	8.22
dm^2	10.03	10.5	9.76

TABLE 7
COMPARATIVE MESIODISTAL CROWN DIAMETERS OF DECIDUOUS MANDIBULAR TEETH
(In Millimeters)

	Burial 2	Jarmo	American Whites
di_1	4.95	...	...
dc	6.30	6.4	5.92
dm_1	8.38	8.1	7.80
dm_2	10.18	10.6	9.83

TABLE 8

COMPARATIVE BUCCOLINGUAL CROWN DIAMETERS OF
DECIDUOUS MANDIBULAR TEETH

(In Millimeters)

	Burial 2	Jarmo	American Whites
di_1	4.90	...	...
dc	6.13	5.9	...
dm_1	6.73	7.5	7.07
dm_2	9.08	9.8	8.84

REFERENCES

Adams, Robert McC.
1958 A Survey of Ancient Watercourses and Settlements in Central Iraq. Sumer, 14:101-03.
1965 Land Behind Baghdad. Chicago: University of Chicago Press.
1966 The Evolution of Urban Society. Chicago: Aldine Press.

Adams, Robert M. and Stuart Harris
1957 A Note on a Canal and Marsh Stratigraphy Near Zubediyah. Sumer, 13:157-63.

Al-Barazi, Nuri
1961 The Geography of Agriculture in Irrigated Areas of the Middle Euphrates Valley. Baghdad: Al-Aani Press.

Biggs, Robert D.
1966 The Abi Salabikh Tablets. Journal of Cuneiform Studies, 20(2):73-89.

Brown, James A.
1967 Dimensions of Status in Burials at Spiro. Paper presented at the Meeting of the American Anthropological Association, Pittsburg.

Burrows, Eric
1935 The Ur Archaic Texts, Ur Excavations Texts, Volume II. London: The British Museum and The University Museum, University of Pennsylvania.

Buringh, P.
1960 Soils and Soil Conditions in Iraq. Baghdad: Ministry of Agriculture.

Campbell-Thompson, R. L.
1919 Excavations of the British Museum at Abu Shahrein, Archeologia. London: Society of Antiquaries.

Carbonell, Virginia
n.d. The Dentition of the Kish Population 3000 B.C. Unpublished 1958 Master of Arts Thesis, University of Chicago.

Dahlberg, A. A.
1960 The Dentition of the First Agriculturalists. American Journal of Physical Anthropology, Vol. 18, No. 4:243-56.

Davenport, William
1960 Jamaican Fishing: A Game Theory Analysis. Yale University Publications in Anthropology No. 59. New Haven: Yale University Press.

Deimel, Anton
1922-24 Die Inschriften von Fara, Wissenschaftliche Veroffentlichung de Deutschen Orient-gesselschaft Nos. 40, 43, 45. Leipzig: J. C. Heinrich.

Deimel, Anton
  1923　Das Betriebspersonal der Tempelacker zae Ziet Urukaginas. Orientalia, 6:1-32.
  1925-47　Sumerisches Lexikon. Rome: Pontiflical Biblical Institute.

DeLougaz, Pinhas
  1938　A Short Investigation of the Temple at Tell al-'Ubaid. Iraq, 5:1-11.
  1940　The Temple Oval at Khafajah. Chicago: University of Chicago Press.
  1952　Pottery from the Diyala Region. Chicago: University of Chicago Press.

Diakanov, Igor
  1959　Society and State in Ancient Mesopotamia: Sumer. Moscow: Government Printing Office.

Fernea, Robert
  1959　Irrigation and Social Organization Among the El Shabbana. Doctoral Thesis, University of Chicago, Department of Anthropology.

Genouillac, Henri De
  1922　Textes Economiques d'Ouma. Paris: P. Guenther.

Gould, P. R.
  1963　Man Against His Environment: A Game Theoretic Framework. Annals of the Association of American Geographers, 53:290-97.

Guest, Evan
  1966　The Flora of Iraq, Vol. I. Baghdad: Ministry of Agriculture.

Hall, H. R. H. and Leonard Woolley
  1927　Al-'Ubaid, Ur Excavations, Vol. I. London: Oxford University Press.

Hallo, W. W.
  1957　Early Mesopotamian Royal Titles. American Oriental Society Series, Vol. 43. New Haven: Yale University Press.

Hatt, Robert
  1959　The Mammals of Iraq. University of Michigan, Museum of Zoology. Miscellaneous Publication No. 106. Ann Arbor.

Helbaek, Hans
  1960　Ecological Effects of Irrigation in Ancient Mesopotamia. Iraq, 22:186-96.

Jacobsen, Thorkild
  1960　The Waters of Ur. Iraq, 22:174-85.

Khalaf, Kamil T.
  1961　The Marine and Freshwater Fishes of Iraq. Baghdad. Ar-Rabitta Press.

Legrain, Leon
  1936　The Archaic Seal Impressions. Ur Excavations, Vol. III. London: Oxford University Press.

REFERENCES

Lloyd, Seton and Fuad Safar
   1947   Eridu: A Preliminary Report of the First Season's Excavations. Sumer, Vol. 3.
   1948   Eridu: A Preliminary Report of the Second Season's Excavations. Sumer, Vol. 4.

Mahdi, Nuri
   1961   The Fishes of Iraq. Baghdad: The Ministry of Education.

Nikolsky, M. V.
   1905   Drevbosti Vastocnyja. Petrograd: P. Gopike.

Oppenheim, A. L. (Ed.)
   1947   The Assyrian Dictionary. Chicago: University of Chicago Press.

Pearce, John R.
   1961   Symbols, Signs, and Noise. New York: Harper and Co.

Pederson, P. O.
   1949   The East Greenland Eskimo Dentition. Meddelelser Om Gronland, Vol. 142, No. 3.

Poyck, A.
   1962   Farms Studies in Iraq. Wageningen: Landbouwhogeschool to Wageningen.

Quastler, H. C.
   1955   Studies in the Human Channel Capacity in Information Theory: The Third London Symposium (Colin Cherry, Ed.).

Safar, Fuad
   1950   Eridu: A Preliminary Report on the Third Seasons' Excavations. Sumer, 6:27-38.

Salim, M. S.
   1962   Marsh Arabs of the Euphrates Delta. London: Althone Press.

Sanders, William T.
   1965   Cultural Ecology of the Teotihuacan Valley. The Pennsylvania State University, Department of Sociology and Anthropology. University Park.

Struever, Stuart
   1968   Flotation Techniques for the Recovery of Small Scale Archaeological Remains. American Antiquity, Vol. 33, No. 3:353-62.

Udy, Stanley H.
   1959   The Structure of Authority in Non-Industrial Production. American Journal of Sociology. Vol. 64, No. 6. Chicago.

Voute, Caesar
   1957   A Prehistoric Find Near Razzaza. Sumer, 13:135-56.

Wittfogel, Karl
    1938   Die Theorie der Orientaischen Gesellschaft. Zeitschrift für Sozial Forschung, Vol. 7, pp. 90-122; reprinted in translation *in* Readings in Anthropology (Morton Fried, Ed.) New York: Thomas Y. Crowell and Co.
    1957   Oriental Despotism. New Haven: Yale University Press.

Woolley, Leonard
    1934   The Royal Cemetery. Ur Excavations, Vol. II. London: Oxford University Press.
    1939   The Ziggurat and Its Surroundings. Ur Excavations, Vol. V. London: Oxford University Press.
    1956   The Early Periods. Ur Excavations, Vol. IV. London: Oxford University Press.

Wright, Henry T.
    In litt.   An Archeological Survey in Southern Sumer.

www.ingramcontent.com/pod-product-compliance
Lightning Source LLC
Jackson TN
JSHW070313120426
100741JS00007B/45